GRANTA

THE MAGAZINE OF NEW WRITING / 82

Life's Like That

with Simon Gray, Lynn Barber and Jayne Anne Phillips
PLUS: Tim Judah on the last Jews of Baghdad

Street of Lost Footsteps

By Lyonel Trouillot
Translated and introduction by Linda Coverdale

Lyonel Trouillot's harrowing novel depicts a night of blazing violence in modern-day Port-au-Prince, and recalls hundreds of years of violence stretching back even before the birth of Haiti in the fires of revolution.

An Empty House By Carlos Cerda

Translated by Andrea G. Labinger

An Empty House gives English-speaking readers a memorable portrait of Chile today: honest, brutally realistic, but with a redemptive touch of lyricism and hope.

Imaginary Caribbean and The Caribbean Imaginary By Michèle Praeger

This book poses a provocative question: When the Imaginary occupies the place of the Real, as in Caribbean culture and European projections of that culture, how does the Real position itself?

Macadam Dreams By Gisèle Pineau

Translated by C. Dickson

A cyclone sweeps Eliette into her past in this novel about the wayward violence of love and nature in Guadeloupe. Gisèle Pineau unveils the cataclysms that have devastated Eliette's life: first, the cyclone of 1928, and now Hurricane Hugo.

The Modernist Traveler

French Detours, 1900–1930
By Kimberley J. Healey

The Modernist Traveler considers figures whose writing about travel rebelled against a literary tradition of exoticism, adventure stories, and novelistic travelogues. These writers initiated a modernist strain in travel writing and a shift in the literary establishment and the culture.

Need for the Bike By Paul Fournel

Translated by Allan Stoekl

Need for the Bike conducts readers into a personal world of communication whose center is the bicycle, and where all people and things pass by way of the bike.

University of Nebraska Press

publishers of Bison Books
www.nebraskapress.unl.edu

GRANTA 82, SUMMER 2003
www.granta.com

EDITOR *Ian Jack*
DEPUTY EDITOR *Sophie Harrison*
ASSOCIATE EDITOR *Liz Jobey*
MANAGING EDITOR *Fatema Ahmed*
EDITORIAL ASSISTANT *Helen Gordon*

CONTRIBUTING EDITORS *Diana Athill, Gail Lynch, Blake Morrison,
Andrew O'Hagan, John Ryle, Lucretia Stewart*

FINANCE *Margarette Devlin*
ASSOCIATE PUBLISHER *Sally Lewis*
CIRCULATION DIRECTOR *Stephen W. Soule*
TO ADVERTISE CONTACT *Lara Frohlich* (212) 293 1646
PRODUCTION ASSOCIATE *Sarah Wasley*
PUBLICITY *Jenie Hederman*
SUBSCRIPTIONS *Dwayne Jones*
LIST MANAGER *Diane Seltzer*

PUBLISHER *Rea S. Hederman*

GRANTA PUBLICATIONS, 2-3 Hanover Yard, Noel Road, London N1 8BE
Tel 020 7704 9776 Fax 020 7704 0474
e-mail for editorial: editorial@granta.com
Granta is published in the United Kingdom by Granta Publications.

GRANTA USA LLC, 1755 Broadway, 5th Floor, New York, NY 10019-3780
Tel (212) 246 1313 Fax (212) 586 8003

Granta is published in the United States by Granta USA LLC and distributed in the United States by
PGW and Granta Direct Sales, 1755 Broadway, 5th Floor, New York, NY 10019-3780.

TO SUBSCRIBE call toll-free in the US (800) 829 5093 or 601 354 3850 or e-mail:
grantasub@nybooks.com or fax 601 353 0176
A one-year subscription (four issues) costs $39.95 (US), $51.95 (Canada, includes GST),
$48.70 (Mexico and South America), and $60.45 (rest of the world).

Granta, USPS 000-508, ISSN 0017-3231, is published quarterly in the US by Granta USA LLC,
a Delaware limited liability company. Periodical Rate postage paid at New York, NY, and additional
mailing offices. POSTMASTER: send address changes to Granta, PO Box 23152, Jackson, MS 39225-
3152. US Canada Post Corp. Sales Agreement #40031906.

Printed and bound in Italy by Legoprint on acid-free paper.

Design: Slab Media.
Cover photographs: Robin Grierson. Front cover taken at the Dorset steam fair, 1994;
back cover at the Knowle Hill Rally, 2002

ISBN 1-929001-12-6

CLASSIC BOOKS. FRESH LOOKS.

*Introducing the timeless new design
of Penguin Classics.*

Confessions of an *English* Opium Eater
has never looked so addictive.

 82

Life's Like That

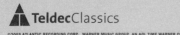

THE SMOKING DIARIES

Simon Gray

Simon Gray, London, 2002

A birthday

Well, here I am, two hours into my sixty-sixth year. From tomorrow on I'm entitled to various benefits, or so I gather—a state pension of so many pounds a week, free travel on public transport, reduced fees on the railways. I assume. I'm also entitled to subsidiary benefits—a respectful attention when I speak, unfailing assistance when I stumble or lurch, an absence of notice when I do the things I've been doing more and more frequently recently, but have struggled to keep under wraps—belching, farting, dribbling, wheezing—I can do all these things openly and publicly now, in a spirit of mutual acceptance—thus am I, at sixty-five and a day—thus he is, at sixty-five and a day, a farter, a belcher, a dribbler and a what else did I say I did, farting, belching, dribbling, oh yes, wheezing. But then as I smoke something like sixty-five cigarettes a day people are likely to continue with their inevitable, 'Well, if you insist on getting through three packets, etc.—' to which I will reply, as always—actually, I can't remember what I always reply, and how could I, when I don't believe anyone, even my doctors, ever says anything like, 'Well, if you will insist, etc.—' In fact, I'm merely reporting a conversation I have with myself, quite often, when I find myself wheezing my way not only up but down the stairs, and when I recover from dizzy spells after pulling on my socks, tying up my shoelaces, two very distinct acts—no, four very distinct acts, each separated by an interval longer than the acts themselves. Naturally, like most people of sixty-five and a day I only grasp my age, the astonishing number of years I've completed, by these physical symptoms—within me the child, about eight years old, rages away—I wish it were all reversed, that I had the appetites, physical stamina, and desirability of a healthy eight-year-old, and the inner life of a man of sixty-five and a day as I imagine it to be from the point of view of an eight-year-old—calm, beneficent, worldly-wise and brimming with tolerance, not to mention forgiveness. Yes, I need to be in touch with my inner adult, is the truth of the matter, who has always been lost to me except as an idea. But the truth is that I'm nastier than I used to be back when—back when I was sixty-four, for instance, when I was nastier than when I was sixty-two and so forth, back and back, always the less nasty the further back, until I get to the age when I was pre-nasty, at least consciously, when the only shame I knew was the shame of being found out, which was when I was, well, about eight I suppose.

Two friends

What's the date? Well, it's Friday midnight the week before Christmas, and this is what happened this evening—at about the time when Victoria and I were vaguely preparing to cross the road to dinner at Chez Moi, there was a ring on the doorbell. We froze, she in her study, I in mine, waiting for the bell to ring again or for the bell ringer to go away—we have a policy, since we were mugged on the pavement outside the house, never to answer the door in the evening unless we know for certain who's there. The bell didn't ring again. 'Any idea who that might have been?' I bellowed huskily (a pretty exact description; my voice, when used normally, is low and broken from fifty-seven years of smoking but when raised it comes out husky). 'Did you get a look?'—sometimes she pops into the bedroom when the doorbell rings, and peeks down from the window—no, she said, she'd seen a shape at the frosted glass in the front door, but couldn't tell anything, not even the sex, it had only been a glimpse, really, from the top of the stair. 'Well,' I said, 'Did you get a sense? Did you hear the footsteps? Could it have been a policeman?' I have a dread of policemen at the door, bearing bad news, a hangover from the years when my children were at that sort of stage—Lucy's first car, Ben's tendency to stray into unprotected areas, unprotected from him, in some cases.— Yes, it could have been a policeman, Victoria said, but then it could have been anyone, as she hadn't heard anything. But I was suddenly convinced that I had, that I'd heard the heavy tread, with something slow and deliberate in it, of a policeman. Though now I come to think of it, it would have to have been a policeman from another age, a policeman from Dixon's age if not Dixon himself, as the policemen of these days don't have a heavy tread, for one thing they don't wear constabulary boots, they wear light, smart shoes that probably cause them to pitter-patter lightly along, in twos or threes or even little packs of four or five, towards some pop star whose sex life they're investigating. Clearly, then, if I'd thought about it, the heavy tread I had heard hadn't belonged to a policeman, but not having thought about it and now actually assuming that our bell had been rung by a policeman, actually picturing him in his helmet, heavy jacket enveloping blue trousers, and his large boots—we crossed the road to Chez Moi and saw, as we entered, Harold [Pinter] and Antonia seated at a table facing the door, in the second room.

'I just came across a moment ago, and rang your bell, to see if you wanted to join us,' Antonia said. 'I saw somebody through the glass at the top of the stairs, so I knew you were in.' We reminded her of our policy of never answering the door until we know who was at it, without of course explaining that I'd mistaken her unheard tread for that of a policeman's from a distant epoch, but it struck me as unusual, not to say unprecedented, for her to have rung the doorbell, and there was something in Harold's manner, subdued and soft in his greetings, not the usual welcoming growl or bark—

'The thing is,' he said, almost as soon as we'd sat down, 'I've got some news. I might as well tell you, in fact I've just discovered— well, today in fact—that I've got cancer.'

He went through the stages of the treatment that lay ahead for him—that he would begin it two days after Christmas, then there would be a break of three weeks during which the poisons would be at their business of attacking the cancer, then another all-day session followed by another three weeks, by which time there would be, he noted matter-of-factly, certain physical changes, his face might alter in shape, his hair might fall out— 'But of course you know the procedure,' he said to me, 'from Ian. How's he doing?'

'Not too well,' I said, and gave him the information Ian [Hamilton] had given to me, just last night actually, and also in Chez Moi, at a table around the corner from the one we were now sitting at—I tried to be crisp and impersonal, and stopped myself saying, 'But of course his isn't anything like yours, his is far worse'—which would be true in as much as I understand the matter, Harold's cancer being local, in his oesophagus, Ian's being all over the place, in his liver, his lungs, probably now also in his lymph—but I didn't think he'd want me to offer consolation by stressing the direness of Ian's plight—direness of Ian's plight! Christ! What a phrase—I've never used it before in my life, where did it come from, direness, plight, when I mean that actually I think he's dying.

How will Harold manage? He'll manage well, I think. With endurance, resolution. Grit. He has a lot of that.

Simon Gray

My holidays

I talked to Rollocks for a short while, first about the moon, which is three quarters full, or a quarter empty, depending on your temperament, and then about cricket, the tragic decline of West Indies cricket, then what it is like to find ourselves in the computer age—Rollocks is perhaps five years younger than me, but older in terms of dignity, bearing, manner of speech—and then he brought me a specially chilled Diet Coke. The bar is empty, apart from Rollocks, who never presides over any customer but myself, as far as I can make out—his hours begin at eleven p.m. and end at seven a.m., and his function is to provide all-night service to a clientele who tend to be in bed as he arrives, and to be about to rise as he leaves. I can't say that the clientele is all elderly—quite a few are much younger than me—but they seem to settle into elderly habits, early days, early nights—I don't imagine that they even notice that everyone else does as they do, or that they do as everyone else does, but often, when I walk around the grounds at half past midnight, I find every light in the apartments and cottages is out, and the hotel takes on the aspect of a large nest, humming with sleep. Then later there are Rollocks and I in the bar, where we too follow a pattern— a short conversation, he brings the Diet Coke, I write. Last night I wrote a letter to Harold. I don't remember now quite what I said— I know I mentioned Rollocks, and then went into a little bit about the hotel and I wrote about the weather, and the mosquitoes, all of this uneasily, as I was trying to find my way towards the central issue, the state of Harold's health—wondering how the treatment was going, how his appetite was, whether his temperature had dropped, etc.—and from there I went into my own feelings when I'd been ill to the point of death five years ago, that I'd found it unbearable to be with people because they seemed to me to be coming from another country, or rather that I'd been exiled to another country and they were paying me brief, troubled visits, then back they went to where I'd once belonged—and then I found myself refining—or possibly coarsening—this thought by adding that actually I'd felt I was under arrest for a rather sad crime, that in some sense the exile was, or seemed to be, a moral one. I'm not sure that this was an appropriate line to take—how can it be helpful to a man perhaps mortally afflicted to have it suggested that he might actually be in the throes of committing some social offence? Well, I've already posted the letter—I know I've posted it, so why did I suddenly start looking for it—I actually picked up my hat as if the letter to Harold I know I've posted might nevertheless be under it. Why did I bring the hat down anyway? It's a straw hat, I wear it to keep the sun off my head, and although I'm outside, it's two in the morning, no sun, just a quarter moon, as I believe I've already—

So a little pause, to light a cigarette, a sip of Diet Coke, calm restored. I've put the hat on my head—Ian's hat actually, that he wore to cover the effects of chemotherapy and has been passed on to me— not quite true—that I claimed a few days after his death, when I was told that he'd wanted me to have something. He probably meant from his library, but I immediately asked for his hat, on which I keep far too attentive an eye, clasping at it when it's windy, fearful I might forget it when I've taken it off on the beach, now wearing it at night in the bar—I'll have to get over this, I'm bound to lose it, it's in the nature of straw hats to detach themselves from you eventually, much better to accept its loss now and adopt a more sensibly careless attitude to it, thinking that I can always get a new one.

I had to get up at six-thirty this morning for a pee. On the way back to bed I popped on to the terrace for a quick gander at the breaking dawn which, as it turned out, wasn't breaking, the light was grey, and the pale trees and the shrubbery shifting about irritably in a sharp wind, the only signs of human life a strange and stooped figure on the beach, moving spectrally between a couple of beach beds under one of the charmingly shaped (like a coolie's hat) straw and wooden-poled little edifices that provide a circle of shade only a few feet from the sea—there are only three of these shelters, which are not only delightful to look at but delightful to be under—a small shelf for drinks encircles the pole, altogether a home from home—and they are much prized and competed for. Now the rules of the hotel, I should explain, regarding beach beds, chairs, etc. are really quite simple, indeed there is only one clear rule, when it comes down to it—first come, first served, but on a day-to-day basis—in other words you can't keep your cherished location for the length of your stay, you have to establish your claim to it every morning—thus the spectre in the 6.20 a.m. gloom—he was staking his claim for the day, though he seemed to be doing rather more than that, stooping now over this bed, now over that, kneeling at the table by the pole, bowing to the sea—he was wearing the hotel dressing gown, a short number with greyish blue-and-white stripes, institutional, a prison or hospital sort of thing that nevertheless in the context conferred on him a sort of authority, and made it seem as if he were performing a ceremony of a ritualistic nature, a blessing perhaps. I peered closer and realized that he was elderly, older than me even, and by quite a bit, and that what he was doing was elderly business, exactly the sort of thing that I've been doing for a few years now—and it gets worse and worse—when I try to sort myself out somewhere, picking things up, putting them down in order to pick something else up for reasons unknown, putting it down, stopping to work out a puzzle to do with, for instance, the whereabouts of a towel that one had thought one had adjusted a moment ago, but now seems to have vanished from the scene of the action, on and on it goes, fiddling, fussing, farting around—and superstition comes into it somewhere, the fear that if one hasn't got every detail—there he is, edging a bed inches sideways from one end, going to the other end and inching it back again, pushing it forwards, pulling it backwards, standing to inspect it, making a further adjustment. Is this one for his wife, slumbering in their room, unaware that her husband is fretting and fiddling at inches and angles for her sake, would she even notice when she came to the beach the exact arrangement of her bed, and how could she notice, really, as there was nothing specific for it to be exact to, unless of course she'd provided him with exact instructions—my bed is to be precisely at such an angle to the sea/sun when we come down at eight a.m. sort of stuff, no, these impulses were coming from *within* him, and mine come from within me, from the synapses or whatever they are that control these matters, going into a muddled repeat mode, doing almost the same thing again and again, the deep-laid purpose, if there is one, is never to finish the inessential task. No, that's not true, getting out of the house is sometimes essential, when I have to meet people or go to the dentist across the street, but getting out of the house—making it from my study to the pavement without going back for something it turns out I haven't forgotten can take ten to fifteen minutes, which I fill by performing inessential tasks again and again—put my spare spectacles in the case for safety's sake, take them out again straight away for future convenience's sake, decide to swap spare spectacles for the ones I'm using, decide to swap the spare spectacles I'm not using for the ones I've just made spare—I become increasingly desperate during all this, crying out, 'What am I doing? Why am I doing this?' generally culminating in a scream, a husky scream, because of my smoking, 'God, I hate myself!' So I found myself hating the old guy who seemed really to be doing a studied and detailed imitation of me. I watched him walk a few steps away from the benches, stop, turn, crouch clutching his knees (I can't do this, joints too stiff), peer at the bench, then back for some more rearranging, then away only a few paces this time, and back, at it again. Finally, he made it to the path above the beach that will take him back to his snoozing wife—or mistress, young, vibrant, preparing herself for a pre-breakfast frolic, while her man—'my man'—is out there, not hunting-gathering, but fiddling and faddling for her sake. Perhaps the realigning was really to give himself angles from which he can peer between her legs or down into her breasts. But I don't think so. There was nothing of the eager scamper, the driven scuttle, in the way he groped his way through the greyness, across the lawns towards his room—or somebody else's room, his legs looked as if they didn't care much where they took him, as long as it was somewhere very close. As he tottered around the palm trees and out of sight, I had an impulse to zip—a word I like to use for my own totter—down the stairs, across the lawn to his nest, snatch up his towels, zip back up here, thus providing Victoria and myself with four towels instead of the usual two, and further providing somebody else with the opportunity of marking out the most desired spot on the beach, and further providing the possibility of the most magnificent row after breakfast when he and his wife come to loll in their rightful place, and find two others, I'd hope of the same age, but of different nationalities, two elderly French versus two middle-aged Scots would be best, but really I would accept any combination—

The impulse didn't pass. I took it to bed with me, and nourished it a while as I lay with my arms wrapped around my wife, who was deeply asleep and mumbling slightly.

Simon Gray

What I read on my holidays

Now that I've written this, I'll spend the rest of the day reading. I feel a strong need for what in my Cambridge days, my Leavis days, was considered a life-enhancing book, though I'm not sure what sort of book a life-enhancing book would be, when it comes to it, or even what enhancing means when connected to a book—I suppose it must have spiritual implications—the only writer who actually changed my life for the better in any practical and measurable way was Hank Janson, who gave me what I had for a sex life when I was twelve years old—at that age I had no idea of what was to be found between a girl's legs, but partly assumed, mystically assumed, it would be a prettier, daintier, more feminine version of what was to be found between my own, and I couldn't imagine, of course, how they could interact, hers and mine. So Hank Janson—the titles alone drove my blood wild—*Torment for Trixie*; *Hotsy, You'll Be Chilled*—and on the cover a vivid blonde, blouse ripped, skirt hitched up to her thighs, struggling sweetly against chains, ropes, a gag—and in the top right corner set in a small circle, like a medallion, the silhouette of presumably Hank himself, trench coat open, trilby tilted back, a cigarette hanging from a corner of his mouth.

His real name was Francis Stephen or Stephen Frances, one or the other surfaced in the newspapers when he was on the run in—when would that have been, roughly? The year Hank Janson was on the run, well, it was when I was fifteen or so, and as I was born in 1936: 1936 + 15 = 1951. Yes, that's about right, 1951. Now what the thing was about Hank Janson was that he was—

Start again. Hank Janson.

I kept my Hank Janson library squirrelled away in different nooks and crannies of my bedroom, some under a loose floorboard, and as an extra security measure, I tore the covers off and concealed them between the pages of the books, so I naturally assumed that this secret cache was entirely unknown to my mother, who never mentioned that she knew about it except once, obliquely. She came into the dining room where my brother Nigel and I had just started our breakfast—a meal my mother cooked before dressing for the day—generally she wore a flapping dressing gown over an almost transparent nightie, so I suppose, on reflection, I could have found out what was to be found, or rather not to be found, between a girl's

16

legs by dropping to my knees—but of course both Nigel and I kept our eyes averted, from each other as well as from her, as she flung herself into and out of the dining room talking constantly and comically or reproachfully, pausing to gesture with her cigarette, laughing at something she'd said—

Now the thing about Mummy, Mummy and me, well, actually it was I who she frankly—

Frankly, I was the one she loved to fondle, the one she made sit on her lap, whose legs she stroked, whose hair she ruffled, the nape of whose neck she kissed, etc., and so forth, while Nigel and his father (well, our father, but I tended to see them as a twosome) stood or sat by with the appearance of disdain for all these displays of full-blooded passion—yes, that was it—Mummy and I were the adoring couple, Nigel and Daddy were a pair of disapproving relatives—great-uncle and uncle perhaps, though that doesn't work out—oh yes, it does if you see Daddy as Mummy's uncle, and Nigel as mine, everything slots into place, anthropologically speaking—is anthropology the right science for these delicate matters, or should we be thinking of psychiatry here—well, these days, of course, one should be thinking of column inches in the *Mail on Sunday*, with myself portrayed as Mummy's toy boy, and Nigel and Daddy as the jilted lovers bonding. There is one memory, though, that abruptly and discordantly intrudes itself into the family idyll. There I was, hunched on the lavatory, brooding over my latest Hank Janson, when the door burst open, and there was my father.

'Get out,' I ordered, speaking from a self I didn't know I owned.

'Sorry,' said my father, and got out.

When I eventually came out of the bathroom on to the landing, I could hear their voices from the bedroom, he was talking quietly, with brio, a lively mutter, not his usual tone or style at all, and she was gasping with suppressed laughter—the obvious effort to maintain low audibility being from tact, I like to think, although they both knew the acoustics of the house well enough to know what carried where. I don't know exactly what I anticipated—scenes, showdowns, confiscations certainly, worst of all a long morbid conversation, anyway not parental laughter, my doting Mummy laughing at her wanking (this word didn't exist at the time, at least in my circles) son, so I was at first mortified, then relieved, then mortified again but in a—not comfortable, of course not, but—but secure sort of way. Loved. I can't remember how I sidled into view at breakfast time, so I assume it was as usual, Mummy's long legs scissoring her in and out of the dining room—Daddy didn't have breakfast with us, he had it in bed—this was the marital routine, Mummy down at seven to make a cup of tea, take it up to Daddy with the newspapers and the post, then she'd slip back into bed, then downstairs to make our breakfast, then in term time Nigel and I off to school, he to St Paul's, I to Westminster, and Daddy, shortly afterwards, off to the Belgrave Hospital, near the Oval, where he was the pathologist. We lived in Oakley Gardens, Chelsea, now a swank address, but then a slummy, no, not slummy, a down-at-heel professional classes neighbourhood at a time when the professional classes, particularly doctors, were overtaxed and underpaid, and my father, for instance, hard-pressed to pay our school fees. England of half a century ago, depleted by war, only just emerging from rationing, restricted in travel (sixty pounds per annum per adult), long orderly queues on the pavements outside the butcher's, the fishmonger's, the sweet shops, I could go on listing the deprivations of this victorious nation, because they were all around us, affecting every aspect of our lives, but of course they were, for Nigel and myself and all those of our age and younger, the natural conditions of life, as were the daily civilities—the calm, the sense of safety. There was a working-class estate, the Peabody Buildings, directly behind the small backyards of the houses along our side of Oakley Gardens, and there was Chelsea Manor Street with its 'bombed outs' living on council estates, and a small cluster of prefabs at one end—so there was a continuous if accidental mingling of classes—but I never once, in the seven years we lived there, heard an obscenity on the street, let alone a violent gesture, though occasionally, when going up Chelsea Manor Street to swim in the public baths, Nigel and I would be encircled at an unintimidating distance by a group rather than a gang of working-class boys of our age or older, and jeered at for being posh—and that was it, the class war, as experienced by the two Gray brothers half a century ago, when there really were visibly defined classes, working/lower, lower-middle, middle, upper-middle, and upper—

But enough history, enough sociology, back to 47 Oakley Gardens, some time in 1951, to the breakfast that followed my mortification on the lavatory, Daddy upstairs in bed with his tea, post and papers, Mummy now downstairs, flying about in her transparent nightie, cigarette hanging from the side of her mouth—but no, that's not the breakfast I'm after, it's a subsequent breakfast, some weeks or possibly even months later. She stalked into the dining room, head held high—an ominous sign—in her hands a plate for Nigel, a plate for me, she flung the plates down with a flourish, drew on her cigarette with a flourish, released a long cloud of smoke. 'That filthy man Hank Janson has run away,' she said. 'Did you know that?'

Impossible to describe the effect of those two words—Hank and Janson—coming from her lips. It was mysterious, omniscient, terrifying. How did she know? How? In retrospect, I can see that Mummy being my mother, and having heard from Daddy about the presence of the book (he couldn't have seen the cover, given my posture) over which I'd been bent, with warm wings brooding, as the Jesuit poet, Gerard Manley Hopkins, once described his own solitary labourings—no, no, it was God in the poem, God who did the brooding, with warm wings, ah, my dear! Nothing to do with my sort of brooding at all, although some critics have hinted that the strain of Hopkins's celibacy might have given rise to the explosive, ejaculatory nature of his verse— Now what was I? Oh, yes, Mummy and her 'That filthy man Hank Janson has run away!'

'Where to?' Nigel said at last, thus seeming to demonstrate not simply a lack of surprise, but the possibility of a vast reservoir of knowledge—at the very least of some of the circumstances that would have caused Hank to run.

'He's wanted for writing lewd and disgusting and obscene books,' our mother replied, at an angle to Nigel's question, 'Wanted by the police.' And by me, too, for the same thing. She jabbed her cigarette at us, and left us to it.

There followed a brief squabble as to whose horde she'd unearthed. 'Not mine,' said Nigel confidently, 'I've only got one, and it's behind the wardrobe, I've pushed it so far back I can hardly get at it myself.' He'd done this on purpose, he explained, because he was trying to give up Hank Janson because he was trying to get into the St Paul's rugger colts, and because he was preparing to take communion. 'Well, it's not me,' I said, although it obviously was, my Jansons squirrelled into so many corners that Mother would have needed little inspiration to turn up one of them within a minute or so, once she'd decided to search—or perhaps she always did a search, a routine search, but didn't grasp the significance of what she turned up until her husband reported to her what he'd observed of their son on the lavatory and the *Daily Mail* reported to her that the writer Janson was on the run—these days, of course, he would have been protected by Index on Censorship, PEN, Amnesty International, Writers in Prison.

In fact, he made it to Spain. I know this because I sat next to his agent—he'd been my agent too, for a brief period—on a London bus one afternoon about thirty-five years ago. I can't imagine the context in which Janson's name came up, we certainly didn't know each other well enough to trade information about our youthful sexual habits—anyway he told me that Janson had fled to Spain, where he had written novels about the Spanish civil war which always contained one scene of bondage. Not of the former playful, fanciful kind, in which there was merely male dominance over sweetly rebellious femininity; the Spanish bondage was gritty, nasty, cruel—political, in other words—heroic Republican guerrillas, female rather than feminine (beautiful nonetheless), brutalized by Franco's thugs, beaten, raped, murdered. He (the agent) had been astonished by the change in tone and style, but the thing was, he said, that the passion in the politics was quite genuine—these novels, which he'd written under his real name—Stephen Frances or Francis Stephen—were serious works, properly researched and constructed, with bits of dialogue in Spanish, and one or two—I think he mentioned a trilogy—had been published in hardback. Stephen Frances or Francis Stephen still lived in Spain, prospered there in fact—it was where he'd always wanted to go, just as he'd always wanted to write the novels he was now writing, so actually he was grateful for his enforced exile, grateful that he'd been hounded out of the dark little office in Soho where he'd dictated the saucy and ebullient works of his early phase to a middle-aged woman who was now his wife—no, I don't believe this last bit, I've added it on to my memory of the conversation—why? But that his amanuensis was middle-aged, yes, that makes perfect sense, I can accept that, though it's far more entrancing to think that she was in her twenties, sitting with her legs crossed, skirt hitched, stocking-top visible, a blonde curl tumbling over her forehead, bent over her pad as her pen flies across the page—and Hank, his feet propped on his desk, hat tilted to the back of his head, cigarette hanging from the corner of his mouth (like Mummy), rapping out his sentences—'fought like a wild cat'—'her arms up behind her back'—'bound them tightly together with the stockings I'd unclipped from her suspenders'—'lay there on the floor, panting, eyes flashing fury'—'stared down at the two softly heaving mounds'—'gentle slopes of'—'as she opened her mouth to scream I'—'fastened it behind her neck with my—' He was a small man, the agent said, with crinkly brown hair, and I'll bet he married his secretary, whether he told me he did or not, and they live in a grand little villa outside Malaga, perhaps. I'm glad he came out on the Republican side, though the handcuffs aspect of his writing seems more Falangist—but really there is probably little connection between a man's sexual obsessions and his political inclinations—think of Kenneth Tynan, theatre critic of the Sixties and Seventies, a prominent supporter of all left-wing and libertarian causes, who devoted the last decade of his life to spanking women, thinking about spanking women, brooding endlessly about spanking women—but perhaps that is libertarian, though probably not left-wing, because whatever you think about spanking women—

A few yards from where I'm sitting, writing this, is a very fine-looking, stiff-backed old gentleman, with fine white hair and a calm and steady gaze. His smile is cryptic and serene. He is holding a magazine, which he now and then consults, but mainly his gaze is fixed ahead, making it seem not only calm and steady, but inward-looking, as if his past were some vast landscape that he can keep unfolded, his to survey and command. His wife is possibly younger than he, perhaps a decade younger, but then his stillness and nobly contemplative air make him seem ageless, while she looks as if she's been the same age for most of her life—perhaps since she met him, took control of all the trivial problems of his days and nights—she's stout, stubby—yes, a little stub of a woman, with a small, ugly, determined face, hair cut brutishly short, her eyes bulging slightly, her brow dark and heavy—not exactly angry, rather furiously anxious—she has dreadful varicose veins, knobs of them on her calves, she stumps about in flip-flops, baggy shorts, tending to her seraphic husband, bringing him plastic cups of water, removing the magazine as soon as he loses interest in it, which is almost immediately, putting it back in his hands, helping him out of his chair and into another chair—tending, tending, furiously and anxiously tending, occasionally talking to him in abrupt sentences, sometimes with a whiny tone, sometimes eagerly, pointing out, for instance, that the hotel isn't a hotel, it's composed of small chalets, each one containing a bedroom and a bathroom and a balcony—he gives her a condescending and rather empty attention while she utters these imbecilities—after all, they are inhabiting one of the chalets themselves, and the one they inhabit must look pretty much like all the other chalets, how dare she disturb this distinguished consciousness to so little purpose, is the thought that goes through one's mind as off she goes, to find him an unwanted towel, or take his walking stick from the back of the chair, propping it beside him or putting it between his legs so that his hands can fold around its top—and then once or twice she presses affection on him. Victoria reports that she saw her once bend suddenly, while she was fiddling about his person, and kiss him full on the lips, then fiddle a bit more before kissing him fully on the lips again—this from a little dog of a stumpy woman to a man contemplating the eternities within. Once I saw her take him by the hand and lead him gently to the edge of the lawn, then down the path that leads to the opening to the beach, then several yards across the sand, the two of them toddling hand in hand, it was most poignant, the childlikeness of it. I've just glanced over his shoulder as I passed (deliberately, I must admit) behind him and saw the cover of the magazine that he was holding passively in his lap. It's called *Bravo Spain*, and is evidently a travel/tourist publication, clearly without meaning to him, and it occurs to me that he has Alzheimer's, or one of its variants, and that all her dogged, furious tending, her changes of tone and sudden open and passionate and tender displays of affection are attempts to compensate externally for all he has lost, and no doubt is still losing within— how hopeless it all is, really, there's no getting away from it when one sees such things—the things people do to the very end and then past the very end—and, you know, I can't imagine them married, or young, or in middle age or even the year or so back when he started to go, and when I try, the question persists unworthily, 'Whatever did he see in her?' to which she provides the answer in virtually every one of her actions... If I look elsewhere there is affection to be seen among the many elderly couples in this hotel, hand-holding, caressing, and at night dancing to the unmusical bands and groups—a different one for each night of the week—

It's half past one in the morning, I am at my table, Rollocks is laying the breakfast tables, the sea growls and rustles a few yards away, and I wonder how Harold is. There was a piece in the paper this morning—Saturday—we get the papers here a day late, so it was Friday's *Times* or *Telegraph*, announcing that Harold had cancer of the oesophagus, and then giving a brief account of his life and achievements that read as if it were a compressed combination of a promotional release and an obituary—ghastly to come across it, even though I'd been warned by someone who phoned from London yesterday. I'm not going to write tonight, I shall sit here sipping my Diet Coke, smoke a cigarette, listen to the sea. First I shall write down one word at the beginning of the next line on my yellow pad, and start from there tomorrow. The word I shall write is—

Books

Oh, yes. So books. What books? I left London in such disarray that I couldn't believe we'd get to the airport, let alone to Barbados and the hotel—when it came to packing books I flung what was nearest to hand on to the bed for Victoria to pack, and then, of course, when she was unpacking them and I saw from our balcony all those ideal spots for reading—on the lawns, on the beach, in the bar where I'm writing this, on the balcony itself—well, there's a biography of Richelieu, the only book I brought with some deliberation. I picked it up with pleasure until I twigged that I didn't want it at all, the book I'd chosen with a degree of consideration was the wrong book, I'm not in the slightest bit interested in Richelieu (well, I am—but only the slightest bit), the chap I'm keenly interested in is Talleyrand, who began his political career by taking holy orders, receiving Voltaire's blessing almost simultaneously, and went on to survive the catastrophes of France, in fact could be found near the centre of the catastrophes of France from the end of the Ancien Régime through the revolution, through the Empire, then through the Restoration, then through the Republic—he should have been executed once or twice every decade—'a shit in silk breeches,' Napoleon called him, perfectly accurately, it seems to me, but Napoleon ended up on St Helena, in the custody of a mean-spirited (or straight-laced, depending on your point of view) English civil servant while old Talleyrand was around to welcome Louis the Eighteenth, Napoleon the Third, how did he do it, is what I want to know, playing with fire almost all his life, burning everybody but himself? Now this is a pathetic account of Talleyrand's life, everything I know about him has gone into a fog, which the book on him would have dispelled if I'd brought it, rather than the book on Richelieu, about whom I'm content to remain in a fog—in fact, apart from a general outline of his life (much muddled by my having seen four or five film versions of *The Three Musketeers*)—about the only hard fact I remember is that he suffered from piles, towards the end of his life could scarcely rise from his bed, and when compelled to do so by reasons of state, would have to be carried. There is a very important book—that's what we say these days when wishing to draw attention to what we believe to be a good film, book, play, exhibition, we say that it's 'important', as, for instance, an 'important' new play by so-and-so (me, for instance), we usually say it in an important manner, our voices becoming grave, heavy, episcopal, so what exactly do I mean when I write that there is a very 'important' book about piles waiting to be written—I think I mean that piles might be found to have affected the course of history now and then. No doubt Richelieu, given his steely mind, his patience and his ambition, would have made the decisions he made if he'd been piles-free, but Napoleon at Borodino, a few hours before the battle which led on to the disaster of Moscow, lingering in his tent, hoping his piles would quieten down so that he could be out and about on his horse, which he couldn't bear to mount—you see how one could go on from there—for want of an ointment—there's one currently on the market called Anus-oil, or very nearly that, which is quite soothing, I believe—for want of a tube of Anus-oil the battle of Borodino was lost—drawn, actually, I think, but a strength-sapping draw, and so the unplanned diversion to Moscow—the rest is history. Yup. Now to move with piles into a different field, take Gary Cooper in *High Noon*, a film recognized as a complete turkey when it opened for try-out showings in the Midwest, audiences laughing, jeering, walking out as jaunty, heroic, sunny, even Gary Cooper strode down the streets of his little town, a parody of the classical Western sheriff—the reason he looked so implausible, however, was that all through the shooting he'd been crippled by piles—every step a torment, which he'd tried to disguise by assuming a bogus jauntiness whenever he could manage it; generally he could do one take in this mode, and that was the take the director felt obliged to use. Well, after the first try-out showings, and the public's response, the producers were in despair, should they can the whole affair and leave Gary Cooper to dwindle into the Hollywood twilight, another star who'd ended in a feeble and melancholy twinkling down? They repaired to the editing room to see if they could find any scenes that actually worked, hoping to build from there, but useless, useless, all they had as alternative was Gary's piles-driven gait, simultaneously cramped and bow-legged, his face grimacing in agony, his eyes tortured—until somebody—either the director or the editor, though I suppose it might have been the producer—suddenly saw that in the problem lay the solution. They spliced all the scenes in which Gary's piles were at their most inflamed, and looked at what they'd got— the nobly tortured, stoically enduring sheriff that marked a significant if not actually an important turning point in the history of the Western—downhill, in my view, being the only person I know who found the film phoney and inflated on my first viewing and before I knew the facts, but my opinion is neither here nor there in this account, which is concerned with pointing out the crucial part played by piles in the transformation of the film from out-of-town turkey to an Oscars all-round triumph, with a treasured place—allotted to it by the usual collection of people I'm inclined by nature to disagree with—in the history of the cinema, etc.—though it should be added that further acknowledgement must be made to the magical powers of the editing room, where they added the magnificent theme song sung by Tex Ritter, and the shots of the ticking clock—you can see that it's just been stuck in, the clock, because it's completely bald, so to speak, no human form comes near it, no shadow falls upon it, we just cut to it whenever the director needs to jack up the tension— but mainly the success of the film has to be attributed to Gary's piles, just as Napoleon's failure in Russia has to be attributed to piles— and there are many other stories to be unearthed, I truly believe. What about Coleridge's piles, for instance—discover if there's a connection between the piles, the laudanum and the great hallucinatory poems, 'Ancient Mariner', 'Kubla Khan'—the laudanum, taken to escape the pain from piles, giving him the hallucinations that inspired the poems—was the man from Porlock his dealer, possibly, come to report that his supply had run out, so no more inspiration, no more Kubla? I could go on in this vein— Oh. I've just come back from a swim—as I was cavorting towards shore, doing my very favourite thing in life, rolling myself underwater, down and down, then bobbing up again, then lolling on my side for a while before dipping back down—I have many of the instincts, though none of the grace, of a porpoise, I believe—I saw a kindred spirit, a recumbent porpoise, toes turned up, arms stretched out, head cushioned on the water. It was the wife of the man with Alzheimer's, the Alzheimer widow, as I've come to think of her, not fussing and worrying and scowling, but taking her ease in the ocean, lolling to the manner born—she got out, quite a difficult manoeuvre on this beach, as there is a steep shelf, and the waves can tumble you about, mixing you into a rush of pebbles and sharp little rocks—but her sturdy varicosed legs carried her up over the shelf on to the shore, where she picked up a stone, took aim, I thought at first at me, but she swung it well away, across an unpeopled patch of water, with accuracy and skill—it skipped and skipped, it must have done four long skips, then a sequence of shorter ones before going under. She watched it do this with close attention, then turned, and stumped off up the beach. The little incident gave me great pleasure, even more when I passed her a few minutes later, her damp head pressed on Mr Alzheimer's chest. He gazed smiling over her head, benignly unresponsive—then she set about sorting him out, pushing his sunglasses further up his nose, exchanging his magazine for a book, getting him a cup of water—

It is raining—more accurately it's just finishing raining, all the colours washed out, the beach, the trees, the lawn, looking dun-coloured, drab. In spite of the rain the predators were down in the early hours, marking their beds and chairs with towels that are now soaking— but of course the old hands know that this doesn't matter, when the sun comes out the towels (they're green) will dry out in minutes and there will be their beds waiting for them, all prepared—we've had our own spot, at the back of the lawn, separated from the sea by a path and a low wall—not really a wall as the top is separated from the bottom by evenly spaced little pillars, which leave evenly spaced little gaps, through which you can see the sand, the sea, the rafts and boats, people swimming and of course those four prized spots, one of which I saw the old guy fussing over at 6.30 the other morning. I consider ours to be the best spot in the hotel, really, as you not only have this view in front, but also you can keep an eye on all the people on the lawn—and it's become accepted among the lawn community that these are our places, two beds, one low wooden table for Victoria's beach kit, and a white stool-like table for my cigarettes and ashtray—yesterday a group of three arrived from London mid afternoon, and took the last three beds, which were directly behind us, okay beds but lacking our versatile view. There was something about them that made me immediately uneasy, a woman of about my age, small, and ginger-grey hair, a pretty freckled face with a shrewd and determined look to it—she had an orange hat which she put on and took off regularly, according to some plan to do with how much sun was good for her head and hair, but she seemed to be doing it almost to the minute, as if she'd worked it out mathematically—I pegged her as the ringleader, a woman of steely calculation, designated moves—beside her was a rather slovenly young woman—early forties, probably a daughter, wearing an unbecoming pink hat, cloche-shaped, that pushed her ears down—couldn't really see her face, she wears very large dark glasses, but her body, white, soft and formless, spills all over her bed, and her green bikini bottom has a touch of the nappy about it—there is also a useless-looking man, husband and father, I assume, who comes and goes to report on his success or failure in accomplishing missions appointed by the other two—he came back to say to the daughter that he hadn't been able to find her sunscreen, went off to look for it again in the small zip bag to be found, the mother said, on a shelf in the cupboard, that's where she thought she'd put it, had he thought to look there—he was already on his way. When Victoria and I went for a swim the mother was training her gimlet eyes on a book—I couldn't catch the title, it blends too much into the background design of the cover—but as I say I had my doubts, my suspicions, and cast a look back at them as we stepped on to the sand, and again just before we plunged into the sea—a lovely swim, lovely and long, out to the rafts, towards the next hotel along, an unhappy looking place, on the skids I bet, with only one bed occupied, listless waiters standing with their trays hanging down by their sides, and then back to our beach, sliding under the moving ropes for the buoys—I'm very bad at this, always misjudging, coming up so the rope scrapes my back or catches my heel, infuriating as I'm mildly allergic to the algae that accumulates on the rope, and so get stripy little rashes on my back and heels. It's inexplicable, as I swim easily under water, love to be there, under water, and it's also infuriating because Victoria glides under them with a few effortless movements of the hips and arms—it's probably to do with my being over-buoyant (stomach full of bubbles from Diet Cokes, probably). I should force myself to dive deeper, not just go a few inches under as I immediately, but without realizing it, bob a few inches back up—but going under the ropes, even when there's a stingy rash to show for it, is part of the fun. So out we came from the sea, full of high spirits and the joys of the sea, had a brisk shower under the palm tree and then sauntered across the lawn to our beds, where I noticed immediately my small, white stool-type table had gone, the ashtray lying upside down on the grass, contemptuously discarded. Of course, my cigarettes and lighter, my personal markers, I'd left on the table at the bar, so theoretically, legally, down to the meanest letter of the law, but against every conceivable spirit of it, I had no clear entitlement, beyond the fact that every one of the lawn's occupants knew that the table was lodged in our territory, and belonged to us—specifically to me. I looked towards the group behind, straight at the boss, and then at the small, stool-type table placed where no small, stool-type table had been placed before—there was a tall full glass on it, a straw in it—then looked again at the boss. She had her orange hat on, her eyes, lifted from the book, stared straight at mine, unblinkingly bold, not to say hard, her lips twitched imperceptibly, her eyes went back to her book, fastened there, as with her free hand she lifted her orange hat from her head and put it beside her drink.

So. So I knew. I told Victoria I knew. This morning I rose at half past seven (thinking 'but what's the use?'), peered down from the balcony through the rain, and saw draped over the backs of our beds three green towels. On the white stool of a table was a small bag, presumably waterproof, and on the other table, the small wooden one, some tubes of sun lotion. I trudged through the rain to some beds further down, laid the three green towels on the two beds and the chair, put some unreadable paperbacks (literally, they've been used so often as markers, on wet days and dry, that now the pages are stuck together, saving them from being found unreadable for the usual reasons), trudged back to the room, dried myself, joined Victoria in bed, where I lay with my arm under her sleeping head—thinking on the one hand of Auden's utterly ghastly 'Lay your sleeping head, my love/Human on my faithless arm'—what is 'human' doing here, what other kind of head would his love have—better not go into that—'faithless arm'—'*faithless* arm'! etc. (the worst thing about Auden, I'm coming to realize, is that his lines stick—how come I can quote reams of him, and only fragments of Hardy? And then to misquote Eliot?) and on the other hand how to punish the squatters on our rightful beds, in a hotel where no dog-turds are available owing to an absence of dogs—there is a cat, a nice cat, marmalady, but a touch withdrawn—and, oh, monkeys, there are monkeys at the top of the garden, by the tennis courts, but wouldn't I arouse suspicion if I were to be seen scraping up monkey turds, especially if they turn up later under the green towels of the squatters?

I'm looking at them now, orange hat, pink hat and useless husband, sitting in a row, in our places, facing the sea, reading their books—almost certainly trashy books, from the rapt expressions on their faces—pink hat has just taken off her pink hat, to release a pack of hair so coarsely and bogusly ginger that it must be natural, nobody could do that to their hair deliberately, not at that sort of age, in this sort of hotel—

Mrs Alzheimer is sitting a bit behind them, she is doing a watercolour. Mr Alzheimer is sitting bolt upright beside her, his face wearing its usual expression. On his feet, a pair of enviable blue canvas shoes, beneath them natty white socks that come up to just above his ankles. He has nothing to read in his hands, which are folded calmly into his lap. I think she is talking as she dabs her brush on to the pad. I think I'll get up and stroll behind them, perhaps I'll hear a snatch—

Of course I couldn't loiter, so I only got one sentence. 'Well, why don't you work at it then?' she said, quite ill-naturedly, but I couldn't tell whether she was talking to Mr Alzheimer or herself. I must find Victoria. Time for a swim.

A package

I'm a bit shaken. Distressed would be a better word. This afternoon was mainly more rain until about 4.30, when the rain stopped, the sun almost came out, we were thinking of another swim when the telephone rang. It was the receptionist to ask if I was Simon Gray. I said I was. There was a package, she said, just delivered. I went down and collected it, puzzled—disconcerted even—the only person who would send me a package of anything would be my agent, Judy Daish, and she would certainly have phoned to tell me it was on its way, and furthermore have told me what was in it—anyway I'd asked her not to be in touch unless she had some good news, which means, if you think about it from another angle, that I'd been in receipt of a steady flow of bad news—

The package was, in fact, a large, brown envelope, which contained a small white envelope in which there was a letter from Harold. He was writing in response to my letter of a week or so ago—tapped it out on his Olympia portable, he said in his opening sentence, warning me of typos and spelling mistakes to come—it was a page and a half long, and on a separate sheet of paper there was a poem called 'An old man looks at a cricket match'. The first part of the letter contains a few comments about this and that in my letter and then comes—the centre of the letter, at the heart of it, an account—a terrible account of the state of his health, a concentrated paragraph of pain and bewilderment, typed out on his Olympia portable, with poignant little typos but all his misspellings corrected, the words crossed out xxxx and rewritten—

Now I must tell myself that Harold has not tapped out on his Olympia portable an announcement of his death. He has merely put down, with characteristic clarity, the ordeal that he is undergoing at the moment—the fact that he cannot eat properly, cannot drink (even water) properly, that trying to do either causes him great discomfort, and is sometimes physically impossible. The sentence that most disturbs me—us—Victoria and myself—is that his doctors are completely baffled that this condition should have returned, and more ferociously than before.

I shall stop now. I might go on with this in the morning. I might not—when it comes to it, there isn't much to say—the thing about a close and long friendship—friendship, what an odd word that suddenly looks, as I write it down.

So that's the word I see when I sit down at the table this morning. Friendship. Looks more normal in the daylight, flowed easily out of the nib, and so I can put down brotherhood, and look at it. Hood, what does it mean, the hood in brotherhood? Well, I suppose the ship in friendship has something to do with making—it has an Anglo-Saxon feel to it, schiffen or schlippen to do with making, could it be?—I was very bad at Anglo-Saxon, considering it a waste of time because it involved a lot of learning, no chance at all of flannelling through the exam, which, as a consequence I nearly failed (this was at Dalhousie University, Nova Scotia). I wish now—as is always the way with these things—that I'd worked at it, so that I could, for instance, know rather than guess that the word *schiffen* means to make, or is a past participle, made—and so avoid having to check it when I get home—I don't believe I'll be able to get hold of an *Oxford Concise* here in Barbados—so I'll have to settle for the guess, and turn my attention to the hood in brotherhood, about which I haven't a clue—fatherhood, motherhood, brotherhood—sisterhood—other words with hood as a suffix, I can't come up with a single one, but then I am in Barbados, the morning is balmy, my mind a muddle of passingly agreeable thoughts, and dark ones lodging deeply—hood, hood, come on, come on—riding hood, Little Red Riding Hood, why would a little girl walking through the woods to visit her granny be wearing a riding hood, and what is a riding hood?—inasmuch as I can visualize it, I see it as dark and sinister, as sported by the three horsemen of the Apocalypse, for instance, or the Ku Klux Klan. Is there something in the story I'm failing to remember, an explanation of Red Riding Hood's wearing a red riding hood, it can't be that Hood is her surname, Red and Riding her Christian (given, they try to compel us to say, these days, in case we offend a Muslim) names—highly unlikely, Red is a name for Irish-American baseball players, Riding as a middle name? Well, I suppose it's possible, no odder than my own, come to think of it, Holliday, Simon Holliday Gray. Simon Riding Gray? I like it—Simon

Riding Holliday Gray?—but it's a translation, isn't it, now I come to think of it, it has a German or Slavic or Scandinavian feel to it— the woodsman, the granny—*Grossmutti?*—the wolf, the wolf waffle, no, that was luftwaffe, wolves come into the Nazis somewhere, I'm sure of it—no good going on with this, again wait until I get home, there'll be a book, quite a few books, no doubt, giving the antecedents of nursery stories, as well as all kinds of analyses, Freudian, etc.—disclosing what the wolf really intends when he says, 'All the better to eat you with, my dear,' to L. R. Hood, or Ms Hood—abandon these futile speculations and take the full word 'brotherhood' in all the meanings it has for you, leave it at that, which is quite enough.

But of course I've started thinking about Piers, over a decade younger than Nigel and me, and dead—how long is it now? four years, five years, that long? The unfairness of it. Though what is fairness— On the day that he was born—

Born. Whenever I remember it, it's always in a slack sort of way, Nigel then about twelve, myself ten and a bit. We're playing cricket on the pavement outside the house, and my mother—*our* mother— comes out. She is wearing a hat, looking elegant and in a hurry. She stops, though, to announce with a smile that she has just given birth to a baby boy, we're going to call him Piers, isn't that exciting news, now she's off to meet Daddy, we haven't seen each other for a long time—this is how the scene idles through my mind, and though it's self-evidently wrong, it's always seemed right enough in feeling. Actually, as I think about it properly, I now see that it's a conflation of two memories, the later one, to do with the announcement of Piers's birth mixed up with the early one, when I was about four and a half, Nigel six and three quarters therefore—we're playing in the snow outside our grandparents' house in Montreal, 4047 Vendôme Avenue, our aunt Gertrude is in attendance somewhere but I can't see her in memory, all I see clearly is Mummy, dressed in her fur coat, carrying a small suitcase, walking hurriedly past us, her face averted. We ran over to her, she stopped, we asked where she was going, she said she was going to get some milk, she really couldn't stop, she said, smiling a smile that meant something terrible, and off she went. Then we were told by Gertrude to go inside, where Grandma was waiting to tell us that the milk, so to speak, was back

from top to bottom: Nigel Gray, Simon Gray (middle) and Piers Gray in 1946

in England, with Daddy. Gertrude was a small, thin, wiry woman, with a sharp voice, often irritable or exasperated, doing her best against the grain of her temperament and possibly ambitions, to look after her brother's two children, for whom she had little natural affection, I suspect, but towards whom she had a strong sense of duty. Grandma, apart from being short, was quite the opposite, a roly-poly, playful, laughing—sometimes hysterically laughing— magnificat of a grandmother, who perpetually sucked peppermints (to conceal the sherry on her breath, I now know) who adored me, and whom I adored being adored by. She used to tickle me until I nearly fainted, bundle me about the bed, and hold me into her breasts, enveloping me with her wonderfully pepperminty smell, with its magic additive—Grandpa.

Stopped there this morning. Can't write tonight. Too much of the sun, though of course I sat in the shade as always, but then I must have spent a total of two hours in the sea, the sun beating down on an unprotected and salty head, so I'll just sit for a while, drink a Diet Coke, smoke a few cigarettes, go to bed. Try not to think too much. Probably can't anyway. The inside of my head feels soft and thoughtless, with a muzzy ache going round its rim. Leave a space for tomorrow. Then Grandpa.

Grandpa. He was in his late sixties when we came to Canada. He was short, he had sticking out ears, he was bow-legged, he always had his hair crew-cut, bristly grey it stood in a bundle of stubbles straight up from his head. His Scots accent was still as strong as the day he and his wife—Good God, I've just this second realized I don't know Grandma's Christian name, let alone her maiden name—left Greenock for Canada at the turn of the century. He was a personal secretary to a steel mogul, working in Toronto, or was it Ottawa? from Monday to Friday, returning to Vendôme Avenue late on Friday night, an event much dreaded by me as I occupied his bedroom, and he would carry me from his bed to a sofa in the sitting room, which I found frightening, or to loving slaps and tickles on Grandma's bed, which I found entirely satisfactory, of course, especially snuggling into the doting comfortableness of her—the dread was of the actual removal, the rough, almost violent picking-up, the stiff, indifferent carrying, as if I were logs, the abrupt dropping down—joltingly, if it was on to the sofa, more complicatedly unpleasant, if on to Grandma's bed, never near her, but at the foot, or on the side, in both cases close to the edge. There was no communication between us that I recall, no warning before he jerked me from sleep, no warning before he dropped me—

The truth is—was—that poor old Grandpa wasn't wanted in the marital, and I was, and it was a shortish journey from the sofa to his marital, and my little legs made it often, and what did he have but his bachelor's bed, kept insultingly warm for him by me. He tried his best, though, during the short weekends and vacations, to be a grandpa, taking us on Saturday mornings to a palatial soda fountain, for ice-cream sodas and milkshakes, and spending half-hours with us in the garden on Sundays, throwing baseballs and Canadian footballs to us—probably rather stingingly now and then when throwing to—at—me. He was a gruff man, reserved, seething with unreleased energy, his bow-legged gait rapid and forceful, 'full of vim', as Grandma used to say, with one of her long, tipsy giggles—well, of course he was full of it, with nowhere to put it, being Scots, Presbyterian, faithful, honourable, etc.—except once, into me, with a strap. He'd been in some other room—his bedroom, perhaps, lying, staring at the ceiling, no, no, it was evening, that was the point, a Saturday evening, past my bedtime, I was frolicking on the bed with Grandma, the game being that she would order me to bed, i.e. the sofa, I would pretend to go, then dart back, slide under the bed, reappear where least expected, allow her to catch me, tickle me into helplessness, be ordered to bed—we were at it for hours, it must have seemed to Grandpa, tormenting hours for him, blissful for me, and jolly, jolly, jolly for old Grandma, the wife he was never not in love with, every second of his life since he'd clapped eyes on her at a Greenock bus stop. He erupted into the room, wielding a strap. He seized me by the nape of my neck, ran me into our shared bedroom where he swung me about with one hand, flailed at me with the strap with the other, yelping out half-sentences to do with teaching me to go to bed when I'm told—time I learnt—Grandma stood at the door, swaying, pleading, crying out with the blows that it was her fault, we were only playing, stop James, please stop. And Gertrude, shocked and silent, grappling with different duties and devotions—to the nephew to which she was an unwilling guardian, to a father she revered, to a brother she worshipped—of course, I didn't really know what she was grappling with, didn't know then (too busy with yelps, screams and sobs of my own) and I don't know now. She'd had a fiancé, a pilot shot down in the first year of the war, but the only photograph she ever showed us was of herself and our father, children at a lake, both grinning in bathing suits that in her case really looked like a suit, he in one with straps over his shoulders— Gertrude gave us our breakfast, lunch and tea, took us to the doctor and the dentist, walked us in our early days to school, read to us in our early days at bedtime, but of Gertrude I know almost nothing— in fact I don't know even that she was an unwilling guardian, she might have come to care for us deeply as Mummy sometimes claimed, when feeling called upon to defend the decision to take us to Montreal after war had been declared and lots of U-boats were on the rampage and then to bring us back just before the war's end, still lots of U-boats, but the question here, whether our parents wanted us back or Gertrude and our grandparents wanted us gone, I no longer have a hope of answering, Mummy in later life propounded one or the other, according to her mood—'No wonder they wanted to get rid of you, is *this* how you behaved?' sometimes separated by no more than a few sentences from 'We had to risk bringing you back when we did, we were missing out on your childhood, you see,' her eyes filling with tears, her voice shaking with what often turned out to be laughter—so that—so that really—

Grandpa taught me to swim in the lakes one summer, when I was five. He'd taught Nigel in the summer the year before, that summer he taught me. Held me firmly under my stomach, encouraged me to kick and to strike out with my arms—this wasn't for graceful or stylish swimming, strictly functional, for survival—the moment when he let me go and I didn't for once flounder and sink, but remained in the water, held up by my own mysterious forces and moving an inch or two was the most ecstatic of my life. So Grandpa gave us our swimming, Gertrude gave us our reading, Grandma gave me all the love I needed—and more. 'All you can eat—and more!' reads the sign outside some of the hamburger joints in the States— but the comparison doesn't hold, to be offered more hamburgers than you can eat induces nausea. More love than you need—well, there's no such thing, in a Grandma's case, my Grandma's case. My appetite grew by what it fed on, needing more cuddles, rollings about on the bed, swallowings up in round flesh and rich pepperminty and something-else smells—and a jealous Grandpa to boot.

We were sent back to England some months before the war ended, but I remember almost nothing about it—of the leave-taking, last cuddles etc., nothing of the trip to New York, or of being put on the boat by Grandpa and Gert, of the journey itself nothing, until I come to my mother's face, appalled, as she took in the two thugs, crew-cut, ears sticking out, with Canadian accents, who'd come back in place of the English moppets she'd checked up on outside 4047, Vendôme Avenue, on her way to get the milk.

From Grandma, Grandpa and Gert we got Christmas cards and birthday cards, five dollars inserted, until we'd grown up. I visited them once when I was in my early twenties, stopped by for lunch on my way from London to Halifax, Nova Scotia. Grandma was in her mid-seventies, and though there was no question of my getting any rollings about on the bed, or ticklings and hysteria, there was still something in her eyes when she looked me over from top to toe, and then took my hands in hers and gave them a long, suggestive squeeze. 'Oh, I can tell from these you're a writer,' she said, 'these have never done a day's work in their life, and don't intend to.' And she turned her round, shiny old face up towards mine, and laughed into it a great gust of peppermint and what I could now identify as sherry, which made me feel quite dizzy, really, and a little loose at the knees. Apart from that, I don't think she spoke much. Grandpa sat at one end of the table in the kitchen, I sat at the other, his two women sat between, one on either side, though Gert didn't do much sitting, she either served, or stood waiting to serve, a Black Cat held between fingers that trembled. Her face was gaunt, her eyes sunk, her voice hoarse, she seemed very ill, but of course I didn't know her well enough to ask after her health. Grandpa and I did most of the talking, he asking thoughtful, Scots-type questions in his strong Scots accent about the make of the aeroplane I'd flown in from London, the state of the English economy, which I answered with lies and guesses and other Cambridge mannerisms. I didn't think of how he'd once thrashed me with his belt—perhaps he did, though, and wistfully. The three of them died a couple of years later, within months of each other, from unrelated illnesses, although they were probably connected deaths in the sense that whichever had gone first would have been the crucial prop removed, the other two would follow, of necessity. Gert was the first, of cancer, in her early fifties, Grandpa next at eighty-six—working almost until he died, his employers under the impression that their Scots dynamo was still in his sixties, then Grandma of liver, I suppose, a bit more lingeringly and expensively than the other two, although Grandpa's life savings were almost entirely used up on Gertrude's medical bills, which were enormous. He must have believed that property was theft, or a waste of capital, or provided career-debilitating security—anyway, for whatever reason, he rented every house they lived in, including 4047 Vendôme Avenue, and he died penniless. Grandma's bills in a nursing home were paid for by their son, my father, who, having moved back to Canada himself (Halifax, Nova Scotia) was able to afford them. I suddenly find myself remembering other stuff about our time in Montreal, to do with Gert and her Black Cat which was cork-tipped, and about smoking, that I was a heavy smoker in Montreal by the time I was seven, but I don't have the desire this evening—a lovely evening, sun hovering before sinking, a light breeze, the sea a trifle turbulent from an earthquake somewhere or other, I'm going down to the beach.

Just back. The red no-swimming flags are up. I decided to ignore them in favour of a bit of rough and ready surfing, using my stomach as a surfboard, well, surftub, getting a kind of bum's rush on to the beach, where I rolled on to my front, heaved myself to my feet, lunged back into the waves. I did it lots and lots of times.

The dreadful thing about this most necessary (so I believe) holiday is that I can't afford it. I'm overdrawn at the bank, in debt all over the place, have pretty well no income. On the other hand I don't really mind. Some years back I would have minded. But some years back I could have afforded it. Even the bar bill, when I was a four-bottles-of-champagne-a-day man. But that was some years back. Now I don't have a bar bill, worth speaking of. But even though it's not worth speaking of (Diet Cokes, fruit juices now and then) I can't afford it. But as I don't mind, why think about it? Think instead about the—

Alzheimers? really? What about them? Yes, the thing is that there they were, the two of them, this late afternoon, sitting at the far end of the bar, where it opens out to an expansive view of the sea, the waves crashing a few feet below, against the rocks and the wall. They were facing another couple, elderly, English, with a table not exactly between, because the other couple were sitting at it, the Alzheimers quite a bit away from it, which gave the impression that the Alzheimers, formal and stiff, were being interrogated. Or that they were doing the interrogating. My plan (which I executed) was to drift around them in a roundabout fashion, picking up any audible scraps of chat. I had to get quite close to hear anything, as the sea was loud, the voices low and the conversation, when the non-Alzheimers were speaking, free-flowing, unstructured, and when you could hear it, nearly meaningless. In fact, the first sentence I understood was spoken by Mrs A. Her voice had a bark to it—her social voice, I suppose—and she has a tendency to 'ink' her 'ings', as for example, now, when she said: 'You weren't thinkink of stayink there, then?' They chattered back that no, they'd had a good look around, it hadn't suited them, but they'd liked the pool, the grounds—all this about a hotel that's recently opened to incredulous applause on the island: applause because it's smart, handsome, comfortable, and so forth, incredulous because it's plonk in the middle of Barbados, miles from the sea, and who wants to be in Barbados if you can't be up to your waist within minutes of leaving your room. 'I wouldn't stay there,' said Mr A, in a clear judicious voice, 'not if I can be staying here. All this—' he gestured with his stick, stiffly but quite dramatically towards the vast and billowy etc., over the rim of which the sun etc.—'all this! And we've got a pool,' he stabbed upwards with his stick—'into the bargain.' Mrs A looked at him with controlled lasciviousness. 'That's right, he didn't like it at all, did you, Willard?' Willard, whose accent I now identified as Canadian, confirmed that no, not at all, he hadn't liked it, wouldn't stay there for a single night. 'Nice lunch, though,' he added, 'Worth going for a lunch.' So. So. Mr Alzheimer hasn't got Alzheimer's. Not only is he capable of speech, he's capable of opinionated speech. Of course, the fact that he's Canadian might have given rise to the misunderstanding, in that one sometimes feels, not that Canadians can't remember, but that they look and behave (some of them only, of course, and even they only sometimes) as if they haven't got that much to remember—not burdened by too much history (Europe), nor animated by too much aspiration (US) might be a rush-to-judgement historian's way of looking at Canadians, though about the quickest, funniest, wisest man I know is Canadian—though actually he's Jewish and basically he comes from Poland—his father was a rabbi who specialized in circumcision (he developed the knack shortly after arriving in Halifax, Nova Scotia, and discovering that there was a shortage of rabbis in this field)—in 1938 he was only just restrained by members of his family from returning to Poland because he'd had enough of Canadian anti-Semitism—which doesn't mean that he preferred the German variety, only that he hadn't much of a nose for the future. But to get back to Willard—no, there's nothing to get back to, really, except an entirely fresh burst of speculation—Willard is a super-rich Canadian recovering from a stroke—how about that? suits the rearranged facts—and his wife, the late Mrs Alzheimer, is probably, given her displays of almost gloating physical affection, only recently his bride—so Willard is a widower, and she—given also the impression she conveys of long familiarity—possibly an employee—secretary, perhaps? Long-time nurse of the long-time ailing now-defunct first Mrs Willard—or—or—

Well, there's another guest we should take a look at, turned up this morning in a red cap, white blouse, red pantaloons, red woollen socks, and black sandals—turned up on the beach in this outfit, a man of about fifty, a New Yorker from the sound of him, and quite definitely the sort of chap most easily described by the sort of word one isn't allowed to use any more—faggoty, queer, pansy, etc.—there are distinctions between them, I know, but he sort of blends them all together—oh, hag-fag probably gets it all in a hyphenated one, as he hangs out with a dwarfish and dour middle-European lady, who, a few days ago was hanging about with a young—well, much younger than she is—rather jolly woman who one would have taken for her niece if they hadn't spoken to each other in English, with thick but distinctly different accents. Hag-fag, by the way, had a natty little camera with him, which he pressed into the hands of one of the waiters, then perched himself on the wall, the sea behind and virtually under him, and posed for a picture of himself. Just himself. In his red socks, black sandals, red pantaloons, white blouse, red cap—his hag abandoned under a palm tree on the beach—I'm going to stop this. I'm coming to the end of the pad, we go home the day after tomorrow (Monday) so I shall leave the remaining half page open for last minute pensées—or leave it blank, perhaps.

As Mr A passed me in the bar after lunch he pointed with his stick to the ice bucket which contained a bottle of water, and said, 'I can see you're a man who knows how to live,' thus reviving memories of myself of six years ago, sitting at the same time of day with a bottle of champagne in the bucket. Mrs A was nowhere in sight. So Mr A—from immobile and mute, to garrulous and roaming. I found more grace and nobility in him when he had Alzheimer's.

When I was changing into my swimming trunks in the bedroom, I caught my naked self in the mirror. Great stomach drooping, like a kangaroo's pouch, though without the opening at the top, thank God—when I stretched my arms out, their pits seemed to have dewlaps, or would wattles be the word? Old. Old's the word.

Came across a discarded section of *The Times*, several days out of date—a medical supplement, in this issue dealing with cancer of the oesophagus, Harold's cancer. Horrible reading—hideous statistics. Hope Harold doesn't come across it, or he'll think he's a goner. Why would they publish statistics of that sort—presumably the medical profession knows them, and current and future patients will be demoralized by them—they certainly can't be helped, can they? Then saw in today's (yesterday's) *Telegraph* a review of Harold's sketches at the National, in one of which he also performed—reviewer said Harold had lost a lot of hair, looked frail, had also lost some of his commanding presence—was this necessary? Could he simply not have reviewed the sketch, Harold's acting—but today's today, even in yesterday's *Telegraph*, and we don't do that these days.

Every night there's a lizard, light grey lizard, about three inches long, on the wall of our terrace, chasing a black moth around the lamp. Every night they go around and around the lamp, in loose, zigzaggy circles.

Beside me on the table as I write this last sentence on the back of the last page of the pad, there is an envelope addressed to Rollocks containing some money and a note thanking him for looking after me. I add that I look forward to seeing him next year. Well—

A death by smoking

Well, here I am, back in London, dizzy and faint from jet lag, or possibly from all the usual remedies, etc. that Victoria has pressed on me to counteract jet lag, or possibly from all the cigarettes I've smoked to make up for the cigarettes I couldn't smoke from the time we passed through security at Barbados airport to the time we got out of Gatwick—a matter of twelve hours, most of them spent conscious, not smoking—most odd that I never mind, in fact scarcely notice, not smoking when I'm officially forbidden from doing so, but the moment I'm a free man I smoke virtually double to make up for the long period of obedience. Ian was probably killed by cigarettes, a fate he accepted stoically enough—a wry shrug, a little grunt of laughter—until it was on him. Even then he accepted the logic of it, as a natural consequence of a self-destructive and therefore unnatural habit, but to the end he couldn't or wouldn't stop. Another friend of mine, another close, good friend died from cigarettes—emphysema, in his case—but he tried to stop as soon as he became ill—he spent the six or seven years in which his lungs shrivelled fighting, and losing, the battle against his addiction, thinking that it would follow the same pattern as his battle against alcohol, in which he'd ultimately triumphed. A heroic tussle, it had been, his tussle against alcohol, entailing many squalid capitulations along the way—he was a great presence for me when I had to stop drinking forever, never ever patronizingly the forerunner, always treating me as I longed to be treated, as the only man who'd ever had to give up alcohol—so he died dry, sober, full of hatred for the old drinking self that had wasted twenty years of his life, and still waging a pitiful last campaign against his smoking self—giving up on his deathbed. It was a chosen death, as a matter of fact, he was offered either a few months lingering helplessly, rasping out short, stabby breaths, or a double or so ration of morphine and an immediate release. It was a decision he made in clear consciousness, to that extent an enviable death, but it was slightly marred, in my view, by his wife's odd sense of style. As he was slipping from the scene, she pressed into one hand a glass of whisky, and between the fingers of the other, a lighted cigarette, thus turning him in the last moments of his life, when too enfeebled to resist but still conscious enough to be aware, into an advertisement for the two things that had destroyed his life. Though I suppose if he'd been photographed and circulated, he might have served as the ghastliest of warnings— look what I've done to myself, and with both hands. She described the doing of it, the getting of the lighted cigarette between his fingers, the curling of his fingers around the glass—she'd poured the whisky in after she'd got the glass firmly settled, she said—I asked her with what tenderness I could muster why she'd done it, well, she said, well, that's how she remembered him in his heyday, when she first met him (both in their mid-forties, divorced, with children) for her he'd been the most glamorous, flamboyant, chain-smoking, whisky-guzzling—and that's how she'd go on thinking of him, that's how he'd like to have gone out, didn't I think so? 'He wouldn't have been seen dead—' I wanted to say, but couldn't, as actually he had been, pretty well—also she was brimming with grief, exhilarated with it, as people sometimes are when they assist a loved one to cross the line, and she had a theatrical background (her father had been famous in musical comedy) and so what could I say—well, volumes, really, but I didn't, hoping that a brief silence would also be a deep and eloquent one. 'I knew you'd approve,' she said, confirming Wittgenstein's remark, which I usually think is nonsensical, that our understanding of the world depends on the way we interpret the silence around us. And mine wasn't even around her, it went down the telephone line, straight at her—but can we say that she misinterpreted it, and thus failed to understand the world, or at least the world inasmuch as I wanted her to understand it, hence *my* world? Am I saying that she misunderstood my world because she failed to understand my silence—but can a silence be mine, or yours, or his or hers? A silence down the telephone is the telephone's silence, open to any interpretation, and she decided to interpret it in terms of her world (i.e. her grieving impulse to create a glamorous last image of her dying/dead husband) which leads me to assume that he must have been silent when she arranged the cigarette and the drink in his hands, incapable one assumes of vocal consent or protest. El Cid springs to mind here, strapped dead on to his horse to lead the charge that drove the Muslims from Spain, played in the film, both dead and alive, by Charlton Heston, who defined the distinction between these two states by being noisy when alive, mute when dead, but actually more eloquent dead than when alive. And you could say that my friend was eloquent in death, but it wasn't his own eloquence, it was his wife's, who offered it up for an interpretation that I completely understood and that I could meet only with a silence of my own which she completely failed to understand but assumed she'd interpreted correctly—though think of it this way, if she'd asked me to interpret my own silence with a simple question, i.e. 'Why are you being silent, Simon?' most likely I'd have said, 'Oh, I'm only being silent because—because um—I can't think of anything to say—um—just thinking—imagining him there—dying, dead, a cigarette between his—and a glass of Scotch, was it, why Scotch, by the way? His drink when he drank was vodka or gin, though admittedly when those weren't available anything alcoholic would do, I remember his breakfasting once off the dregs of his last bottle of gin and about a quarter of a pint of port, mixed into a coffee mug—' and so from there we would have escaped from the attempt to understand each other's world through the interpretation of each other's silences, by swapping anecdotes about the beloved dead when in his heyday as a smoker and a drinker. *Requiescat.* □

ANUBIS
Paul Murray

Here in space you don't often get the chance to meet women, so Taylor and I are pretty excited when we get the signal from over Tau Ceti direction: two female bipeds, mating-age, in what looks on the screen like one of those vintage Aulaab roadsters. It's been months since we've so much as spoken to another living soul—months of just me and Taylor and of course the damn asteroids, rolling endlessly across the monitors like herds of petrified buffalo over some invisible plain—and to be honest, by this point Taylor is beginning to get on my nerves. A little Taylor goes a long way, and by this point I have had a lot of Taylor. Actually it's not even strictly speaking accurate to say that Taylor and I are pretty excited, because when I first go to tell him about the signal he just looks at me with that blank look he has.

'Two female humans, mating age,' I say to him, making my hands into laser guns and firing them and blowing imaginary smoke from the fingertips.

'Oh,' Taylor says, with the blank look. 'What are you going to do?'

'What do you think I'm going to do,' I say. 'I'm going to hail them.'

'Oh,' he says again, and then: 'But, what about the mission?'

'The mission?' I say.

'Well, yeah, I mean,' he says, swivelling his chair in the direction of the monitors, on which the little green lumps representing asteroids are rolling, rolling.

I give him a kind of a weary look as if to say, Two females, Taylor, for God's sake, and then I do actually say, 'Technically, Taylor, this is a part of our mission.'

'Right,' he agrees. But at the same time he picks up the Manual and starts flipping through it looking for our mission statement. Already I can feel my good mood ebbing away and being replaced by irritation, and as we very rarely meet women out here and so I am not that frequently in a good mood, this irritates me even more. I pull the Manual out of his hand and tell him that as commanding officer I call the shots in this ship, and the shot I am calling right now is for us to hail these ladies and exchange data about the region with them and then depending on how things are going maybe see if they'd like to have a little dinner. Am I making myself clear, I ask Taylor. Taylor says yes sir and gives me his dutiful yes-sir look, which frankly annoys me even more than his blank look. 'And let's not have any screw-ups this time,' I say meaningfully before leaving the room.

Back in my quarters, I soon find my good mood returning. I put on a clean shirt and a blazer and then thinking what the hell I take some medals from the box on the shelf and pin them to my chest. Humming a tune to myself I go up to the bridge and activate the communicator and hail the Aulaab roadster, which is now within a couple of parsecs of us on the starboard side.

It takes a few moments for a connection to be established, and as I wait I gaze out into space, or rather it gazes in on me. I have to confess that it makes me a little uncomfortable, space, I mean. It makes me uncomfortable that there should be so much of it—so much nothing. So much nothing, looking down its nose at you because you are something; peering down at you in amusement as you labour along under the burden of your somethingness, much as a lion might peer down at an ant. It doesn't seem right to me, this arrangement. It lacks balance. No matter how many runs I've made out this direction, it still gives me the heebie-jeebies.

So occasionally I make decisions which, if you were adhering to the letter of the law, might be considered strictly speaking outside our mission brief. I mean if you were going by the book, you would have to side with Taylor in the view that we should not be trying to break from Procedure in order to get invited over for coffee or a drink or perhaps something more substantial with these ladies, whoever they are. But what I say is, if you were out here for months on end you would not be going by the book either. If you were stuck on a tiny ship in the middle of all this damn nothingness with no one but Taylor to talk to, which frankly many of the asteroids would be better company, you would be hailing people first chance you got, and you would be damn glad to see the communication console blinking as it does now and a wave of static passing over the glass and all that space being replaced by a pretty blonde in a purple jumpsuit.

The blonde has a button nose and these dimples when she smiles that immediately chase my morbid thoughts away. She issues the standard Universal Protocol Greeting; I give her the standard UPG response. Then I ask her what a good-looking girl like her is doing out in this godforsaken neck of the woods. She laughs and says that she and her associate are monitoring asteroid distribution patterns as part of a study of the Thin Gravity phenomenon. I don't know what she's talking about but I tell her What a coincidence, because Taylor and I happen to be in the asteroid business ourselves. Taylor has just arrived on to the bridge behind me. He has somehow gotten his shirt buttoned into his jacket. I point this out to him and he starts fiddling with the buttons and getting entangled with his tie and basically making the whole thing worse. To be honest I have no idea how Taylor even got this post. I suspect there was some serious string-pulling.

The blonde is called Regina, and from what I can make out of the bridge behind her that Aulaab she is driving is a high-class piece of machinery. Leather upholstery, one of those McIntire rotators—that stuff can fetch a pretty penny, if you know the right people. Lurking in the background, I see now, is the second mating-age female. She has steely-grey hair like the undercarriage of our ship and two big louring eyebrows which not to be unkind but they are for all intents and purposes one eyebrow. Also I am wondering if the computer has made a mistake about her being mating-age.

'And who's this, your sister?' I say to Regina.

'This is my first officer, Veronica,' says Regina.

'How do you do,' I say to Veronica. Veronica stares at me without so much as a twitch. I turn back to Regina and tell her that we've run into a little problem, which is that we've totally run out of antimatter for our antimatter drive. This of course isn't true; ships don't run out of antimatter, not at this particular point in history. I mean this place has its problems, but a scarcity of antimatter is not one of them. As such, asking for antimatter is kind of a code. It's like calling in to your neighbour for a cup of sugar; it's understood to be merely a pretext for getting something else. By the same token, when Regina, blushing ever so slightly, tells me that their ship is *heaving* with antimatter, so why don't we come over and help ourselves, this would again be sort of a figurative use of the word, given that antimatter does not have weight or volume in the conventional sense. This kind of flirtatious to and fro is quite common in space conversation. It's because of all the nothingness, it tends to bring out people's more intensive urges and emotions.

I give her a wink and say we'll be right over. We sign off and Taylor trudges reluctantly after me to the trans room. 'Time check, Taylor,' I say, as we're waiting for the transporters to charge. He doesn't reply. I look round and see him staring at me, or more particularly at the holdall I have just taken from the storage unit, with an apprehensive expression. 'Time check, Taylor,' I repeat.

'Two hours twenty-six minutes,' he mumbles.

'That's more like it,' I say, stepping on to the telepad. If he thinks he is going to make me feel guilty, he has got another thing coming. All this talk about mission statements and legality and exploiting people is pretty disingenuous on Taylor's part. He couldn't tell you our mission statement if it was written on the back of his hand. No, the real reason Taylor is acting apprehensive and reluctant at this point is that Taylor is not good with women. He is clumsy, at the best of times he is clumsy; and when he is in the vicinity of a female mating-age woman, that clumsiness becomes a thousand times worse, such that I think it would probably be physically quite dangerous, being in a sexual intercourse situation with Taylor, and sometimes I even feel a little guilty, taking him along, although to the best of my knowledge he has never gotten as far as actual sexual intercourse with anyone. Basically the thing about Taylor is that he does not like being a man. Or rather, he does not know how to be a man. And I agree, it's not something they can teach you in Training. It's more like a dance, you can either pick it up or you can't: and that's the beauty of it, I tell him, that is the strange beauty of it. Because there are moments, if you are doing it right, when you get completely caught up in it: and all the asperity of this universe, all the coldness and the forward-rushing of time and the never-ending bombardment of sensations that is like standing in a meteor shower, all of that conjoins in an instant to create a surge of something so rich and white-hot that it is almost too much to bear; you can really see the point of it, at moments like that. But that is not how it is for Taylor. If life is a dance, then Taylor is a man with two left feet. In fact, he is a man composed entirely of left feet. Life is a dance and Taylor is top to bottom made from left feet and even as we stand on the telepads and the transformer hums with gathering power, I am trying to limit the damage incurred by going on a double date with him.

'Did you read the Manual?' I say.

'Of course,' he says, which is what he always says.

'Did you?'

'Yes,' he insists, with a wounded look.

'So I suppose that means there aren't going to be any screw-ups this time, are there,' I am about to say, but then the transporters lock and engage and there is the familiar deep-down sense of relief as we are split apart into a zillion different molecules, and then the familiar sense of panic and entrapment as we are re-gathered into a single time and place, in the trans room of the Aulaab.

Regina is waiting for us, practically bouncing up and down with excitement. She has changed from her purple jumpsuit into a low-cut silver jumpsuit which shows her attractive physique. Behind her, Veronica has not changed into anything and is glowering at us like our boots are covered in dog faeces and we are treading the dog faeces all over her ship. A single glance is enough to confirm everything I thought back on the bridge, viz., that she is a classic man-hater. 'The grey-haired one's yours,' I whisper to Taylor out of the side of my mouth.

'Great!' Taylor whispers back. Sometimes I almost feel sorry for him.

Regina has the antimatter ready for us in a little plastic case with a picture of cats on it. 'But we're just about to eat,' she says, 'so if you boys wanted to stay a little longer...?'

'We wouldn't be inconveniencing you?' I say.

'Not at all,' she says.

'Shouldn't we be getting back to the ship?' Taylor says.

'No,' I say. 'We'd be delighted,' I tell Regina, and she leads us down to the Dining Area.

Dinner itself is an ordeal, as always. I have to keep a constant eye on Taylor. Put him in a room with a woman and he forgets everything, and I mean everything. For instance, when Regina boots up the CyberChef and asks him what he wants, he goes totally blank. For a good thirty seconds he stands there going uh, uh, until I step in and say that we'll both just have a club sandwich. That bails us out of that one, but the grey-haired man-hating one is already suspicious and she keeps asking awkward questions. 'That's a funny kind of a ship you've got,' she says, squinting at me. 'It came right up out of nowhere. One minute our radar is empty, the next there you are popped up right beside us.'

'Probably just the asteroids, Ma'am, interfering with the sensors,' I say, taking a bite of my club sandwich. 'So,' I say, 'you ladies are doing some work on Thin Gravity?'

'Yes,' Regina says, and goes into a long and very complicated explanation involving Wallace space and curved densities. I put my hand over my chin and nod and go, 'Mmm, mmm.'

'And what about you?' Veronica says sharply. 'What are you doing in this sector?'

'Looking for quartz,' Taylor says, before I can stop him.

'Quartz?' Regina says, her pretty face puckered up in puzzlement.

'Ha ha,' I say. 'Quartz. I should have warned you ladies that First Officer Taylor here is quite the comedian. Quartz indeed. Imagine the two of us spending months on end in the middle of nowhere looking for worthless quartz. Ha ha ha. No, the two of us are what you might call archaeologists. Seeking out remnants of lost worlds, lost civilizations.'

'Out here?' Regina says, puckering up again. 'In the asteroid belt?'

'You'd be surprised,' I say. 'The past is everywhere,' I add in a moment of inspiration. Everyone seems impressed by this and things begin to pick up. On the other side of the table I overhear Veronica ask Taylor where he's from, and I relax a little, as this is something that Taylor and I have practised rigorously beforehand and by now he has it more or less by heart. His childhood by the Bluestacks, his beloved dog Finn, his mother's home-made bread, fishing for carp in the mountain lakes. The last time we timed it it ran to about seventeen minutes, so—after catching his eye—I hastily finish off my sandwich and turn to Regina and say how about a guided tour of the ship. She agrees eagerly and I relax a little more and think that this time we might actually be getting somewhere.

First I have her take me down to the engine room. To the neophyte, this might not seem like an obvious arena for the making of sweet music. To those of us who have made a study of women, however, who have explored the mysteries of their language and desires, their seemingly whimsical yens and foibles, the engine room is pure gold. All that heavy machinery, all that compressed power waiting to be unleashed at the touch of a button—never underestimate the aphrodisiac effect of a good engine room. And your Aulaab, of course, has one of the finest of its kind. The little touches are what really make it, the little flourishes—this finishing, for instance. 'This finishing is magnificent,' I say to Regina. 'What is it, jet? Obsidian?'

'I'm not sure,' Regina says. 'Veronica takes care of all this stuff.'

She giggles meaninglessly, the antimatter drive glowing night-time blue against her face. We pass on to the tractor add-on they use to break up asteroids. I draw imperceptibly closer to her; without stopping talking, she backs infinitesimally nearer to me. It's these subtleties of motion and of interconnection, which really throw someone like Taylor, that I love about this place. To the onlooker we will hardly seem to have moved, but we are dancing a dance here: a dance sensible only to the two of us, which will cancel out temporarily the coldness of all that space. The two of us are experts and we complement each other beautifully. And the ship complements us too: the ship, the very engine parts presently caressed by Regina's demonstrative hands. Because although the technology might not to the modern point of view be much more than balsa wood and rubber bands, you can still see the craft that went into its making, you can still sense beneath the primitiveness the same subtle poetry at work—a kind of secret knowledge behind the stuff you actually see in front of you, that if you get close you can feel getting into your head and making it swim, like the scent of flowers hooshing up to hit you in a room that has been unopened for thousands of years—or like music, like very distant music. In Ancient times, for instance the times of the Egyptian astronomer Ptolemy, they believed the universe was composed of a series of spheres, which when they struck off each other made a sound like chimes. Earth was at the centre, then the sky, the planets, the constellations—each one a sphere inside another sphere, and if you listened very closely you were supposed to be able to hear it: the universe like a clockwork toy, creating this dimly audible music. They were completely wrong, of course. But you can see what they were getting at when you are with a woman like Regina, when even though there is no music, it feels like there is. And that's why a ship like the Aulaab would fetch crazy amounts of money, if only you had some way of towing it back.

By now it's clear that Regina and I understand each other, and that at some level she may even share my sense of urgency. We have a cursory look into the arboretum and the Quantum Lab: then we find ourselves in her bedroom. 'Although I don't know that there's anything to interest you here,' Regina jokes nervously.

'There's plenty,' I say with a smile; from the corner of my eye I see her pass her hands quickly up and down her body. Romantic overtures aside, there is actually plenty to interest me in her bedroom. In one corner is a halogenarium: I tap on the glass and see the little gaseous clouds come to life, combining into new and breathtaking colours as they pass through each other. By her bed there is an elegant Quasar lamp, releasing light in slow rolling waves. And there on her worktop is what looks like an—

'Espresso maker?'

'Yes, do you want some?'

I turn it over in my hands. The curving hexagonal top, the mirroring curve of the base, the molecules of silver metal bound together with such conviction, such force of belief. 'A Coffee Boy, right? European model? I'm guessing, what, 2776? 2780?'

'I don't know,' Regina says.

'Probably more like 2780,' I decide.

'I just picked it up in a department store,' Regina says, shrugging. She takes it out of my hands and sets it back down on the counter. 'You know an awful lot about coffee makers.'

'Hobby of mine,' I say. 'Regina, you wouldn't happen to have a Tums, would you? I think I may have eaten that club sandwich a little too quickly.'

'Let me check...' With a look of concern, she goes into the en suite bathroom. I put the coffee maker in my holdall and also a nice star-clock. I'm looking at the halogenarium and wondering how it would transport when Regina comes back with a box of antacids and I decide that there are more pressing matters at hand.

She has reapplied her lipstick: it contains some kind of miniature sequins that sparkle there on her lips, like flakes of mineral in a handful of clay. 'I hope you're not coming down with something,' she says.

'Oh no,' I say. 'It's just that—well, to tell you the truth it's a little strange, having someone to talk to after all this time. I mean someone I can really...talk to. I suppose it gets me a little overexcited.'

A dimple appears where she is trying to conceal a smile: 'It must be hard, being an archaeologist,' she says, wandering over to the far wall. 'Spending all your time with lost civilizations. It must be lonely.'

This isn't the first time I've had this conversation, and I have an excellent speech about how although you do necessarily spend a lot of your time digging up relics and dead things, what you ultimately learn from them is that while the accoutrements of life may change, people themselves, even over thousands of years, stay pretty much the same—that the way they live, the way they (pausing momentarily) *love* remains constant, so what you as an archaeologist end up with is a sense of (a) the indomitableness of the human spirit and (b) how great it is to be alive as opposed to dead, and how we should all really make the most of it. At first glance this may seem rather high-flown and not really to the point: however, those of us who have actually made an effort to comprehend women know that the whole endeavour will rise or fall on these seemingly insignificant details. Essentially what's happening here is that the woman is seeking assurance that the person she is about to bang is not just some schlub who will not appreciate it—that she is not, as the phrase goes, casting pearls before swine. You could of course argue that she is kidding herself, given that she is just going to bang this person and not marry him, and as such it doesn't matter whether he's a schlub or not. But this would be to miss the point: which is that the two of you are dancing a dance, that you are seeking out that underlying, inaudible music, even if you don't necessarily know it, even if you can't say it in so many words. And usually this speech is something I do exceptionally well, beautifully even. But just as I am about to begin, Regina pushes a button on the viewer, opening it on to the black wastes outside: and confronted by those billions of miles of emptiness, I find the words fly out of my head, and I just say, 'Well, you know, it pays the rent.'

'But it must be sad,' Regina reflects. 'I mean all those things you learn about, they're gone forever. So it must be like, the more you know about them, the more gone you realize they are.'

'Mmm,' I say. Generally the response at this point should be something about how although there is no getting around the fragility and transience of life, being an archaeologist also gives you a sense of life's permanence, in that you realize that life is constantly repeating certain archetypal situations, and also you realize how great and affirming it is to get to take part in these archetypal situations, the unspoken subtext being that I personally am very skilled at these archetypal situations. But suddenly I'm finding it difficult to concentrate. It's the damn space—it's like I can feel it pressing down on me, bending me out of shape, even though I know that this is not the case, space being a vacuum. I try to change the subject by complimenting Regina on her physique and asking if she has ever trained as a gymnast or a professional athlete. But she is like a dog with a bone. Staring out of the viewer she starts asking me questions about what civilizations we've studied, and how they came to an end, and how can a whole civilization just come to an end. Soon I am beginning to actually genuinely experience painful indigestion. It is a coldness, a hollowness—as if space were now inside me, as if I had unknowingly ingested it with the sandwich and now it was expanding, and the more she talks the more it expands and the stronger the urge becomes to abandon the operation and flee out of her room back to the transporters—when there is a shriek from outside and Regina and I look at each other and then we both run back to the Dining Area, where Taylor has obviously made some sort of significant screw-up because the aggressive grey-haired woman has left her linguine and is standing with her back pressed up against the CyberChef holding a kitchen knife, presumably to defend herself from Taylor, who is sitting at the table with the apologetic expression that I am all too familiar with.

'What's going on in here?' I say, attempting to take control of the situation and make it look like whatever the problem is, it is Taylor-specific and nothing to do with me. 'Regina, get away from him,' Veronica gasps to Regina.

'What is it, Veronica?' Regina says, my poor sweet innocent Regina.

'These people,' Veronica sort of hisses through her teeth, 'these people, I don't know who they are but they are not human. They are not human.'

'Not human...?' Regina says slowly.

'Hold on there,' I break in. 'Time out. Those are pretty hefty accusations to be throwing around at people. Why don't we all just take a minute and calm ourselves down, and then we can work out—'

'He said to me,' Veronica sort of yelps to Regina, pointing at Taylor with the knife, 'he said—he said he grew up underwater! He told me his mother had fins, and that the, the dog made him bread—'

'Well you see, Taylor,' I attempt to intervene, 'it's important to bear in mind that Taylor tends to express himself in a way that at times can seem—'

'He told me,' Veronica says, 'he told me that I had "nice ducts".' She draws a racking breath, then bursts into tears.

'Nice ducts?' repeats Regina, looking to me in bewilderment.

'Ladies,' I say, 'this is all just a big misunderstanding.'

'They are impostors!' Veronica is shouting, even though Regina is now standing right beside her.

'If you'd just let me explain,' I say.

'Get off our ship!' Veronica makes a lunging gesture at me with her knife.

From bitter experience I know that once you have reached this point, with people reaching for weapons, there is really no coming back. The rational thing to do would be to cut our losses and go, while we at least have the clock and the Coffee Boy. But I am not thinking rationally at this point. The poisonous hollowness inside me is spreading. Am I going native? Is this how these people feel all the time? I don't know: I don't care. All I know is that it is more important than ever that I have sexual intercourse with Regina. She is the serum; she is the antidote. So instead of leaving I keep trying to fix things.

'What we have here is a simple crossed wire,' I say. 'First Officer Taylor just gets a little confused. He's a war hero, you know. Battle of Heliopolis. Took a few knocks to the head. Just give me a couple of minutes with him. I'm sure we can straighten this out.' I smile glassily at the two women huddled together by the CyberChef and back out of the Dining Area to the corridor outside.

'"Nice ducts?"' I say, after the door is closed.

'I meant——' Taylor begins impetuously, his expression melting into a hotchpotch of shame and self-righteousness and excuses.

'"Nice *ducts?*"'

'I meant her, her pods...'

'Oh, her pods, oh I see, that's just great, Taylor.'

'I meant...' Taylor is about to start blubbing himself, by the looks of it.

'Just tell me one thing, Taylor. Did you read the Manual before we left the ship?'

'Yes,' Taylor says vociferously, staring at the ground.

'Did you, Taylor? Look at me, Taylor.'

'I did,' he says, voice cracking. 'I mean I skimmed it.'

'You skimmed it,' I say sardonically. 'You skimmed it.' I'm really angry now, because Taylor's sin was so venial and avoidable. 'Because you realize what you've done, don't you? You've scuppered the whole operation. The whole thing is screwed now, simply because you won't take the time to learn off a few simple facts.'

This is not the first time this has happened, either. This is not even the second time or the third time. But instead of accepting culpability, instead of being a man and actually facing up to what he has done, which would be something at least, Taylor starts shouting about how that's not what the Manual is for, how what the Manual is for is accidental chance-type encounters on our mission, which our mission by the way is to recoup quartz from the asteroid belt, not to cruise around trying to sleep with loose women and then steal their belongings to sell on the black market. 'Keep it down, you idiot,' I urge him. But he doesn't keep it down: he just goes right on trying to tell me my job and generally making a lot of noise to the effect that I am Public Enemy Number One and he, Taylor, is some sort of a paragon of virtue, which I'm not even going to dignify with an answer except to say in passing here that (a) it's all right for him, Mr Rich Kid, with his money and connections, but some of us actually need to make a living and that (b) it's also all right for him in that he *likes* space, he *likes* all this emptiness, probably because it reminds him of the inside of his head, but to anyone with even an ounce of feeling it's totally unbearable and if he thinks I'm going to spend the rest of my life out here trailing around the ends of the universe he's got another thing coming. To him, however, I simply stick to my original point, which is that he hasn't read the Manual, which he hasn't, and when he won't shut up I finally tell him that I have no choice but to demote him to Second Officer. This only elicits a smart remark about how can I demote him to Second Officer if there's only two of us on the ship. 'All right, Third Officer,' I say. 'Are you happy now? Would you like to keep going, Mr Third Officer? Would you like to see how much further down you can go?'

'I don't care,' he shouts. 'I can't do this any more. Taking things from—taking advantage of these women who are going to die?' He swipes the holdall from my hand and holds it up accusingly.

'Give that back, Taylor,' I warn.

'Can't you see it's wrong? Don't you even feel sad?'

'Of course I feel sad, you idiot. Naturally I feel sad. In an ideal world of course I'd prefer that Regina and all those other girls didn't have to die. And those little critters in the halogenarium, for that matter, and all this nice furniture. But that's the way the cookie crumbles. I didn't make the rules. Anyway, can't you see we're doing them a favour? We're bringing a little happiness into their last hours, aren't we? And what are we taking in return? Nothing, except a few bits and pieces that they're never going to use again. Where's the harm in that?'

Taylor doesn't say anything, so I say cajolingly, 'Now, just give me back the holdall and let's go back in there and see if for the next twenty-six and a half minutes we can't behave like normal human beings.'

'No,' says Taylor.

'Taylor—'

'No!' he yells, and jerks the holdall away so that the top, which has not been closed fully, comes undone, and the Coffee Boy flies out, bounces along the ground and rolls over the carpet into the small hand of Regina, who is standing in the doorway with a chalk-white face. 'We're going to die?' she more whispers than says.

'No, of course not,' I say, at the same time that Taylor is saying, 'Yes, I'm afraid so,' which is Taylor for you, put him in a hole and he just keeps digging.

And so here we are again, with the explaining and the tears and the hysterics, when Regina and me could have been spending Regina's final hours making sweet music together and Veronica could have been, I don't know, polishing her jackboots, or doing something about that eyebrow. Because there is really no good way to break this kind of news. As a consequence of double-dating with Taylor, I have had occasion to try it from several different angles by this stage and it always works out the same. Tell somebody their universe is shutting down and it is basically all downhill from there.

'I hope you're happy,' I say to Taylor, who is sitting beside me once again at the Dining Area table. He stares at the crust of his club sandwich without replying. Behind us, Regina is making strange gulping noises, like a cross between sobbing and the dry heaves. Veronica, on the other hand, seems more angry than distraught. In fact, she is acting like the whole situation is my fault. She brushes her eyes and asks me for the nth time:

'How can a universe just shut down?'

'They just do, Ma'am. The decision is nothing to do with us, I assure you.'

This only makes her worse. 'The decision?' she says. 'Whose decision?'

I look at Taylor. Taylor looks at me. This is all kind of a sensitive area.

'Is someone controlling...' she spins around with her arms out. 'Do you mean to tell me that someone's controlling this? Are you telling me our universe is in someone's control?'

'Well, I can't say for sure how the whole system works,' I say. 'I mean it's all pretty complicated, as you can appreciate.'

I am hoping that she will be satisfied with this, but she keeps boring at me with those unblinking eyes. I sigh. 'Probably the best way to put it would be—have you ever felt like you were being watched? Like your life was just a ball in some kind of crazy pinball machine?'

Veronica nods slowly.

'Well, that would be the basic set-up,' I say.

She turns away slowly with her hand over her mouth. 'Dear God,' she whispers.

Regina retches into the waste disposal. Taylor shakes his head.

'Like I say, though, it really doesn't have anything to do with us,' I repeat for what it's worth. 'I mean, I am asking you not to shoot the messenger here.'

'It's just going to end?' Regina's head is still in the sink, which gives her voice an eerie metallic reverberatory kind of sound. 'It's just going to...?'

'Because we're here by chance more than anything else, see, the energy generated by this universe ending opened up what you might call a wormhole between this continuum and the continuum which myself and Taylor are from, allowing us to sort of scoot back and forth between the two—retrieving minerals, quartz mostly, back in our universe people are crazy for it—'

'Your universe!' Regina's head pops up and she wipes goo from her mouth with the back of her hand. 'You could take us back with you!'

I shift about on my seat. 'Well, no,' I say. 'No, I'm afraid that won't be possible. I don't want to get bogged down in a big long explanation, but the two universes are basically not compatible.' I stop and cough. I hate talking about this stuff, it always sounds like

I am making it up. 'Our universe, you see, it is really pretty stripped down. I mean matter, form, so forth, we wouldn't go in for that so much. It's more a case of, uh, consciousnesses, of pure energy—wouldn't you say that's how it is?' I appeal to Taylor for a little support here. Taylor just shrugs and toys with his sandwich crust. 'Well, anyway, that's how it is. Though I know to look at him it's hard to believe Taylor here picked his face from a catalogue,' I add, attempting to lighten the mood a little. The two of them just stare at me. I sigh. 'Certain kinds of inorganic material, for instance quartz, can be transported through the wormhole. But two female human-type ladies like yourselves—it just doesn't work.'

They retreat into a stunned silence. There being nothing more we can do here, it seems to me that the best thing now would be to leave the ladies to grieve in peace. I kick Taylor under the table and am slowly and unobtrusively rising from my chair when Regina sort of shrieks: 'Why did you come here, so?'

I flex my arms backward as if I have just stood up to yawn. 'Pardon?' I say.

'Why did you come here?' she repeats, blocking the door, her fists bunched and her upper lip all quivering and shiny. 'And don't give me that about needing antimatter. What do you really come for? Just to watch us die? Just to, just to laugh at our primitive society?'

I don't know why it is that whenever people find out you're from another continuum, they always assume you're there on some sort of high-minded ticket to study them and probe them and laugh at their primitive society. Maybe they've had bad experiences in the past. I don't know. Once they've come around to that way of thinking, though, it's next to impossible to persuade them otherwise. The Manual is pretty explicit on that point. You're better off just keeping your mouth shut and getting out of there ASAP. And yet I don't move. It's like Regina's eyes are a tractor beam, holding me in position. I stand there not moving and in the strange stillness of the moment I notice all of a sudden how one edge of Taylor's sandwich has been shaped exactly to the shape of Taylor's mouth. It's like an exact duplicate. I am still marvelling at it when I start noticing other things as well. I notice the constellations through the viewer are like impossible-to-follow dance steps, printed in silver on black felt. I notice Regina's dimples are there when she cries too, like little stars, and her body is now frail and squashy and mortal-looking inside the silver jumpsuit and I think of our dance and what might have been and suddenly I feel an unfamiliar but totally overwhelming desire for her to understand me and for me to understand her and for the two of us to understand each other and not keep going as we are going, not-understanding each other.

'Look,' I say, 'I know you are upset. Believe me, we feel as badly about it as you do. We may not be humans. We may not technically speaking even be life forms. But that doesn't mean we don't have hearts. And this is not exactly a walk in the park for us either. We are just trying to make a living. We have a mission, just like you. The wormhole spits us out five hours from the shutdown, we sail around collecting transportable matter to take back to our universe. Along the way, we make contact with any sentient beings we should happen to run into. We're not supposed to, but we do. We get lonely. If you think this is easy for us, spending all our time living in the past, passing months on end in the death throes of someone else's universe, going around the same five crappy hours again and again and again, you are wrong. We get lonely, and we want to reach out. Of course we feel terrible about the shutdown. But what can we do? We are just two superior beings far from their own continuum, trying to make ends meet.'

For a moment after I make this speech, nobody speaks. Taylor stares at me with new eyes. I feel a sense of tremendous well-being and lightness, as if a weight has been lifted from my shoulders. This is the first time I have told the truth, or at least some of the truth. Who'd have thought it could feel so good? My hollowness has melted away; I feel a new sense of connectedness with the universe and ready to make a fresh start with Regina. But then she says: 'In the *past*?'

I pretend I haven't heard her. I extract a slice of tomato from the sandwich on Taylor's plate and chew it thoughtfully.

'What do you mean, the same five crappy hours?' Regina says. 'What do you mean, again and again and again?'

I chew and cough and scuff my gravity boots together.

'Are you saying you've been here before?' Her voice is rising in pitch and, as it does so, wavering and shaking. 'Are you saying the shutdown…has already happened?'

I swallow the tomato. 'Technically, this would from where we're standing be the past,' I admit. 'This universe actually went up about a thousand years ago, our time,' I add, in the new climate of transparency.

'A thousand *years*...?'

You might think, once people discover their universe is ending, that anything after that would be pretty much academic. But you would be wrong. This whole area of the past is what really gets them, without fail. Finding out they're yesterday's news, they're out of the loop, that everybody else has been there and dealt with it and moved on long ago. I can't claim I understand it. Now, though, I am wishing I had not said anything. Regina and Veronica look as if someone has whacked them with an iron bar. They look at each other like they have just this second been teleported here from some totally other place and they have no idea where or who or what they are.

'A thousand years...' Regina whispers again. Her eyes fall on the Coffee Boy on the table. 'That's why...that means...' She covers her face with the cuffs of her jumpsuit and I know that she has put two and two together, and she has also at the same moment put a different two and two together, and then she has put the two fours together to get a big ugly eight from which yours truly does not come out looking so good. Taylor has sunk lower and lower into his seat, like someone has finally found the valve to let the air out of him.

'I really am sorry about all this,' I say.

'Just go,' Veronica says heavily. 'Just take what you want and get out of here, you jackals.'

'Really, though,' I persist. 'Because what we're doing is based on a deep admiration and respect for your culture. I know it's hard for you to see any kind of silver lining here. But if it's any consolation, there is still a whole lot of interest out there for this universe. In fact it's not an exaggeration to say that people are crazy for it. Quartz, calcite—all that stuff is very popular. And something like this Coffee Boy, why, back in our continuum this is a priceless artefact. You know? This is the sort of thing people take their kids to see. And what we are all about is seeking out and preserving remnants of this civilization and reminding everyone what a great civilization it was. Like they did with Ancient Egypt, for example. To us, this universe is a place of mysteries and wonders, the way Ancient Egypt is for you. You know, space,' I gesture out of the viewer at space, 'is sort of like a pyramid, and this,' holding up the Coffee Boy, 'is like one of the offerings the Egyptians left in there for the mummies, you know, for the dead to take with them to the other side—'

'The dead,' Regina says quietly. 'That's us.'

'Well, I don't know that I'd put it quite like that,' I say, because although strictly and technically speaking she is right, in another very important sense right here and right now she is not dead; and there is still time, if she were so inclined, for us to explore this second very important sense. But she is no longer listening: neither of them are. They are standing at the viewer and looking out through the glass with sorrowful and at the same time hungering expressions, and I know that they are thinking of ducks and suns and buildings, junipers, quarks and blueberry muffins, hydroelectric plants and sausage dogs and all the other features of life here that we have read about in the Manual; they are looking out at the vastness of space and thinking, how can all this just come to an end—as if all this nothingness were some sort of guarantee of permanence, when what you would think logically is the exact opposite. 'I should've got married,' Regina is saying, 'I should've had kids'; and if you ask me, that is this universe all over, it's regret regret regret, it's would've and could've and should've and not a damn thing you can do about it.

Now as it enters its final minutes, I see that the inky blackness is taking on a faint green phosphorescence along its curvature. Discreetly placing the Coffee Boy back in the holdall, I stand up and thank them for the sandwiches and tell Taylor that we ought to be on our way. But Taylor does not move. 'Taylor,' I say.

'I'm not going,' Taylor says.

I look at him. 'What?' I say.

'I'm not going,' he repeats, laying his hands flat on the table. 'I'm staying here.'

I had thought by now that nothing Taylor did or said could possibly shock me any more. But I have to hand it to him, he has really pulled this one out of the bag.

'Are you out of your mind?' I say to him. 'This place is shutting down.'

'I don't care,' he says nasally, looking at his hands. 'I'm staying.'

'Is this because of the demotion?' I say.

'No,' he says emphatically. 'It's not. It's because I'm sick of feeling like a pickpocket at a, at a folderol.'

'A funeral,' I correct him.

'Whatever,' he says. 'It's not *right*, what we do. It's wrong, can't you see that? Even if we stick to the mission, it's still all wrong.'

'That's your personal subjective opinion,' I say. 'Are you saying you're going to get yourself shut down for some personal opinion?'

'I don't know,' Taylor says. 'I just know that for once I want to live these last minutes like they were meant to be lived, and not sneak out before the end like some time-hopping bottom-feeder.'

'What's that going to achieve?' I say. 'Taylor, this is totally pointless and stupid.'

But Taylor just turns his face to the glass and says, 'I like it here.'

This is pretty rich, considering he has never even properly read the Manual. But it's the kind of thing that can happen after you've been out here a while. You start getting these funny notions. It's something to do with all the forward-rushing time and this weird state of being a very small and site-specific something in the middle of a ton of basically nothing. You catch the melancholy of the place just like you might catch a chill.

I make a last-ditch effort to change his mind. I tell him that technically speaking this is mutiny and a court-martial offence. However, as he is going to die anyway I am aware that my threat does not carry much weight. I ask him how I'm supposed to pilot the ship without him. He just shrugs. 'Fine,' I say. I go to the door and at the door I turn around to see if he has moved. But he is still in the same position, hands laid palms down on the table, head turned to look out of the viewer. Maybe he is trying to impress Regina and Veronica, I think. If he is, they don't appear to have noticed. They are standing also looking out through the viewer at the phosphorescence that is gathering like an arm to choke the life out of the encircled wastes. 'Well, I'm going,' I say. No one replies.

I find my own way to the trans room and teleport back to our own ship. Obviously it wasn't true, what I told Taylor about needing him to pilot. I can do it without him, the same way I could do it without those two fuzzy dice that hang over the console. I step into the navigation chamber and do a time check. There are only a couple of minutes left. I have two options. I can power up the engine and sail five hours back into the past, in a new sector, and return to scanning asteroids. Or I can call it quits and head for the wormhole. What with the Coffee Boy and the clock, I have enough of a haul to justifiably call it quits. So I tack around and make for the wormhole, as all around the strange green light, which of course is not light, whitens and intensifies.

I am thinking as I go what a relief it will be to get back to the other side. At the same time, I am wondering how it would feel to be suddenly extinguished. To have all that force of time behind you, all that valedictory rush of a whole universe shutting down: that must really feel like something, I think. I pick up the plastic case with the kittens on it that Regina gave to me and I wonder what would have happened if I'd stayed on the Aulaab with Taylor, and for an instant I have a picture of him and Regina and Veronica, all naked and sweating and getting it on. Then that goes and I have a picture of the three of them dancing in the Dining Area to some Earth-type music, as detailed in the audio section of the Manual. Suddenly I am seized by an overpowering urge to turn the ship around. But I ride it out. It is just me being emotional. Space does that to you. It's all the nothingness. You can't help getting het up about things. Stay out there long enough and you'll do anything to make being something actually feel like being something, as opposed to just a different shade of nothing. But in the end it doesn't make any difference. The music has got to end some time. And when it does, you'd better be ready to get the hell out. The wormhole yawns up ahead, so very black. Behind me in the freakish new light the asteroids roll, like tumbleweed through a ghost town. □

ENVY
Kathryn Chetkovich

Kathryn Chetkovich

This is a story about two writers. A story, in other words, of envy. I met the man at an artists' colony, and I liked him from the first story I heard him tell, which was about how he'd once been jilted by a blind date, after which he went right out and bought himself some new clothes. He was working on his third book when I met him, but he had no particular interest in talking shop. He read the paper and watched sports on television. He was handsome in a shy, arrogant way, dressed safely but deliberately in his white shirts and black jeans.

He was, I soon learned, struggling.

There may be women out there who do not love this beyond all else in a man, but I'm not one of them.

He played pool after dinner in the barn-like common room of the colony, and I would watch him through the window of the phone-booth door as I made my nightly call to my parents across the country in California. My father, who was eighty-one and not in good health, had recently fallen. He had damaged his back and shoulder, but he was reluctant to go to the doctor, and my mother was becoming frantic with worry and exhaustion. The anticipation of those ten-minute phone calls—during which I did nothing but listen, and even that not very well—dominated my days.

The booth itself was tiny, barely big enough for its folding chair, shelf, and payphone. The air felt pre-breathed and thick with the molecules of other people's long-distance calls, of their quarrels and appeasements. A small, squat window was positioned at eye level if you were sitting down, and through it, while my parents' distress poured into my ear, I could see a slice of the man, a helping from his waist to the middle of his thighs, as he played pool. I watched him set his legs, wiggling them into place. As my mother spoke in the tense, coded voice that signalled that my father was in the room with her, I focused on the cue sliding forward and back across his body like a bow. As long as I kept my eye trained on that cue, I told myself, I would not get sucked through the tiny holes of the receiver.

One afternoon, on the threshold of the building in which we both had bedrooms, I ran into the man and, partly in a bid to keep him talking, told him about my parents and my uncertainty about what I should be doing to help them. His own father had died after a long illness, he told me, so he had some idea what I was going through.

Just then a staff member came by and complimented him on one of his novels, neither of which I'd heard of—a fact that helped to equalize the discrepancy between his two published books and my none.

We both watched her walk away again, awkwardness rushing in to fill the space she left behind. He looked back at me. 'You have to do your work,' he said. 'That's your first responsibility.'

He meant, of course, my writing, and he spoke with a confidence I had never managed to feel about those hours of daydreaming at my desk, stringing together decorative little sentences to describe small, made-up events. Work to me always meant a job you were paid to do, necessary labour that someone else depended on.

He may have been struggling, but he knew what his work was. That was the first thing I envied about him.

When my father, after at last agreeing to see the doctor, was immediately scheduled for major surgery, I made arrangements to fly back to California. I left my computer and most of my belongings behind to ensure my return to the colony, and I bought a copy of the man's second novel to take with me. Over the next week I read it in various locations—on the plane, in the hospital cafeteria, at my parents' breakfast table. This life of waiting for what was going to happen in my father's life now seemed like the only real one to me, and the book like a token I had managed to smuggle out of a dream.

There were moments, reading, where the recognition was so strong, and the life on the page so vivid, I could feel my pulse speed up.

This book is good, I thought with joy—the way you can when it's the work of someone you don't really know and expect you never will. Because it's the very fact of not knowing the writer that gives you that proprietary thrill, that frees up the book to belong to you.

But I did know him, at least a little, so I also felt, intermittently, the stabs of dread familiar to all writers—that here were sentences, paragraphs, whole pages I not only admired but wished I had written.

And I suppose pride was also in the mix, because this man whose perception I envied had possibly liked me. I saw myself reflected, if in an incomplete and distorted way, in that possibility, the way you can see the ghost of yourself in a store window through which you can also see a real woman examining a shoe.

So from the start he was both man and writer, real and something more than real, to me. I had liked him as soon as I met him—a current rippled across my skin when he walked into a room—but something stronger kicked in once I met him on the page, naked and decked out in phrases I would never have thought of.

My father, having undergone a second, unanticipated operation, was still in the hospital when I returned to the colony. I spent four of the five-plus in-flight hours of the trip certain that the plane was going to crash, a conviction that every casual observation—the ominous silence from the cockpit, the flight attendants' huddled conversations in the galley—seemed only to confirm. Maybe this was just residual anxiety from having been on high alert for the previous few days, or maybe I was not at all sure at that point where I truly belonged and had simply found a colourful way to express that dilemma.

To fend off the guilty suspicion that I was abandoning my father, I reminded myself that I was returning to work, a choice that he, in all his years at the office, had taught me the value of making. But the moment I walked into the colony's dining room that night and my glance snagged on the man, his white shirt and Oscar Wilde hair, I knew it wasn't just my work I'd returned for.

I was falling for another writer, and I recognized my descent by its peculiar calling card: the fear of what I wanted. In my remaining week at the colony, confident that nothing would actually 'happen' between us there, I engineered as many coincidental meetings with him as I could. Because we lived on opposite sides of the country and would probably never see each other again, I felt crestfallen, and safe.

My father remained in the hospital, not so much recovering as trading one complication for another, for the next two months. Once I got back home, I visited him every day and never got over the feeling, as I searched for a parking space and walked to the entrance and made my way down the wide squeaky hallway to his open door, that I was pulling myself along like a reluctant dog who might one day slip my collar and make a break for the car. I was afraid of finding some new test under way in my father's room or some new piece of equipment—evidence of more bad news. When a doctor would come in armed with nothing more ominous than a clipboard, I was afraid of that, too—afraid that my father would not be able to come up with the answers to basic questions like what hospital he was in or who the president was. Even though I routinely have trouble remembering what day of the week it is and can almost never name the date, it terrified me to see my father muddled by this kind of mild confusion. His had always been a sharp and certain mind, an accountant's mind; 'sometimes wrong but never in doubt' was one of his favourite sayings.

One day as my brother and I were leaving my father's hospital room, I broke into tears—sudden, gulping sobs that overtook me and made it hard to breathe.

My brother put his arm around me and asked me what I was afraid of. Dad was not about to die, he assured me.

'I'm not afraid he's going to die,' I found myself saying. 'I'm afraid he's going to live.'

I was afraid that my father was going to get what we all wanted: better enough to go home. And that once there he was going to take the rest of us down with him, starting with my mother.

During that time, the fact that my husband and I had recently separated and I had neither a family of my own nor a full-time job behind which to hide left me exposed to my parents' needs, which were sizeable. I tried to regard the time I was spending with one or the other of them as a job I would later be glad to have done, but this gladness was often undermined by my resentments and foul moods, by my running tally of the sacrifices I was making and the uncomfortable fact—hard to admit, even to myself—that I wasn't getting any writing done.

Then one day in my mailbox there was a letter from the man at the colony.

Of course I wrote him back right away, labouring for hours to strike an appropriately offhand tone. I drove my letter to the post office for faster pickup, and began waiting impatiently for a response. Before long we were corresponding, with a double-edged satisfaction that seemed destined to mark everything that happened between us. It was a simple thrill to see an envelope addressed in his hand in my mailbox—and then I would open the letter and begin answering it in my head, and the thrill would get complicated.

In the letters I wrote him, I was compelled to see my life as it must have looked from the outside: a lot of driving and errand-running, a lot of empty, necessary hours at the hospital. Meanwhile, his letters,

Kathryn Chetkovich

chronicling his successes and failures at his desk, where he was at work on a novel about family troubles, reminded me of the writer's life I myself was failing to live.

I knew, from his descriptions of them, that his days were no easier than mine. He was still struggling, throwing away much of what he'd written, and I took a furtive solace in that. But occasionally he would report having had a good day, and I would feel, under my encouraging cheer, the shudder of panic you get when a friend deserts you by joining AA or leaving a bad marriage. It was one thing for him to be sitting down to it every day while I was not; but to hear that he might be getting somewhere made me feel abandoned and ashamed. He was pulling ahead in the great race of life, and he was throwing my own stasis into unbearable relief. Fortunately, over the next two months, such days were rare enough to discount.

Eventually my father came home to a house that had been fitted for his wheelchair-bound return: doors taken off their hinges, rugs rolled up, and a hospital bed installed in the den, with a baby monitor so my mother could hear him call. My reluctance to visit him got worse once he was home. At home bad things might be happening and no expert, no breezy young man with a stethoscope, was there to take charge. There was only my mother, with her fraying nerves, and later a willing but under-qualified aide and a nurse who visited a couple of times a week. In the hospital there had at least been the grim herd comfort of other ill people and other worn out families.

And of course the hospital was a place you could always leave. In the hospital my father was someone else's responsibility. At home, he was ours.

One night, encouraged by a recent letter and feeling at loose ends at home, I called the man. I was anxious and uncomfortable the whole time we talked, but as soon as we were off the phone I couldn't wait to talk to him again. We talked periodically after that, but it felt like the sort of dangerous pleasure you eventually have to swear off, and I couldn't shake the feeling that each conversation brought us closer to the inevitable one in which we would agree to stop talking altogether, so I mostly tried to enjoy the idea of calling him without actually doing it, all the while reminding myself that there was a good chance that we would never speak again and that even if we did, it certainly wasn't going to lead to anything.

As my father was ostensibly getting better, to the point where he was able to drag himself around the house behind a walker, he was also clearly getting worse. It was hard to get a firm sense of exactly what was wrong, and for a while I was frustrated because he seemed simply unwilling to make the necessary effort. But he couldn't: he was too tired and discouraged; he was in too much pain. Finally he agreed to go back to the hospital. As soon as he was there, crammed into a corner of the busy emergency room, he looked up at my mother with exhaustion and relief and said, 'We made the right decision to come back here.' As if his body had just been waiting for the signal, organ after organ began to shut down over the next few days. Even so, he fought to stay alive. He elected to go on a ventilator, after which he had to be heavily sedated and eventually slipped into unconsciousness. His body by then was wrecked.

Two weeks later we finally decided to disconnect the machine that had been breathing for him. The doctor warned us that it might take him as long as a week to die. The nurse we liked unhooked him from everything except the heart monitor and the morphine drip before she left for the day, and another nurse took over and wheeled him to a temporary room down the hall. My brother and I took the first shift, sitting on opposite sides of the bed and holding his hands. The television was on and we watched it absent-mindedly. After the cramped busyness of the ICU, the room we were in seemed peaceful, in a makeshift way, but my father did not. It seemed to me that he was no more resigned to dying than he had ever been, and I couldn't bring myself to say the encouraging things that seemed called for, urging him to let go and to trust that everything would be all right. But if he was waiting to hear these, he didn't wait long; an hour later, he was gone.

I drove to the shopping centre that afternoon under cover of buying groceries and stopped to call the man from a payphone. I think he may have told me the story of the day his own father died, but I don't remember for certain. What I remember is just my relief that he was home, that when the phone rang, he answered. I remember standing outside a pizza parlour, watching the cars glide in and out of their spaces, listening to his voice.

I had told my mother I would stay with her for a while, so I moved my clothes and books and computer to her house, and began trying to write, without much success, in my father's study. In the days immediately following his death, my sister and I had sorted and cleared what looked like the most current piles. It felt at the time as though we were working with the determined haste of people trying to beat a storm or nightfall; now night had indeed fallen, my father's death had become real, and I lacked the courage or energy to examine, much less remove, any of his things. In the centre of his otherwise cluttered desk I cleared a small space for my work, and when I stepped into the room and saw it from a distance, it looked not unlike one of those mysterious crop circles—an emptiness created for no known reason.

I knew this was a strange time for me, living in my parents' house again for the first time in twenty years, but it was probably even stranger than I realized. I had a sense that my friends were listening in a particular way when we talked, forming opinions. I recognized that attitude of the concerned outsider; I have employed it often enough myself.

The man, too, seemed worried about me and surprised me by inviting me to come and visit him in New York. I still didn't know him well enough to feel comfortable with him, and I often felt nervous when I picked up the phone to call him. It was odd in one way and not odd at all in another to find myself sitting across the table from him in the apartment he had described to me in his letters. We talked for hours that first night, pushing the words back and forth while each of us tried to figure out what the other was saying underneath them. Finally I took my dishes to the sink and he came up behind me and, after all those months, put his hands on my shoulders.

Over the next two years, as we visited each other for weeks and then months at a stretch, the man and I settled into a routine that included a lot of satisfying time together and a number of anguished fights.

During the day, imagining him hard at work on his novel, I tried to work myself. My collection of short stories had finally been accepted and published by a university press the fall after my father died, and much as I thought I was prepared for the polite silence that greeted that publication, I must have been more disappointed than I realized, because I now found myself questioning my efforts more ruthlessly than ever. It sometimes took me a whole morning to get to my desk; once there, often I would turn on the computer and distract myself by opening a book or answering email or fussing over a small editorial job. When I did finally manage to turn my attention to writing, I worried that the play I had begun working on was a mistake and that I should go back to writing fiction; on the other hand, I reasoned, if I really wanted to work on a play, a play was what I should work on—but then with every line I saw fresh evidence that I was going down the wrong road, and every step was taking me farther from the one thing I knew how to do: write stories. Except that by now I worried that I had already forgotten what I once knew about that, too. I hadn't written a story in what seemed a long time, and even though I remembered pretty much always feeling as if I didn't know what I was doing, even when I was doing it, I could see now that in fact I had known what I was doing, before, and it was only now that I didn't.

I looked forward to evening, to the sight of the man, who still felt new and mysterious, walking through the door, and I also dreaded that moment because it meant either lying about what I had accomplished or, worse, telling the truth—and it meant having to hear about his day.

Because the man, who had been struggling so agreeably when I met him, had finally found his key, the way in. In the months it took me to produce a drifty fifteen-page story about the end of a marriage, a short play about a woman who sleeps with her best friend's husband, and seventy pages of a screenplay that had the desperate signs of 'learning experience' written all over it, he piled up several hundred pages of his new novel.

It was, alas, good. My own reading told me this, but I had independent verification as well—because as sections were finished they flew almost immediately into print, and just as immediately, the phone would begin to ring with congratulatory messages, comparisons to dead writers and to living writers whose reputations were so established they might as well be dead.

In the middle of this somewhat tense time the man came home one night, feeling frustrated after a couple of hard days, and asked if I would read some pages that were giving him trouble. I was immensely relieved to think that he, too, could produce bad work, and grateful that he was willing to show it to me.

I had the sudden wish to knock him to the floor and hike up my skirt, but I thought I would read the pages first.

He brought me olives and a glass of wine, and I sat down to read. Hoping for the worst and prepared to be encouraging.

'I don't understand,' I said when I finished. 'This is great.'

'Do you really think so?' he asked hopefully. 'You really think it's okay?'

'I think it's perfect. Funny, true, interesting.' I managed to shove the words up my throat and out my mouth. I might have wished for it to be bad, but I couldn't tell him it was if it wasn't.

'Thank you. That's a huge relief. That really *really* helps. *Thank you.*'

You want to see bad work, *I'll* show you bad work, I thought, even as I was privately vowing never to show him another word I'd written.

I was forty, then forty-one, then forty-two years old. I had no children, the husband I had thought I would be with forever was gone, the father I had always assumed would one day really know me was dead, and I had no career to speak of. And now I was with a man who could do this.

The impulse to make love had passed.

When his novel was finally done, the man handed it in, and his editor called every hundred pages or so to say he was loving it, then called to say he was cutting the cheque, and finally called to say he wanted to take the man and me out for a celebratory dinner.

The day of that dinner, after putting in a few unhappy hours at my desk, I went out and bought myself a pair of black slacks and a silk blouse. The evening went well, I thought; the editor seemed to approve, and I felt, as always, gratified by that.

Halfway through the meal, when the editor said something polite about wanting to read some of my work, I did not know what to say, and the man intervened: 'You did read it, actually. You passed on it.'

In one of those bizarre coincidences that is proof of either the universe's intelligent plan or its gratuitous randomness, it happened that this editor was, in fact, the one person in New York who, two years earlier, had read and rejected my book before its publication by the university press. I might have thought, until that moment, that this unhappy fact belonged to the category of shameful secrets whose dark power is neutralized when someone actually speaks them aloud, but I saw immediately that it did not.

The editor, an urbane and gracious man, must have said something urbane and gracious then, but I couldn't hear him over the sound of my own voice in my head: Keep smiling, keep smiling!

Later that night, after the stony silence, the tears, the fury, I had to ask myself: What did I expect the man to do? I wanted it to be his fault, but it wasn't. I was angry about what he'd said, but I would have been angry about whatever he'd said, even if he'd said nothing—because what I was really angry about was having to go out to dinner with an editor on whom my work had made so little impression that he did not even remember reading it. An editor, it turned out, whom I *liked*, whom I thought was not just funny and sweet but smart, and who was going to do everything in his power to make sure the man I was with got the notice he deserved.

Over the next several months, what had at first seemed like a pathologically extreme anticipation of the man's success on my part began to look like nothing more than a reasonable prediction. Advance copies of his book were released, and suddenly he was being interviewed, photographed, written and talked about by, it seemed, everyone. Clearly his book was on its way to becoming not *a* book but *the* book, and every day seemed to bring new evidence that he was on his way to becoming that rare thing, a writer whom people (not just other writers) have heard of.

On September 11, 2001, his book had been out about a week. In the shock of that day, he and I shuttled back and forth between the apartment and the television in the realtor's office down the hall. I felt the sensation of disaster, the weird chill of fear limned by exhilaration at the possibility that the world and all its fixed routines might have changed in a single day.

As we tried, along with everyone else, to think about what had happened and what would happen next, another question went unasked: what would it mean for the man's book? I was sure he was wondering this, and I was too, but I let the whole day go by without mentioning it. In those strange hours when anything seemed possible, it seemed not all that unlikely that the book on which the man I loved had spent ten years working might disappear before our eyes—and yet I said nothing.

I told myself that it would be unseemly, even in the privacy of our apartment, to focus on our petty concerns when thousands of people had lost their lives and the fate of the world itself was suddenly uncertain. But the truth is I didn't mention his book because I didn't want to. Because for one day, at least, for the first time in what felt like months, he and his work had been eclipsed—and I was relieved.

That was the place envy had delivered me to.

My friends, trying to be helpful, had this to say: 'I could never do that, be involved with a writer who was that much more successful than I was.'

But really: why not? Partly, I suppose, because a fellow writer's success makes it that much harder to console oneself with thoughts of what Virginia Woolf called 'the world's notorious indifference'. The world, Woolf said, 'does not ask people to write poems and novels and histories; it does not need them. It does not care whether Flaubert finds the right word or whether Carlyle scrupulously verifies this or that fact.' So when the man was merely gifted but not particularly rewarded, I was comfortable; we were in it together, comrades in a world that didn't care what we had to tell it. But now, what did his success prove, if not that when the gift is prodigious enough, the world *does* need us, it *will* pay?

When the subject of his success came up, often enough a friend would say, 'The great thing is he really deserves it.' Were they kidding? This was precisely what made it so hard. For once, the gods hadn't made the stupid mistake of smiling on another no-talent, well-connected charlatan. No, this was a genuinely excellent piece of work by a man who had dedicated his life to doing such work and was now being rewarded for it. Proof that the system was not essentially corrupt and misguided, incapable of recognizing true merit, after all.

Where was the comfort in that?

One morning, unable to focus on whatever I was working on, I suddenly thought of a passage of his. I got up and walked across the room to pull down from the shelf the magazine in which the passage appeared. This was the wrong thing to be doing, I knew.

Still, I watched myself do it. Heart knocking like a lunatic on a door that will never open, I flipped through the pages. I found it. It wasn't as good as I'd remembered. It was better.

I refused to let myself form the question, but I knew it was in there, all the more powerful for going unasked: If I couldn't do that, what was the point of my doing it at all? With that peculiarly severe egotism of the insecure, I could not believe I would ever be the best, and I could not bear to be anything less.

But why, then, didn't I feel this when reading Wharton, or Faulkner (who crowed that a writer will not hesitate to rob his mother, 'Ode on a Grecian Urn' being worth any number of old ladies)? Why aren't we all still eating our hearts out over Shakespeare? Why does it hurt only to read good work by the living? Why does the pain increase as the distance narrows between ourselves and those gifted others: those we know, those we know who are our age (or worse, younger), those we know who are our age and our friends? Worst of all, maybe, when the enviable other is someone we share our life with.

According to an appealingly commonsensical theory of human behaviour known as Tesser's self-evaluation maintenance model, we all want to think well of ourselves, and one of the ways we enhance our own self-esteem is through our interactions with other people who are doing well. In what's known as the 'reflective process', someone else's success can make us feel better about ourselves; this explains why, for example, we feel good when our favourite sports team— the individual members of which have never met us and probably have no desire to—wins. And it's probably part of what's behind the old model of marriage in which a striving, supportive woman was to be found behind every successful man. In addition to whatever material advantages they promised, the man's achievements were a feather in his wife's cap: a sign that she had succeeded in marrying well.

But this happy scenario holds only for those cases in which the other person is succeeding in an area outside one's own domain. When a rival succeeds, the 'comparison process' begins: we measure ourselves against the successful other and feel diminished. Fortunately, this competitiveness is limited to a small number of areas. Unfortunately, those areas are extremely important; they're the ones on which our sense of self are based.

Kathryn Chetkovich

I came home one evening and the man asked about my day, which had been unremarkable. I asked about his and learned that the British rights to his now-famous book had been sold for a whopping figure, higher than anyone had anticipated. It had been a big day, and he was proud and excited. It was the kind of news you want to call home with, and because his mother was no longer alive and he has no sisters, he had called his sister-in-law.

He hadn't known where to call me, he said, or he would have. But I could see it in his wary, eager face: he wanted to call someone whose enthusiasm he could trust.

The part that was his girlfriend put her arms around him and told him how happy she was, and the other part, the miserable writer within, kept her distance.

Not long after this, we broke up. At the end of a holiday trip to visit family in the west, I told the man I couldn't imagine going back to New York; it was too hard there. I told him there wasn't enough air for both of us in that apartment; I told him I was drowning. He asked me to be more specific, and I told him I just didn't think I was cut out for this life together.

'What life? What are you talking about?' It was late; we were arguing in the dark, on a sofa bed in his brother's house.

'This life. Where you're so...big, and I'm so little.' It made me feel littler just saying it.

'I don't think of you as little.'

The fact that I believed this helped not at all. I was drowning; what good did it do to hear that he thought I could swim?

But breaking up, it turned out, was not the answer, either. I still wanted him, and my pride, already inflamed, now fairly throbbed at the idea that it was my own weakness that kept me from having him. I was in pitched battle with myself, and the wrong side was winning.

A few months later, when I persuaded him to try again, I sensed this was our last good chance at being together. I also sensed, despite my recent conversion to the belief that problems are solved by talking, that this one, born of words, was one that words would never fix. The more I talked about it, the more secretive he would become, and the more guilty and resentful we would both feel.

It became, and remains, the thing we don't talk about.

When the man told me stories about his wife—his ex-wife, but she had a fearsome presence that made her more real to me than I sometimes felt to myself—I would feel a cool draught, as though someone had left the door to the future open a crack.

She had been a writer, too. During the happy, lean years of their marriage they would both write eight hours a day, fuelled, in the starving-artist tradition, by a diet of rice and beans and jumbo packs of chicken thighs. They were going to publish together, the story went; their books would find their way to discerning, appreciative audiences. And when his first book made good on their bargain and hers did not, he tried to wait for her to catch up. She moved on to a second book and on to a second house, alone, where she hoped to work better without the distraction of his success. But the second book wouldn't come together; she couldn't finish it. It wasn't until they had finally separated, for good this time, that she gave herself the gift of putting that work away. As far as he knew, she had stopped writing altogether—except for an essay that had just been published in an anthology, which he learned about and bought one day.

In her essay, as I remember it now, his ex-wife wrote about what it felt like when she and her husband separated. I had a hard time reading this; I was simultaneously so curious to know what she thought of their life together and so afraid to find out that the sentences kept shorting out on me. But I got the gist: she not only stopped writing when her marriage to the man dissolved; for a time, she stopped *reading*.

Well, I was in much better shape than that! On the other hand, he and I were still together. Who knew what I would have given up by the time it was over?

What would have happened, I wondered, if the situation had been reversed, and she had published first? He would have kept on, I'm sure; her success might have been satisfying or frustrating to him— perhaps both—but he would never have given up.

I thought of Alice Munro's 'Material', a story about women and men, writing and envy. In it, a woman comes across a published story written by her ex-husband and discovers in it an affecting, sympathetic portrait of another woman whom, in their real life together, he had mocked and treated callously. 'How honest this is and how lovely, I had to say as I read… It is an act of magic, there is no getting around it; it is an act, you might say, of a special, unsparing, unsentimental love.' But when she sits down later, to write him a letter of praise, the words that appear on the page are these: *'This is not enough, Hugo. You think it is, but it isn't.'* And then she admits it to herself: she blames him, still; she envies and despises.

I've read this story half a dozen times over the years, and when I think of it, I always remember that woman envying her ex, the writer. But when I looked at it again recently, I was surprised to discover that it's not just him she envies but *them*—that is, not just her former husband but her current one. Different from each other as they seem, they have both 'decided what to do about everything they run across in this world, what attitude to take, how to ignore or use things'. What she envies is not something about being a writer, but something about being a man.

My father had been a managing partner—a phrase I had never stopped to consider before—of an accounting firm when I was growing up, and my mother was, therefore, the managing partner's wife. A corporate first lady whose job, in addition to running the house, was to entertain my father's business associates and accompany him on trips.

'Everywhere we went I was his wife,' she told me recently. We were in what is now her house, standing next to a dresser on which was a smiling picture of my father that neither of us was looking at. 'He was never my husband. I hated that.'

'But you weren't in his field,' I tried to explain. How could she possibly think that her situation was anywhere near as bad as mine was? 'You weren't *trying* to compete with him.'

'No, I didn't even have a field.'

She had the purity, the self-righteousness, of unadulterated resentment. Here was the old-fashioned envy I envied—the clean, sweet fury of a woman who had a man to blame. Their life together had been dedicated to his job, and she had had only one choice: she could have left him. But how could she? She had no income of her own and four kids, the youngest of whom, that good-natured albatross, was me. Whereas I—I!—had had all the advantages, and I still felt resentful. Nothing righteous about *that*.

It's tempting to take comfort in generalizations, and I have. I see myself as belonging to a generation of women who were raised to believe that we could do and be whatever we wanted—by women who, by and large, had not enjoyed that freedom themselves (and who perhaps envied their daughters for it). I grew up still wanting all the old things—to be pretty, to be good, to be liked—and also wanting not to care about such things.

But old habits die hard. Maybe it was no coincidence that when I was feeling most outstripped by the man's success and talent, when I was reading those pages of his that I wished I had written, I responded by withholding from him the gift of myself. When he was being lauded and invited, the world praising his intelligence and imagination, my way of evening the score was to shy away from him.

As long as he wanted and didn't quite have *me*, the logic went, we would be even—and I could stop feeling so outdone by what he had that I wanted. But what did that really mean? That if I could not be happy I was ready to make us both miserable. And that my answer to his work was my *self*; he had his book to make the world love him, and I had my sex with which to take my revenge.

It reminded me of something that had happened not long before I met the man. I had written a short play, in which six women are doing what my characters always seem to be doing—sitting around talking. I had written it for a class, because at that point I was having trouble writing anything unless it was for a teacher who would tell me it was good. As it happened, the teacher didn't think this one was particularly good. She thought the stakes weren't high enough, and nothing much happened, and six people was too many for a play that was only ten minutes long.

Afterward, as I was leaving the room, discouraged but not quite convinced, a man from the class came up to me and told me he'd liked what I'd written.

All his plays were about rodeo men and the half-dressed women who were always crying at kitchen tables after they left. I now realized he had a much more subtle mind than I'd ever given him credit for.

'Thank you,' I said.

He suggested that one thing the play might benefit from was the addition of a man, just at the very beginning, to pique the audience's interest.

I told him I'd consider that.

'You want to get a drink?' he asked me.

Kathryn Chetkovich

What are we here for, others or ourselves? Grandiose and overstated as it sounds, doesn't it come down to that? I always thought I would have at least a working answer to that question by this point in my life, but I don't; and in the absence of that certainty, everything feels provisional.

The last time I saw my mother, she and I talked, over a pleasant restaurant dinner that both of us were happy not to have cooked, about what will happen when she can no longer stay in her house. I love my mother. I want her to be happy and safe, free from worry.

And yet what do I find myself doing? Reassuring her that everything will be fine, leaving my nearby brother to look out for her, flying to the other side of the continent, and writing about the guilt I feel.

Another writer and I talk about some of this one night. Before I really knew her, I used to think of this woman as a relentlessly cheerful and optimistic person, so given to looking on the bright side that she wasn't even aware that's what she was doing. Tonight she reassures me, again, about the merits of a draft I've shown her, gushing in a way that makes me want simultaneously to embrace her and to run screaming from the room. But it's a good talk, full of confessed fear and desire, full of the agreement women love. We each order another glass of wine. I tell her, sounding less convinced to myself than I'd thought I was before I started talking, that I'm hopeful that my various crises of confidence may be opening the door to a new, more assured way of working.

When we get to her, she surprises me by revealing that she's been depressed lately. She feels as though all anyone wants to do these days is exercise furiously to stay in shape, and she wants…something else. She's losing track of the point of it all.

The next morning, my phone rings and it's her, telling me that she's just learned that her sister has inoperable cancer. I can hear the fear and grief in her voice, but I can also hear the mobilizing of forces, the list-making and dinner-cooking, the shoulder pressing gratefully to the wheel. She certainly wouldn't have wished for it, but she has a job again; it's clear what it is, it's clear it must be done, it's clear she knows how to do it and that she's good at it. She's suiting up to do what's been women's work since the beginning of time, and it would be hard to argue there's anything on earth more meaningful.

That's how I feel sitting here, anyway.

But then I think again of Munro's story 'Material': 'I envy and despise.' Isn't the most important irony of that story the invisible one at its centre—the fact that it was written by a woman, who gave to her gifted male doppelgänger the qualities and perceptions, the easy knowledge of how to ignore or use things, his ex-wife so envies?

Life, obviously, is about more than this. It's not as though anyone thinks that being a good writer makes you a good person. But it helps. (Isn't this perhaps one reason why women, as a whole, are more apt than men to see writing and reading as therapeutic acts? All that private time spent rendering and transforming personal experience on paper is easier to justify if the writer—and, ideally, reader—is healed in the process.) If you're truly talented, then your work becomes your way of doing good in the world; if you're not, it's a self-indulgence, even an embarrassment.

But how do you *know* you're good, if not by comparing yourself favourably to others (an essentially un-good activity)? And how many women are comfortable doing that?

Here's Edith Wharton: 'If only my work were better, it would be all I need. But my kind of half-talent isn't much use as an escape.'

Here's Joan Didion on the subject of her first novel: 'It's got a lot of sloppy stuff. Extraneous stuff. Words that don't work. Awkwardness. Scenes that should have been brought up, scenes that should have been played down. But then *Play It As It Lays* has a lot of sloppy stuff. I haven't reread *Common Prayer*, but I'm sure that does too.'

Or Dorothy Parker: 'I want so much to write well, though I know I don't, and that I didn't make it. But during and at the end of my life, I will adore those who have.' (Here is perhaps womanly envy in its purest form: one's own worthlessness worn as a hair-shirt reminder to love those who are better.)

It's hard to talk about the category of 'women writers' or 'women's writing' without feeling that you're picking at a scab that will never heal as long as you keep picking. On the other hand, vexed as they are, those categories continue to be meaningful, even if we can't always agree on just what the meaning is.

Most women I know are reluctant to say, 'I am better than her, and her, and her—okay, I'll keep going,' and most men I know rely, when necessary, on some formulation of exactly that. Plus women have not only each other to compete against (in devious and exhausting ways, requiring much track-covering and nice-making as they go) but men to envy; because it's still the case that women writers are compared to each other, and the big (as opposed to, say, lyrical) literary novel persists as an essentially male category. Women's books are still not talked about in the same way men's books are, and women are still sensitive to that.

As I was turning all this over in my mind, I thought again about meeting my boyfriend for the first time. How before I had known anything about him, I had known this would happen—that one day he would write his Big Book, and the world would roll a red carpet to his door. All those months when he was miserably, triumphantly, cranking it out, page by artful page, I had known it—more certainly than I had ever known anything about my own life. (No wonder I had gotten so little of my own work done—I had been so preoccupied with monitoring his.)

Had I been clairvoyant, then? Or was it something more metaphysical: had my fear acted like a cosmic magnet, drawing to itself the object of its obsession (forgetting for a moment that my boyfriend might have had anything to do with his own fate)?

Or had I, in some perverse way, got exactly what I wanted?

I had found a partner who, by being so good—and so successful—at what I wanted to do, had called my bluff. I didn't want to quit, it turned out. I wanted to find a way to keep writing, whether I could ever be good enough or not.

I did envy his talent—the way he could go off in the morning and come home at night with five smart pages, the way he could expertly tease out a metaphor, nail a character in a sentence, and tackle geopolitics or brain chemistry without breaking a sweat. I envied the fact that in airports and restaurants, strangers—readers!—would come up to him and rave about his book; I envied his easy acceptance at magazines that had been routinely rejecting my work for years.

For all that, though, I was startled to realize that I didn't wish I'd written his book, any more than I would have wished to wake up tomorrow looking like the beauty from a magazine cover. What I envied were what his talent and success had bestowed on him, a sense of the rightness of what he was doing. I wanted what women always want: permission. But he'd had that before this book was even written; it was, after all, the first thing I'd envied about him. It was arguably what enabled him to write the book in the first place.

I was raised to admire a life of service, and to this day, I do admire it. When I see someone bend to the task of helping another, I think she is doing the work of all, the human job. But someone else's good deed never stabs my heart the way a good book does. I admire it, but I do not envy it. Whatever else it has done, my envy of the man has helped me see the difference between what I was raised to want, what I wish I could want, and what I do want.

I flatter myself that I'm doing better with it all, that I'm adjusting. The man and I are finally happy and at ease, for the most part, and his book and public stature are a fact of our life together.

But who am I kidding? At home sometimes I don't want to check the phone messages; when I step into a bookstore and see that stack on the new-book table, I can sometimes feel my heart rattling the bars of its cage. I read the reviews and the interviews, but not all of them; I want them to be good, and then I want to forget them. The book itself, which I've read twice, I don't even want to look at now.

That's how much better I'm doing.

And yet I am doing better, because something within me has surfaced: another story. In this new story, every ugly impulse and selfish yearning, the whole insecure unlovable mess, has been given wing. There's no better self to protect any more; the moral high ground has been ceded.

In this story, I don't do the work I was born to, perhaps not even the work I am best at, but the work I have chosen—incompletely, erratically, often unhappily and uncertainly.

In this new story, I write to refute the ex-wife, and to avenge her. She is my enemy and my friend.

I have met the circumstances that are larger than my capacity to be gracious, it turns out. I have come up against the limits of my goodness: someone I love has what I want, and he probably always will. What else is there to do for it? I might as well work. □

WALTER BENJAMIN

WALTER BENJAMIN

Selected Writings, Volume 4, 1938-1940

WALTER BENJAMIN

EDITED BY HOWARD EILAND AND
MICHAEL W. JENNINGS

This volume ranges from studies of Baudelaire, Brecht, and the historian Carl Jochmann to appraisals of photography, film, and poetry. At their core is the question of how art can survive and thrive in a tumultuous time. Here we see Benjamin laying out an ethic for the critic and artist—a subdued but resilient heroism. At the same time, he was setting forth a sociohistorical account of how art adapts in an age of violence and repression.

Belknap Press • New in cloth

ALSO AVAILABLE FROM HARVARD

WALTER BENJAMIN
Selected Writings: Volume 1
1913-1926

Selected Writings: Volume 2
1927-1934

Selected Writings: Volume 3
1935-1938

MOSCOW DIARY

THE ARCADES PROJECT

THE COMPLETE
CORRESPONDENCE, 1928-1940
(Harvard edition not for sale in the British
Commonwealth except in Canada)

harvard university press
US: 800 405 1619 • UK: 020 7306 0603
www.hup.harvard.edu

selected writings

FIVE CATS AND
THREE WOMEN
J. Robert Lennon

Ten years after she divorced him, Albert's wife Lenore brought him a cat. She'd gotten it from the biomed lab at the research hospital where she was a nurse—they had planned to euthanize it. A kitten. Lenore's husband, a doctor, was allergic, and the cat was a longhair, and she asked Albert could he please keep the thing for awhile, those bastards wanted to murder it, she'd come by now and then to make sure everything was all right, and meanwhile she would find it a permanent home. And by the way she had named it McChesney.

He could have said no, he was well within his rights, but he didn't want to seem like a bad sport. Anyway, how hard could it be, cats take care of themselves, right? So he said yes. Sure, he'd take it.

'Thanks, Albert,' she told him. 'I'll get her out of your hair in a few days.'

But it was not to be. Days passed, then weeks and months. The cat settled in. Albert tried to like it, but there wasn't much about the cat to like. It was loud, demanding and unaffectionate. It had no loyalty, no moral organ, no sense of personal responsibility. The best you could say for the thing was that it was well-groomed, cleaning itself often, even compulsively, especially in the summer, which is also when it liked to stalk chipmunks in the grass and bring them inside and play with them in a secluded spot, then forget them when the life went out of them. He kept the cat for something like twelve years, living alone with it in the house he used to share with Lenore.

A guy might reasonably expect a cat of this advanced age to mellow out, quit sprinting from the room every time he sat in a chair, stop sniffing its food bowl for ten minutes before even the first tentative bite of kibble. But no. Like a human being, the cat grew entrenched in its bad habits and developed ones that, though entirely new, were absolutely true to form: for example *refusing to use its litter box*, instead demanding to be let outside so that it could relieve itself in somebody's garden (as if that were somehow cleaner), and the cat did this many times each night, to the point that Albert didn't bother going back to bed once the cycle of opening and closing the front door got under way. At the height of this routine he was getting perhaps three hours of sleep (best described as fitful) a night. His dreams were full of monstrously distorted cat sounds and he half-woke on several occasions during those hours to respond to door-opening requests that proved to be false alarms.

Sleep mattered to Albert; he was a mailman, he had to get up early, he needed the energy to walk.

So, on his day off one week, he went down to the hardware store and bought himself a heavy-duty moulded-plastic pet portal. He pulled the basement door off its hinges and jigsawed the appropriate-sized hole, then screwed in the pet portal and spent much of the next several days directing the mewling McChesney through it; a thankless task, as the cat extended its claws when picked up and coiled itself into a ball of the greatest possible diameter, so that Albert was forced to wedge it through the opening, suffering multiple bleeding wounds on his hands and arms in the process. But in the end the project was a success. The cat seemed to relish its newfound independence. Apparently it had enjoyed the summoning of Albert no more than Albert had enjoyed opening and closing the front door for it. A blissful peace fell over the house and lasted for two weeks.

Two weeks! Over those halcyon days, he and the cat lived their own separate lives, neither needing to acknowledge the other, with only the food and water bowls for Albert to fill and the cat box to occasionally glance into. It wouldn't be a stretch to say that these were two of the best weeks of Albert's post-wife life.

Then, abruptly, they ended. It was two in the morning and quite black inside and out of the house; the moon was new and the stars obscured by August clouds. The cat was asleep on the other side of the bedroom, as it tended to be, preferring Albert's unconscious company to his actual living presence, which was fine by him. The night was still and restful and unseasonably cool. The occasional passing car served only to deepen the surrounding silence and to deepen Albert's sleep.

What woke him then? The click of toenails on the kitchen linoleum? The scent of a foreign beast? A sixth sense? Whatever the case, he was awake. In the dim light filtering down the hall from the street lamp that shone into the kitchen, he could see its low silhouette in the bedroom doorway—another cat. He groaned, and then McChesney was awake, hackled like a stegosaur, and the cats began to screech and hiss and back into corners. Albert switched on the light and saw it: fat and black and tailless by accident, not breed, it had the bony haunches of a male, and as Albert watched, it lifted its leg and sprayed the corner of his bed. Of his *bed*! He threw his pillow at it—'Out! Out!'—and it bounded through the door and scuttled away down the hall. Now he could smell the spray—piss! Cat piss in his house!—and when he went to retrieve his pillow it too had been sprayed, and suddenly the whole room smelt of it, like an unwashed dry underarm, like a stairwell in a parking garage. He leapt out of bed (scaring the living shit out of McChesney, who exited the room as if yanked by crook), gathered the pillow and sheets and blanket and mattress pad into his arms, and shoved them, along with an excessive amount of detergent and bleach, into the laundry; then from the kitchen he grabbed a bucket and squirted dish detergent and water into it, and with a sponge scrubbed the wall and carpet and floor and the frame of his bed, the smell of the foreign cat filling his entire head, until it had filtered down and infiltrated wherever it was in him the essential purest ore of the self was kept, and made that smell like cat piss too. All this from one goddam cat. He cleaned for a good half-hour and still he could smell it, so he threw the sponge and bucket into the backyard and slept on the living room floor.

Next night he blocked the cat door with a cardboard box full of old clothes. McChesney mewled to go out in intervals that seemed flawlessly spaced to interrupt the final stages of wakefulness before they were engulfed by sleep, and in his half-dreams as he drifted, Albert was reaching, swiping, grasping for some unrecognizable thing that looked close enough to touch but in fact was impossibly distant. He woke mostly dead and it took him nine hours to deliver the day's mail.

That night he took away the clothes box and the intruder cat came back and howled again and ate all of McChesney's food and *shat in Albert's left shoe*, and sprayed, this time on the sofa, and so he blocked the door again. This went on for several weeks, until most of his ruined furniture stood in the yard and some neighbour (if he found out which one he would burn his/her house down to the *fucking foundation*) called the cops on him about it. And so the furniture was hauled away (274-HAUL) by a goateed fatty with a twenty-year-old pickup, who charged him forty dollars. But it was all right, the furniture had been Lenore's and he'd wanted to get rid of it for a long time, even if it meant there was no place to sit or eat breakfast.

One night, instead of reporting to bed, he went into the cellar, arranged a folding chair beside the cat door, and sat down. He resolved to stay all night, if necessary, however long it took. When at last the offending cat hopped suavely in, in its posture all the blithe confidence of a mall cop, Albert grabbed it by the scruff and pressed it to his lap. The claws came out and dug into his legs and the lips curled back revealing pitiful fangs. But Albert was oblivious to pain or threat. Giggling, he fumbled with the collar until the tags came into view and he memorized the address: it was on his own block, for Chrissake, wasn't that the place with the kids who threw eggs at his house on Halloween? The place with the motorcycle and the dead rose bushes? The place that caught fire and they put it out but never repaired anything, so there was plastic over the burnt-out window and smoke damage on the peeling clapboards? Oh, man. Oh, man.

He thrust the cat into the clothes box (emptied earlier of clothes) and folded down the flaps and marched out the front door intending to put a stop to this nonsense once and for all, he would tell those people a thing or two, how the hell they ended up in this perfectly good neighbourhood he'd never know, there ought to be some kind of law keeping people like that out, a law against cigarette-stained moustaches and garments with the Buffalo Bills logo on them and rusted-out American cars with no mufflers and mullet haircuts and distended lard-fed bellies with dirty T-shirts stretched over them and children's toys sitting out in the grass with tall weeds grown around them and twisted filthy air-hardened rags caught in the hedge.

But when he got to the address it wasn't them—*they* were asleep behind their curtained windows, the Harley stowed somewhere out of sight. Instead it was the house next door, a trim brick bungalow with flowering plants in boxes on the porch and a spotless moonlit Mercedes parked perfectly straight in the newly asphalted drive. The house was uncurtained and a lamp burned at the rear of a large open living room (a marble sculpture resting on a baby grand piano, abstract oil paintings on the walls), where a thin grey-haired man, outlined by the blue glow of a laptop computer, could be seen bent over a small desk.

The sight of this man gave Albert pause. He stood on the sidewalk with the cat scratching and keening in the box under his arm and considered leaving the man alone, he looked so beautifully content, so *seasoned*, with his trim neck and square shoulders, working on whatever it was he was at work on on his computer. Look: there by his elbow was a steaming mug of coffee, he was burning the midnight oil, probably didn't even know his cat had left the house, might as well give the old fella the benefit of the doubt. But in the end he thought he ought to let the guy know, as a kind of neighbourly service, what his cat was up to; the poor thing might get some disease or hit by a car or tortured and killed by the people next door. So he climbed the tidy stone steps and crossed the porch and lightly knocked. He could hear the grey-haired man's approach. The porch light went on and a face appeared in the door's small window: thin nose, narrow mouth, piercing eyes, around sixty-five, looked like some kind of genius, probably a professor of something or other.

'Yes?'

Albert held up the box and the two men listened for a moment to the sound of the cat exerting itself.

'I suppose you've found Dissy.'

'Dissy?'

'Short for Odysseus. He is, of course, a wanderer. I tremble'—an eye roll—'as I enquire where you found him.'

'In my bedroom.'

'Oh, dear. Do come in.' The door opened wide and Albert entered. He could smell a recently blown out candle, freshly ground coffee (and there also was the blurb of the coffee maker in the last moments of its brew cycle), something else he couldn't quite identify, a smell of human effort. An immaculately clean if lived-in house, not a cat hair in evidence, carved mahogany coffee table scattered with magazines, a wine bottle and other junk, blankets wadded on the sofa, a couple of fancy old chairs bearing embroidered pillows, but all around them dustless corners and art hanging at right angles. 'Yes,' the man said quietly, 'I'm afraid I haven't had time to straighten up.' He took from Albert's arms the shuddering box.

'That's okay. I just wanted to return your cat. He sprayed my house, I have to tell you, I've had to get rid of a lot of furniture, and I was hoping I could convince you, if it's not too much trouble, to either keep him inside at night or have him fixed or—'

'Beg pardon,' the man said, 'Mister...'

'Lippincott.'

'Mister Lippincott, I shall not have my cat "fixed" as you put it when there is nothing per se wrong with him. Nor will I prevent his egress. He must seek lady cats to fuck.'

Albert's eyes were drawn to the piano where the marble sculpture he'd noticed from outside was beginning to resolve itself into the figure of a man, seated upon a stylized tree stump, his head thrown back, his arms behind him, supporting his backward lean. And the stump—it seemed strange—it sort of extended around and obscured the man's knees...

'How would you like it, Mister Lippincott, if you were visiting a lady friend at her residence, and at the very height of your passion you were interrupted, seized by giant rough hands, imprisoned in a box and delivered to some white-coated Mengele who unscabbarded a knife and cut your testicles off? No, there shall be no "fixing", sir.'

—no, wait, that isn't the stump, it's—it's—

'I regret I could not be of assistance, Mr Lippincott, good night.'

—it was the form of a woman, a kneeling woman, kneeling in front of the man, and she appeared, that is, she seemed to be—could it be?—*fellating* the man. Could that be right? Could his neighbour actually have a marble statue of a *blow job* on his piano? So that when he played, say, a Chopin polonaise, he could peer over the score and be inspired by the sculpted image of *oral sex*? Where, he wondered as he was ushered out the door, would a person *get* such a thing? He imagined all the people who had walked past this window and seen the statue without knowing what they saw: the children on their bikes and the little old ladies and the avuncular priests on their way to mass: the poor slobs, infected now with the subtle, subliminal germ of perversion. Would it one day metastasize, he wondered, colonizing the innocent with lewdness and bad taste? But that wasn't Albert's problem: Albert's problem was that his mission had failed.

And so he closed up the cat door for good, and it came to pass that he couldn't stand it any more and had to get rid of McChesney at any cost. So one night he got out of bed and shoved the cat into the pet carrier and got into his car and drove about fifteen miles out to the rural edge of the county and dumped his cat in a field. It was easy. Somebody would find it, he surmised, somebody would feed it and take it in and get along with it just fine. Next time Lenore came by he'd tell her McChesney ran away, and he would put up posters in the neighbourhood, for her sake, but of course it wouldn't make any difference, by then the cat would be with some loving country family and would live in a barn and chase mice all day long, which is what cats are supposed to do.

The next morning he woke feeling great, said hello and howareya to everyone at the post office, drank the weak office coffee out of a styrofoam cup, heard two jokes and told one (the one about the priest, the rabbi and Bill Clinton), walked his route whistling and gave rubber bands to children and ate a fine lunch on the Square and returned home, where he was greeted by a ringing phone.

'Hi, I think I have your cat?'

A chill of absolute horror. Impossible! Somebody must have seen his car, written down the licence plate number, called a buddy at the police station who was able to look up the registration info ('Ordinarily we don't do that kind of thing but if this joker was abandoning his cat I'm willing to bend the rules') and give the caller his name and phone number: and now they were just playing with him, pretending it was all innocent and that the police weren't on the way to his place right now to haul him in on cruelty-to-animals charges. Oh, God, what had he done?

'Hello? Do I have the right number? I found McChesney, is she your cat?'

He later realized he could have gotten out of it, there were dozens of ways: 'Oh, I just got this number, I don't know who had it before,' or, 'We used to have a cat but its name was Walter,' something, *anything*, and the caller would have just said sorry and hung up and probably brought the cat to the SPCA.

But no. He said, 'Where did you find it?'

'She was wandering in the weeds along Bird Sanctuary Road. I stopped to pick some goldenrod, and there the poor dear was. Where do you live? I'll walk over with her.'

'Um, I live downtown.' Thinking how did she *know*? for it was a woman's voice.

Long pause. 'Downtown *Nestor*?'

'Yes.'

'Heavens! That's ten miles! How long's she been lost?'

'Couple of days.'

'Oh, what a tale she must have to tell! Thank goodness she had tags or she might have been lost to this life.'

Tags? The cat had *tags*? Of course: the clinking when it ate out of its bowl. He never thought to check. Idiot! The woman was asking him should she bring the cat over and he said sure, bring it over, and she said, 'All right then,' in a tone indicating she didn't approve of the 'it'. In other words, a cat person.

Albert slumped on the living room floor (he hadn't yet replaced the furniture) with his head in his hands and briefly mourned the past fifteen flawless hours of normal human life without the burden of a pet. Why did people saddle themselves with animals? He could hear himself debating it with an animal lover: 'But man and the animals have been in partnerships of some kind for millennia,' (this animal lover might say, his loosely curly hair framing a tanned bespectacled face, his chambray work shirt reeking slightly of woodsmoke and dog) 'and there's no reason this shouldn't continue today.'

'But you see,' (Albert would reply) 'in antiquity man employed the animals in useful tasks such as the ploughing of fields and the guarding of property, and the animals lived outside, not in the house which is clearly not the place for them.'

'Oh, but many dogs serve as sentries in modern times, and they are quite happy living in the house.'

'You say happy, but you can't know; in fact I'd argue there can be no happiness without self-determination, and a dog depends heavily on his so-called master for the necessities of life.'

'Are you saying that thousands of years—oh! Did you hear that? That was the call of the ruby-crested weed thrush—that thousands of years of domestication, which have bred into these animals an intense affinity for man, have been a mistake? Because I would argue that the domestication of animals is what made civilization possible. Imagine, if you will, how agriculture could have gotten started without oxen to—'

'Yes, yes, okay, you've made your point, but what about the cat, which is what we're talking about here, the cat was never very useful, wild cats aren't social like wolves are—'

'Some of the big cats are social.'

'—Okay, whatever, but domesticated cats sure aren't, they're simply self-interested and don't really want to be with us, and for that matter I don't think dogs really want us either, they only like us because we happen to be there, happen to feed them and let them crap.'

'If you're looking for my approval, Albert, for this cat-dumping plan of yours,' (because that's what Albert had decided to do, to cut off McChesney's collar and try again tonight, this time several dozen miles further down the road) 'you aren't going to get it. Your little McChesney will be devoured by coyotes.'

'Survival of the fittest. Don't you enviro types believe in that?'

'I believe,' the animal lover said, getting up from his giant natural-fibre-upholstered down-filled cushion, 'in tenderness.'

Well, screw tenderness, Albert was going to do it; his life since McChesney was simply too good, too *normal*, and he couldn't live with the damned thing another second. As soon as this woman, this cat person, had come and gone, he was going to get into his car and re-deliver the cat unto its destiny.

It couldn't have been more than twenty minutes before she showed, she must have hung up the phone and jumped right in the car. She was carrying the cat in her arms, not in any kind of carrier or cage, and walked slowly into Albert's house gently stroking its head while gently kind of *squeezing*, the hand soft and deliberate and *practised*, and this would have turned him on mightily if not for the look of smug satisfaction on the cat's face, those dark little lips slightly parted and the pointy teeth exposed. The woman was in fact rather sexy. Although her face looked older than its years—(he guessed she was around fifty but the face wouldn't have been out of place on a sixty-year-old, with its slight greyness and deepish wrinkles and a certain crooked looseness, as if the skin had come free of a few of its moorings but not in a symmetrical way, and the nose splotched and spotted and the eyes deep in the head, but for all that not a bad face, in fact a cute and friendly one)—her body looked far younger, sheathed in a kind of clinging linen caftan, stocky yet smooth, muscular, her rear holding up beautifully, her wide round strong hips and legs and really nice-looking breasts (even with a cat pressed against them), large without seeming heavy.

Immediately he began looking around the place in a panic to find her a chair, but there weren't any, so he had to go to the kitchen and grab a couple of grey metal folding chairs and set them up.

'Actually, maybe I should leave these in the kitchen in case you want to sit down and have a coffee or tea or something,' he said, and she, still holding and stroking the cat and smiling with what seemed slight though genuine amusement, replied, 'Yes, that would be delightful,' and he returned the chairs to the kitchen.

They sat down. He made tea. She cooed at and petted the cat, efforts which were irritating him far more than turning him on, though they were still turning him on. Her name was Semma: married once, two grown-up kids, divorced ('He didn't wish to receive what it was I had to give him') for five years, lived today with three kitties and a room-mate named Lily who owned a loom ('That's right, a loom').

He told her his story and she asked him what he liked most about cats, and he said, 'Oh, I don't know, I guess just the essential, you know, a thing about them that, it's just that certain quality, they seem so possessed of this, and I respect and admire a thing that has this thing, and knows it has this thing and seems to say, "I am the thing I am and this is mine and that's that", and it's really nice to have that kind of presence in your life.'

She told him she knew exactly what he meant and said, 'What I love about cats is their angel-like ability to receive pleasure.'

He thought to say *'Angel-like?'* but did not, instead, 'You like that they receive pleasure, I see.'

'Yes, they take such pleasure in pleasure.'

'So what about them gives you pleasure?'

'I take pleasure in pleasing them. That is the source of my pleasure.'

He said, 'That's very wonderful of you,' and she laughed and said, 'Yes, it is a wonderful thing.'

Before she left she said, 'Here, take my phone number, if you ever need to get away and would like McChesney to have a sitter, you can call me, she loved Bitsy and Wrinkles and Huck.' She handed him the number written on an ATM receipt. He noted that her balance was in the high four figures.

That afternoon he cut off McChesney's collar with scissors and drove out to the Onteo Lake Motor Park to dump her. It was the middle of a grey day and hardly anyone was around. He parked by the woods and tossed the cat out and it ran right into the trees as if content, even eager, to go. He never saw the damned thing again.

The next day he called Semma and said, 'Hi, it's Albert Lippincott, you brought me my cat, and I had such a good time talking with you, and maybe we could see each other, what do you think of dinner?'

She said, 'I would be very pleased to see you, shall we dine in or out?'

'Oh, in, out, I dunno, how about,' he said, thinking sex, 'in?'

'Let me receive you at my house at eight tonight.'

'Great,' he said, 'thanks.'

'What are your dietary needs?'

'No cheese, otherwise I eat it all, are you a vegetarian?'

To his surprise she said she wasn't, she loved meat. 'I love everything about animals, including the flavour of their flesh, which I think the gods made for other beasts to consume, even human flesh which the fiercest animals are meant to eat,' and Albert did not question her about the word 'gods'. She said, 'You should bring McChesney,' and he said, 'I think I should tell you that McChesney is actually sick, dying in fact, which is probably why it, or rather she, strayed so far, she's a little demented, I think she's looking for a place to die, so I've sealed up her cat door. Don't worry, it's not catching.'

'Good heavens, I'm sorry, what on earth is wrong?'

He said, thinking of the lab the cat came from, 'Cancer.'

She said, 'Of what? She seemed so healthy.'

He said, 'It's everywhere, it's what do they say, metastasized? Some days are better than others, she gets painkillers.'

'Oh, I feel pain for her.'

'No need, it isn't your fault, I've come to terms with it really, I prefer not to talk about it.'

'You poor man, I'll show my sympathy by making good nourishing food.'

He arrived right on time, met the room-mate (a long-haired distracted woman of about forty who seemed already to have eaten and who subsequently spent the whole night in her room making fabric), and sat at the table, where cats (also long-haired) repeatedly jumped on to his lap, and he repeatedly pretended to like it.

'Are they bothering you?' Semma asked over their giant filets mignons.

'It's just they remind me of my own cat and her illness.' So Semma got up and put the cats out for the night.

They had dinner and drinks. They spent some time ogling each other while she named each tree and bird that could be found in the vicinity of the house. She said, 'I've been delighted by your company.'

He said, 'You're delighting, too. Ful.'

She said, 'Would you like a tour of my home?'

'Please.' She showed him around, led him to the bedroom. 'This mattress is made entirely of organic and unbleached fibre. Here,' she said, taking his hand and leading him to the bed, 'smell it, it is utterly unadulterated by inorganic chemicals.'

He leaned over, sniffed the bed. It smelled like her, like sex. 'Sure, smells great, here, come smell it with me.' They sprawled across the mattress, stroking the comforter.

'I too am made entirely of organic materials,' she said, and he liked this, this was self-mockery.

'Funny, so am I, we ought to get along fine.' They sniffed one another like dogs and then took all their clothes off. He was right, her body was terrifically smooth and firm, if he squinted she could pass for a husky thirty, but he barely got to touch her. She really worked him over, feeling him everywhere and saying, 'Mmm, mmm,' as if she were the one being touched, and then when they finally had sex (Semma on top, synchronizing the rhythm of her efforts perhaps unconsciously to the jingling thump of the loom's pedals behind the all-too-thin wall) she made the exact same sound as the pigeons that had roosted on the balcony outside his college dorm room, this at a time when he absolutely did not want to be thinking about pigeons. And even then, with her shoulders heaving and breasts sloshing above him, when he tried to put his hands on any part of her besides her knees, she pushed him away and instead ran her fingers through his hair and over his chest and even reached behind her to massage his legs, never pausing in her dovey humming or her methodical pinioning upon him. In the end he just gripped her knees and rode it out. Afterwards she lay on her stomach (rendering inaccessible most of the interesting stuff) and blindly massaged his hip and arm and ribs with strong fingers and said, 'Was that pleasurable for you?'

He said, 'It was great, all that touching you do, I would love to give you that kind of pleasure, what do you say?'

'Oh, but I felt pleasure, very intense pleasure.'

'Sure, me too, I don't mean that, I mean giving you the kind of pleasure you gave me, wow, it was amazing the way you did all that, I mean how about I do that same thing to you?'

'Nothing is more pleasurable to me than pleasing the man I'm with, I hope you mean it when you say you're pleased.'

'Oh, of course, very pleased.'

'Then I'm pleased too.'

They slept awhile and he figured he could give it another shot, so he woke her and they again went at it, this time him on top, except when he put his hands on her breasts she took them off and began kissing and sucking on his fingers, and never once let go of his wrists. Afterwards she said, 'Did you feel pleasure?' and he said, 'Yes, I'm very pleased,' and left it at that.

He soon realized that, if this went on, McChesney's absence was going to be a problem, so he called Semma one night (late, to give the impression that he was all torn up over it) and told her the cat had died. She said, 'I'll be right over, we'll have a burial ceremony.'

'No, that's a bad idea, I feel like—I think basically that this is something I must do alone.'

'You say that because you don't want to be embarrassed in front of me, but you need a friend, I'll be there shortly, we'll find a good spot.'

'Well,' he said, 'All right, sure, that's fine.' He hung up, shouted 'Shit!', went down in the basement and found an old wooden box with latches and a rope handle that some wine had come in; he stuffed it with old clothes and nailed it shut. It had the approximate heft of a dead cat wasted away from multiple cancers. By the time he finished she had arrived.

They took the box out into the bird sanctuary ('She loved birds,' Semma said, though how could she have known that? and was it even true, and if it was, wasn't it true of all cats?) and buried it in a clearing near a pond. Then she embraced him and sobbed exactly once and said, 'Poor Albert, let me please you,' and she undressed him but not herself and did her hand thing for awhile, then stripped off her undies and straddled him on the weedy ground with her dress still on, and pleased him. Then he thanked her and they went to his place and slept, and ate cold cereal for breakfast, over which they exchanged occasional slightly shy (though there was no reason to be shy, really, it seemed like the shyness was all an act that one of them had started and the other had picked up on and gone along with) grins.

A month passed, a month of twice-weekly encounters with Semma, you could hardly call them dates. Then, on a warm October night, probably the last warm night of the year, he got to thinking that she was all right, that Semma. A little loopy, sure, but full of life, life that, frankly, Albert could use a bit of himself. He thought of calling her, but it was late. Too late to call your...girlfriend? Was that what he was about to think? So be it, then—girlfriend. I'll call my girlfriend tomorrow! Then the phone rang.

When he picked it up he heard a woman's voice, not Semma's, toneless, Midwestern, a voice trying to make itself heard between racking sobs, saying, 'Albert? Is this Albert?' and Albert said, 'Yes, hello, who's this?' and the voice said, 'Lily Gallagher,' and he said, 'Sorry, I don't think I know any Lily Gallagher,' and then he remembered: sitting and having a cup of tea in Semma's kitchen and spying on the table a letter addressed to Lily Gallagher, that is to say Semma's boarder, the amateur weaver, and thinking that it was a nice-sounding name, good rhythm, a variety of sounds pinned into place by the L's, like water rushing through a garden hose wrapped around a row of saplings, *Lily Gallagher*.

'Semma's *room-mate* Lily, okay?' the voice managed to say, seeming to calm itself by speaking its name.

And Albert said, 'Lily, yes, sorry, the last name threw me, is everything okay?' knowing things were obviously not okay, otherwise why would she be calling him at all, let alone while crying?

And she said, 'Nah, it's not okay,' and began to sob again, and he said, 'What is it, Lily, is it Semma, is something wrong with Semma?' thinking what a stupid question, who else is there going to be something wrong with, and she said, or rather sort of screamed, 'She's dead! She's dead!'

'What!'

'Dead!'

Albert managed to get out of Lily that Semma had been picking wildflowers by the side of Bird Sanctuary Road in the dark (he thought: picking flowers in the dark? What the hell for? And then it occurred to him that they might be for him, she might have been going to invite him over for the night and thought he might like some fresh flowers around, and he thought, Don't! don't bother!) when a family of four pulled off to the side so that one of the kids could pee, and at that particular point the shoulder was narrow and the driver, who was not familiar with the area and did not realize this, overshot said shoulder and ploughed into the weeds behind which

Semma was standing, and her back was broken and an artery severed, and she was paralysed and lost a lot of blood and by the time they got her to the hospital, she was dead.

'So she's dead now?' he asked, not understanding why this seemed so difficult to believe.

'Yah, right, dead! Sorry! Gotta go!'

Albert said all right, he thanked her and she hung up and immediately he thought: what do I do now? What's expected of me? What am I? The boyfriend, probably one of many for a good-looking divorced woman her age, never met her family, ex-husband or children. He didn't even know if she had living parents or siblings. There would be a funeral, wouldn't there? He would have to go— but for whom? For himself? Did he need proof that she was actually dead? No, he would go for the friends, the family—but he didn't know them, he knew only Lily, and so slightly that he didn't even know if he would recognize her if he saw her on the street, or the grocery store, or the park, anywhere except at Semma's house scampering into her bedroom to weave. And what if he didn't go? Only Lily would notice (or maybe not, she might never have noticed him except for his generalized Semma's-boyfriend presence), and even if she would resent him not going, even hate him, that hatred could only manifest itself—what?—five times for the rest of his life, the grand total of times their paths might happen to cross in town, a generous estimate given that before Semma, he'd never even laid eyes on Lily. No, he wouldn't bother going, it would only make people miserable when they asked him who he was and he told them he'd been 'going out' with Semma or 'involved' with her, which they would inevitably and correctly interpret as meaning they were regularly having sex in the days before her death. Forget it, he'd stay home. And now he got a sudden, awful image of Semma wrapped in rags, wedged into a cheap box, like his fake burial of McChesney, and for a moment felt responsible. She was killed, wasn't she, picking flowers at the spot where she found his cat? And now he thought, what about her cats, those irritating longhairs, will they be put to sleep? And while he didn't mind (not much anyway) being responsible for the death of one cat, his cat, he did not feel good shouldering the death of four cats. And one woman. His girlfriend.

That night, lying in bed, he missed her and found her desire (or rather, it could safely be said, *need*) to please him not annoying or disturbing or sexually off-putting, as he had considered it in the past, but charming, generous and exciting; and he realized that he had been *taking* his pleasure from her all along, he hadn't allowed her to *give* him anything, he had resisted her generosity and allowed himself pleasure only in the physical sensation of sex and never, as she had wished, the emotional sensation of caring enough about somebody to let them give a thing to you without strings attached. And thinking of this he began to weep, and then to sob; and the understanding that he was sobbing not for Semma but for himself, for what a terrible man he was and how greedy and selfish and cold, only made him sob harder, so much that when he finally slept he kept waking up from the involuntary hitching of his chest, and rose the next morning feeling like he hadn't slept at all.

And then he started to miss McChesney. That was unexpected. He hadn't thought about the cat in days, the cat was unimportant, but as the morning wore on, he felt more and more distant from the thoughts he'd had the night before about Semma—felt more and more that she was, in fact, weird and screwed up—and came to feel more and more miserable about the dumping of McChesney, who, as the imaginary animal lover had pointed out, had by now probably been shredded and eaten by coyotes. Now *that* was unjust; somehow more unjust than Semma's death, which after all was the result of crouching invisibly in the weeds by the side of a busy country road with narrow shoulders. But McChesney's end was impossible to regard as anything but a colossal gyp. He'd killed her. All that day he delivered the mail in a funk, and when he got off work he drove out to the woods in the Motor Park and stumbled among the trees calling her name. But it was beyond futile. What cat came when you called? Not McChesney, anyway.

That night he sobbed again, this time for the cat he'd killed, for all the terrible selfish things he'd done in his life, for the feelings he withheld from Lenore, from Semma, from his mother; for all the sadness and anger and shame he'd caused: he curled himself on the floor of his empty living room and sobbed, and called out, 'McChesney, come back!' until the hour grew late and he slept.

A few days later Lily showed up. She was wearing a sort of baggy hooded sweatshirt that he bet she'd woven herself: a kind of amazing pattern, coloured stripes without clear borders so that each seemed to fade into the next. In her arms was a large cardboard box. It contained three long-haired neutered male cats. 'These're fer you,' she moaned, 'Semma always felt bad your cat croaked.'

'Oh! I don't—I couldn't—'

'Nah, it's all right, her brother and kids and ex don't want 'em and I gotta move 'cause they're selling the house.' And she put down the box on the stoop and burst into tears.

'Oh—no, wait, it's all right, I just—Is there anything—Here, why don't you—' he said, and led her into the house and sat her down in the kitchen and made her a cup of coffee while the cats sniffed around, exploring their new home.

She sipped the coffee and at last opened her mouth, only to say, 'The poop trays're in the car.'

'All right.'

And then she began again to cry: and so Albert went to her, held her, patted her coarse grey hair and her narrow bony back, and in about ten minutes they were rolling around naked on the living room rug. He didn't quite know how it happened, it just did. She grabbed his shoulders and then sort of stroked them and then felt his chest, and he felt hers. Or something. Compared to Semma she was so skinny, so quick, her arms and legs first here, then there, then somewhere he couldn't reach; and together they tumbled over and over and hissed and growled. Somewhere in the middle of it he felt tears again coming on—what the hell! he thought, is this crap never going to end?—and to keep them in check he shouted, 'Come!' he shouted, 'Come! Come back! Come back! Come back!'

He never saw her again. How many men, the heartless bastards, would like to say that about a woman they spent a single night with? He tried to call her later that day, but she was gone: she'd been on her way out of town when she came to him, and she had left no forwarding address (he checked at the PO, too). Now, he knows, he could find her over the Internet; how many Lily Gallaghers could there be? But there'd be no point. She isn't Semma. She's probably in California, which is where he guesses women with looms go to live, and he doubts she'd be pleased to hear from her dead ex-landlady's boyfriend whom she boinked a couple days after her funeral. Who'd want to be reminded of that? □

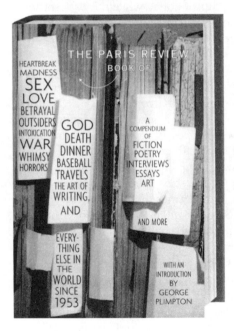

TERMITE'S BIRTHDAY, 1959

Jayne Anne Phillips

Nonie hates the idea of blue cake, she says it looks like something old and spoiled, too old to eat, though it's light and delicate and flavoured with anise. But Termite likes it, and he likes pink cake that tastes of almond, and mostly he likes me putting the batter in different bowls, holding them in the crook of his arm while I bend over him, stirring. I tell him how fast a few drops of colour land dense as tinted black and turn the mix pastel. I make three thin layers, pale blue and pink and yellow, and I put three pans in to bake, shut the door of the oven fast to pretend I'm not making everything still hotter.

'Hot as Hades today,' I tell Termite, and I move his chair so he gets the hint of breath from the window. The radio cord still reaches and he turns the knob with his wrist, slow or fast, like a safe-cracker, like there's some sense to the sounds, the static and the interrupted news.

'Don't try talking to me in radio,' I tell him, but he does anyway. As long as he holds it, he'll be trying to make it talk. I take the radio out of his lap and put it back on the counter, and I hold a bowl of icing down low. I hold the little bottle of blue, no bigger than a doll bottle, in Termite's hand, and we let just three drops fall. Divinity icing makes peaks and gets a sweet crust like meringue. Mine is like sugared air that disappears in your mouth. Nonie says I'm a fabulous cook. I could cook for a living, she says, but not at Charlie's, where she works, or anywhere like it. The egg whites can go bad fast in hot weather but I turn up the fridge to keep the icing cool on the lowest shelf, and we'll eat it all today, this birthday. Nick Tucci will take some home to his kids. Nobody makes those boys cakes. Rat boys, Nonie calls Nick's kids, like she's disappointed in them. Delinquents like cake too, I tell her. You be sure cake is all you're making them, Nonie says. Then she'll say she wasn't born yesterday, like anyone ever bothers me. I tell her no one does. They only look. Looking never bothered anybody.

It's true. It's like I've got a beam out my eyes that backs people off. Now that I'm seventeen and graduated high school, I've got a clear space around me I didn't have before. I wonder if that's like a future, or a place where a future will be.

I remember when Termite came. Nonie is our guardian and our aunt but I'm Termite's sister. In a way he's more mine than anyone else's. He'll be mine for longer, is what Nonie says. Nonie isn't old but she always says to me about when she's gone. She looks so strong, like a block or a rectangle, strong in her shoulders and her back and her wide hips, even in her legs and their blue veins that she covers up with her stockings. Your mother didn't bring him, is what Nonie told me, someone brought him for her. Not his father. Nonie says Termite's father was only married to my mother for a year. He was a baby, Nonie says, twenty-three when my mother was thirty-five, and those bastards left him over there in Korea. No one even got his body back and they had to have the service around a flag that was folded up. Nonie says it was wrong and it will never be right. But I don't know how Termite got here because Nonie sent me away that week to church camp. He was nearly a year old but he couldn't sit up by himself, and Nonie had him a baby bed and clothes and a high chair with cushions and straps, and she had papers that were signed. She never got a birth certificate though, so we count the day he came his birthday, but I make him a birthday when it suits me.

Pale-blue divinity sounds like a dress or a planet. Blue icing does look strange, like Martian food, unless I trim it, so I saved out some white for a lattice over the top, or garlands or flowers. A decorated cake looks like a toy, and people do want it. I'm putting the icings away to keep them cold and I've got my whole face in the fridge, near the steaming icebox at the top. The sweat across my upper lip dries in a sudden tingle and then I hear someone at the door. The bell rings, and it rings in a way I can tell is new.

Good thing or bad thing, I think.

Termite gets quiet.

'Who can that be?' I say out loud, like a charm. Like we're in a TV show about a charming mother and her kid. But we don't have a TV. Termite doesn't like those sounds. Joey always had the TV on at Tucci's, and Termite wouldn't even go inside. Back then, all those summers. He liked to be moving, or by the river, in the tunnel under the cool of the bridge. There's two bridges in town, both spanning the river: the spiny one for cars, all metal ribs and rattles, and the concrete one for trains, wide enough for four lines of track. Once they used all the tracks, Nonie says. Now just two are kept repaired, but the arches of the bridge are just as wide and the tunnel below as long and shady and deep. Termite likes it best. The echoes.

The doorbell rings again, twice. Somebody won't give up.

I push Termite's chair out past the dinette into the living room. I leave him sitting by the piano and through the window in the door

I can see somebody. Brown suit-coat and trousers, in this heat. Tie and button-down shirt. Glasses. I open the door and there's a man standing there with his briefcase in his arms, like he's about to hand it over to me. Not a real old man. Thick lenses in the glasses, so his eyes look magnified. Owl eyes. White-blond hair parted to the side under his hat. Fedora, like a banker's.

'Hello there,' he says. 'Hope it's not too early to stop by. I was hoping I could speak to—' He looks down at the papers he's got on top of the briefcase.

'My mother's not here,' I say.

'—your aunt. It says here your aunt. You must be Lark.'

'You're from Social Services,' I say.

'Yes. I'm the new caseworker assigned to your family. Actually I live two streets over, moved in a week ago. I was on my way to work, so I thought I'd stop.' He smiles in a nervous way. 'That's the good thing about these small towns,' he says. 'You can walk to work. Anyway, I can. I suppose you can walk to the high school.'

'I'm not at the high school. I take a secretarial course.' I've got my hand on the door and I push it shut just a little.

He steps up closer and looks over my shoulder at Termite in his chair. 'This is your brother? Termite. A nickname, I'd guess. What's his real name?'

'Terence,' I lie. I always seem to start lying to these people real quick. Even if I don't have to.

'By the way, my name is Robert Stamble.' He sticks his hand out at me from under the briefcase.

Stumble, Stamble, I think. And from that time on he's stumble, stammer, tumble, someone tripping in my head. Right away, I think he'd better leave. He thinks he means well and he doesn't know anything. I can smell it on him like a hint, like the Old Spice smell of his aftershave. I hate that smell. Dads wear it in Dadville. I look at him closer and see that he doesn't even look old enough to be much of a dad. He's pale pink as the rims of a rabbit's eyes, and blue-eyed behind his thick glasses. Hiding in his suit.

'Nonie's not here,' I say, 'and she says the cheque we get from Social Services is not enough to be harangued or bothered about. If you want to make a home visit, you should arrange it with her.'

'You know,' he says, 'we're very much in favour of in-home care whenever possible, and we want to support you. There may be ways we can help. Physical therapy. Equipment. A wheelchair.'

'He's got a wheelchair,' I say, 'a big heavy one. We keep it in the closet. He doesn't like it, but we use it for his medical appointments.'

He fumbles around, opens the briefcase, shuffles papers. 'Oh. Yes, of course, says so here in the file.' He looks up at me. 'One of the chairs Alderson passed on to the County.'

Alderson is the State Hospital that closed last year, one town over. They shipped the craziest loonies somewhere else and let go the ones that were only taking up space.

Stamble persists. 'Still, don't you find it easier than—'

I get it. He's seen me pull Termite in the wagon. I do most every day. The wagon is deep and safe, with high wooden slats for sides, and long enough Termite can stretch his legs out. It's like the old wagons they used to haul ice or coal. It was in the basement of this house when Nonie moved in, she says it's probably older than she is. 'Termite doesn't like the wheelchair,' I repeat.

Stamble nods. 'He's a child. He should have a smaller chair, one his size. Something portable would be easier for you.'

I think about that. Portable. Coming into port, like on a boat. Termite, bobbing on the waves. I'm watching him through a round window small as a plate. A porthole. We're coming up on a pretty little town by the sea, and Stamble blink, blink, blinks. For a minute I think he's fooling with me, then I realize he's nervous. Where did they get him?

He goes on at me. 'The newer chairs are lightweight. Easy to fold and unfold, take in and out of an automobile, whatever.'

'We don't have an automobile,' I tell Stamble, 'and I've never seen a chair like that around here.' I step back. 'Anyway, he doesn't like the chair he already has.'

'Maybe he needs a chance to get used to it, gradually of course. Does he mind the medical appointments?'

'No, not really. I wouldn't say he minds.'

'Because if he associates a wheelchair only with something he doesn't like, you could maybe change that by taking him to do something he really does like…in the wheelchair.'

I shift my weight and stand so he can't see behind me. Termite stays real quiet. If he knows when to be quiet, I don't know how they can say he doesn't know anything. 'Maybe so,' I tell Stamble. 'I've got to go now. I've got a cake baking.' I'm easing the door closed.

'Hot day for baking,' he says. 'Someone's birthday?'

I nod and smile through the narrow space that's left. 'You can call Noreen,' I say. 'If there's anything.' And the door is shut. I feel the knob turn in my hand and I hear the click.

'Very good to meet you,' I hear Stamble say from outside. 'I'll see what I can do about a more suitable chair.' Then I hear his footsteps going away. Termite has his head turned, his ear tilted toward me, and he doesn't move. I walk across the room to turn his chair back toward the kitchen and then I smell the cake, a sugary, toasted smell with a brown edge. 'Oh no,' I say, and move him back just enough to get the oven open, grab the layer pans with the hot pads. The cakes are a little too brown on top, but not bad. I show him one. 'It's fine,' I tell him, 'a tiny bit burnt, not so you'd taste.' *Tiny bit,* Termite says back to me in sounds like my words, *tiny bit.*

'Don't you worry,' I tell him.

I decorate the cake in three pale colours and keep it in the fridge all day so the icing sets up just right. After supper Nonie tells me to take the plastic stacking chairs out of the shed where they stay clean and I put them beside Termite's chair. I have a little round plastic table I put there too, for the drinks. Nick has mowed the alley. He takes off his work shirt and washes like always at our outside spigot.

'Cocktail hour at last,' he says. He puts the shirt back on and his wet skin soaks it through in spots, but he buttons it up like he's in a formal situation and combs his thick dark hair straight back with his hands. Water drips on to his collar in rivulets.

'Take a load off, Nick. You want some ice tea?' Nonie comes outside in her housedress. She takes off her apron and folds it in pieces, smaller and smaller, like her own flag, her own little ceremony.

'Jesus, is that all you're serving tonight?' Nick Tucci says. 'I work like a dog on the pasture here and you give me some tea?'

'I made a cake,' I tell him. 'A birthday cake. I'll get it in just a minute.'

'Another birthday? Lucky fellow.' He puts the flat of his palm on Termite's head. 'How you doing, Junior?'

Termite never answers Nick Tucci, he just gets quiet and holds still, like he thinks Nick is part of the mower or he carries the sound of the mower inside him. Maybe the sound is in Nick's hand, like a vibration, and Termite hears it. Maybe the vibration is there.

'Junior ought to take up for me,' Nick Tucci says. 'We men got to stick together.'

Nick won't call Termite by his name. He says that's the name of an insect, a bug, not a kid, not a boy, but he's the one who never waits for Termite to talk back. He fixed Termite's chair though. There was this upholstered chair with arms Termite liked to sit in like a nest, and Nick turned it over one day so its bottom showed all strange and naked. He took off the flimsy wooden stumps it had for legs and screwed on silver wheels he said were strong enough for carts that move pianos and refrigerators. He said they were sure strong enough for this dinky kid, and the chair was narrow enough to fit through the kitchen door, all the doors. Nonie says Nick is handy. Charlie, now, he can't fix a sink or a lamp cord. Nonie does all that at the restaurant, but Nick helps her here. Nick fastened a handle on to the back of Termite's chair so we could steer it, and he put a wooden ramp stapled with stair treads leading out the back door, over the stoop and the one step.

Termite was smaller then; he was so small when he started liking that chair that his feet didn't reach to the end of the seat cushion. His legs were always curved like they are, but we used to keep them out in front of him. It was later that he would whine and make noises until we tucked them under, like he didn't want to see them any more after he knew what they were.

Nick sits down in his own chair now, and Nonie sits just opposite, and he fixes her with a look. 'Noreen,' he says, 'I'm forty-two years old.'

Nonie has the blue Fiestaware pitcher that's squat and fat and sweats on its cold round sides, and she pours us three glasses of tea. 'You're a spring chicken,' she tells Nick. 'Good God, you can't complain until you're fifty, like me, and if you're a man, you can't complain then.'

'I got this passel of wild teenagers running around. They got three junkers between them now and I never know where they are.'

'Who says you need to know? You ran around plenty, Nick. You might not remember, but everyone else does.'

'Yeah,' he says, 'I'm still running. All day I feed the wrapper, and every night that cold beer gets colder.'

I think about Nick and the wrapper, how he stands between the belts and lifts the bales from one to the other. The plant makes business forms and the wrapper is the big machine that thuds a few thousand pages into a batch, wraps and seals them in plastic for shipping. Bale in and bale out, Nick Tucci says, his calling in life.

'I could near dive into that beer,' he goes on, 'I get too thirsty to live.'

'You don't want to get that thirsty,' Nonie says.

Termite says exactly what she does, without the words being in it, and he starts moving.

'What is it he wants?' Nonie says. 'Lark, get him a plastic glass and his straw, and get him that little doodad he likes. I swear, he's crazy about that thing.'

'I'll get the cake too,' I tell them.

While I'm in the kitchen I can see them through the window, and I can hear them, but they keep talking like I can't, like they think they sent me to another country.

'What are you doing to do about her, Noreen?' Nick Tucci says.

'What do you mean? She's finished her first year down at the secretarial school. That will give her something, a lot more than her diploma from that high school Zeke doesn't show up to half the time. She's got some financial assistance, for the good grades she always had. Barker girls can even be legal secretaries, if they go all three years. The last year is work-study. Maybe she can get a job with one of the lawyers in town.'

'She just going to sit here for three years, taking care of Junior in the days, and typing at night?'

'What would you like her to do, Nick?' I hear Nonie say. 'Run around with one of your boys, maybe?'

I'm looking for Termite's doodad, the little pitcher he likes. Where has that old thing got to? It's small, pale-yellow porcelain, doll size, easy to lose in a sinkful of dishes. He doesn't like me to wash it at all or take it from him, but he holds it so often I want it to be clean. The fat moon face on the front is winking and smiling, maybe that's why Termite likes the feel of it.

'Jesus, Noreen,' Nick says. 'Someone, sometime, is gonna drive up here by the alley and open the door for her to jump in. Don't you know that?'

I have to move all the dishes that are drying before I find the pitcher in the sink; it's so small it falls through the skinny rubber rungs of the drainer to underneath. I've got it in my hand, washing and drying the face. I can hear them outside, I can hear them perfectly well.

'Uh-huh,' I hear Nonie answer. 'And you think she's just going to ride off and leave Termite sitting here.' There's a beat of quiet like a pause in a song. 'You remember their mother, and I do,' Nonie says, 'but Lark is nothing like her.'

Nick doesn't say anything then, and Termite doesn't say anything either. It's no wonder I think he does understand some of what people say. I hear the bell on his chair. He rings it, just a small, glancing sound, once, and twice, and three times.

Be right there, I tell him, but I say it in my head. I catch myself doing that, when there are people around, like I think he can hear me. Here's his plastic cup and straw, and the handle of the moon pitcher fits around my smallest finger, like a ring. I put the silver-plate pie server in my pocket, the one I found last week in the basement, in the boxes Nonie keeps down there.

The tray with the rim around it is good for carrying things. Plates slide and they don't fall off, but the edge is low enough that the cake still looks pretty, sitting in the middle with dishes and spoons beside. People ought to see something pretty moving toward them. That way they get time to want what they really can have. I like coming out the door with something on a tray. Nonie looks over, and Nick does, and Termite turns too, like he can feel them looking even if he can't see what they see, and then Nick is up and coming over to hold the door. He winks at me, pleased and jaunty. For a minute I see how he looks like his boys, young in his eyes like them, and how his boys might look when they're older, big-chested like Nick, and working at the plant. If they broaden out like him. I guess it takes a man built like Nick to run the wrapper. There's a lever a man has to swing timed just so, and Nick can fix the wrapper too, keep it running. It's as big as a couple of cars parked close, side-to-side; he says it makes a noise like a jet engine pausing to yell Wham! every thirty seconds. A man has to be big to throw that lever and stand in that noise, move the bales on time like he's part of the machine. Nick's boys are all long and thin, and they move fluid as dogs; they have taut ropes of muscle in their necks, like they're always tense or ready, and swells of hard crescent under their nipples. Come spring, Joey and Solly and Zeke work on their cars in Nick's yard. They go without their shirts and their pants ride low on their hips. You can see the perfect run of their spines as they bend over, lean and white, lost to the chest in their engines. They were always hard and skinny, when they were little kids, when we were all little kids. I can't see Nick's boys ever being big and broad as Nick, like a wrestler, or moving so heavy, like he moves now, coming toward me. I can feel his footfalls on the stone walk through my bare feet. Then he's here, making a mock bow before he reaches to take the tray. I'm taller than Nonie now and Nick's dark eyes are level with mine. His forearms are furred with dark, curly hair. I look away when Nick gets too close, when he's a blur at the limit my eyes can see.

'Lark, you're too much,' he says.

'It's just a cake,' I say.

'Yes, it's a cake,' Nonie says. She shakes her head at Nick.

'But look at it, Noreen. Little white garlands in the icing, and the garlands are braided. How does she do that?' He nods over at Termite. 'You were here, Junior. How does she do it?'

'An icing bag with special attachments,' I say. 'Gourmet baking set. I got it for my birthday.'

'My point exactly,' Nick says. 'For your birthday you want some fancy cooking gadget so you can make exotic creations. My thugs want new carburettors, so they can drive even faster and end up in the pokey in the next county, and their old man can come bail them out.' He's carrying the tray in front of me and I follow the hulk of his back. 'Joey's latest thought is to join the Marines. Driving delivery for the plant's not good enough, he wants to see the world. Zeke can't pass tenth grade but he's got him a car put together. And Saul. Now he wants a motorcycle.'

'He want you to buy it?' Nonie asks.

Saul is the middle one, the one most like a wolf, with his green eyes and his thick fair hair, and that dark skin, like Nick's. Solly has been in school with me since first grade over on Lumber Street. They put him back a grade though, for skipping school so much when he was nine or ten. He ended up a grade behind me, even though he's

Jayne Anne Phillips

a year older. Their mother had left before school even happened, when Zeke was barely walking. Nick Tucci bought the groceries. Nonie took care of those boys and fed us all supper at night, then sent us all over to Nick's when he pulled in from work. She used his car to go off to Charlie's for the dinner shift, then closed up and got home around eleven, carried me down the alley from Nick's to my own bed. She says I never stirred, but I remember the leaves on the trees moving, blowing above me at night. There used to be trees along the alley. That was a long time ago. After Termite came, Nonie's friend Elise stayed with him and me at night, after Nick's kids would go home. Nonie went to work and Solly would come back over. Guess you think we're better than TV over here, Elise would tell him, better than Jack Benny. If we weren't doing homework she'd have us 'helping out', running the sweeper, folding laundry, entertaining Termite. Elise brought over a clock radio she got with S&H green stamps, and she taught us card games so she'd have someone to play with. Solly played rummy with her while I read to Termite, or Elise would bring over whatever she wanted to hear. *Gone With The Wind. Little Dorrit. Good Housekeeping* magazine: 'Can This Marriage Be Saved?' Elise said I was better than the radio, better than *Playhouse 90.*

When I was eleven Elise started running the Mini-Mart across from Charlie's. After that I took care of Termite myself. He was little. I could do it as well as anyone. Solly still came by. I know Solly like I know the shelves in my room, and the turn of the walls. There's always been a wild quiet about Solly. It stays in the air near him like a scent.

'Solly doesn't need me to buy him anything,' Nick says now. We've reached our little enclave and he puts the cake on the round table. 'He's been pumping gas and fixing cars down at the Amoco all year. Somebody pulled in with this thing on a flatbed and now Solly thinks he's got to have it.'

'Well, he doesn't,' Nonie says. 'He lives with you and you're his father and you can tell him he can't have it.'

'Sure,' Nick says, 'and I'll see his back real quick. The kid managed to get through high school not half trying. I want him to work this summer, save money, maybe go to college next year.'

'But his grades weren't bad,' I say. 'Solly's smart. He should go to college. Couldn't he play football somewhere?'

'You tell him.' Nick turns and looks at me. 'I'm serious.'

120

'That's not her job,' Nonie answers him. Then, 'She's the one should be going to college.'

There's no college near enough, though. Nowhere I could take classes at night. 'Sit down, Nick.' I'm moving the plates, handing out napkins. I put Termite's moon into his palm. He holds it in his lap, rubs the flat of his wrist across its grimace of a face that's all wrinkles and bulging cheeks, like no face, even a porcelain face, is too small to wink or sigh. Termite moves his wrist across and across like he didn't have hold of it just this morning. I have the cake server, a shiny wedge shape with a carved handle and serrated edge, *Lenox* on the back in tiny script. It has its own velvety envelope to keep off tarnish; there's just a shadow of dark along the blade. I touch the shadow with my thumb. If these are my mother's things, why are they here? I always thought of her walking, moving, some landscape streaming away behind her. Now that I've actually taken something from her secrets, I think of a green lawn holding her, or a coastline where she disappeared, even an alleyway where it happened. A dark bitter alley, cinders and trash. No. Make it an alley like ours, grass, white gravel, summer dusk. I see Nonie recognize the cake server in my hand, but she doesn't say anything. 'I'll cut the cake,' I tell them, 'if everyone will kindly take a seat.'

Termite gives me his little half smile and starts talking. *Take a seat. Take a seat.*

'He sounds like a bird sometimes,' Nick says.

Take a seat is what I say to him when we're in the basement, cooling off, sitting in the old couch that has its springs out right through to the cold cement floor. It's the couch Charlie used for years in the office of the restaurant, a narrow room behind the kitchen where Nonie did the accounts and bills. It's a big couch, long and broad enough for one person on top of another. This summer I realized the use they must have put it to nights when I was a child, and slept at Nick's on a love seat by the living room door so Nonie could retrieve me without disturbing anyone. Or no one but Solly, who was likely curled up next to me. It was this summer too that I started looking through Nonie's boxes. Pretending is a lie I'm tired of telling her by now. Down there with Termite one of the hot afternoons, sitting at the workbench so he could use the big crayons he can hold, I saw how the boxes were stacked, balanced and squared, like they'd been there a long time. Termite holds the crayon tight. Once I get him started, he moves his arm up and down, back and forth, long arcs in one colour across unfolded newspaper, while I draw in my notebook. He doesn't look at what he makes but I watch his colours get darker. Most of the time, I draw him. Standing in space. No chair, no alley. That day I turned the radio loud the way Termite likes it. 'Heartbreak Hotel' was on and I looked over at the boxes. *Well since your baby left you. You've got a tale to tell.* The boxes had always been in that corner, sometimes covered with other stuff. They were big and they were all the same size, plain, like from a moving company, a solid dusty wall stacked four across and four deep. I went over and touched them, careful, like they were sleeping. The song went on about Lonely Street while I wiped off the dust. The boxes were solid and full and hard to rock, taped shut and never opened, addressed to Nonie in somebody's handwriting. I saw where they were mailed from and I decided to go slowly. I know the stuff in the two boxes I've gone through was never Nonie's. No pictures though, no documents, no papers to tell me more than I already know.

Termite is still saying a one-note tone. *Seat, seat, seat.*

'Kind of musical,' Nick says. 'A bird making its own sense.'

'Or not,' Nonie says.

'Termite can imitate almost anything,' I say. 'Things just sound more like music in his version, since there are sounds instead of words.'

Nonie leans forward to help Termite with his cake. He can hold bigger things than spoons—his pitcher, fat crayons. He holds his strips of blue because we wrap them around his wrist. But spoons and forks are too thin and hard. We know exactly how to feed him. Touch, touch, each side of his mouth, neat and fast. Nonie's looking at him and I wonder what she sees. 'You never make things up, though, do you, Termite?' she says.

'No,' I say, 'he doesn't.'

It's a fact. Termite can only tell the truth. I know she means she wishes, she wishes, he could say something more than the sound of what he's just heard. I pretend he knows more, backward and forward for miles.

'Good cake,' Nick says. 'And this cold tea is mighty nice, evening like this. The air is goddam still, heavy as lead. That storm coming in. Tomorrow, or the next day. Rain all week, they say. Maybe it'll clean up the river a little. I don't like such a brown muck of a river.'

'Lord, Nick.' Nonie laughs. 'That river was always brown.'

'Not so, Noreen. The river was cleaner years ago. You could see into it. In the dark it was olive green. I remember.'

'In the days it was—' She goes on at him, making fun now.

'Sapphire,' I chime in. 'It was sapphire. Bright, stone blue.'

Nick Tucci gives me a look, then he nods. 'Knocked your eyes out,' he says. 'Standing there under the rail bridge, watching the water. Oh, that blue river.'

We're laughing, and Termite hunches his shoulders, throws his head back to look up into the plum-coloured sky, like the river is up there somewhere. *That blue river.* He says it in high and low sounds, and the sky over us could be a river, bruised and deep as it looks. I reach over and tilt his chin down. His head is heavy and his neck muscles are not so strong. He throws his head back again, right away.

'He's got his opinions, has Junior,' says Nick Tucci. 'You tell them, Junior.'

'Leave him be, Lark.' Nonie's eyes get wet when she laughs hard. 'He's taking a sounding. My god, that sky does look like it could fall. Should be a full moon tonight, but we won't see anything behind clouds like those.'

I can see Termite's nostrils move, a vibration so slight, like the gill of a fish moving when it breathes, and I hear him smell the air like he's drinking it. I wonder does he see the clouds at all, does he feel the colour instead, or does he think a river is like a sky, so he looks up? Why would he think that? Because it's true, he could think the sky is like a river that doesn't stop. Nonie would say he just reacts to us, our laughing, our shouting, whatever. She'd say I give him things to know, even if I don't know what those things are.

Then I think of the candles. 'Not much of a birthday, is it Termite? I forgot about candles.'

'You don't need candles every time, Lark.' Nonie feels the pockets of the apron she took off. They're all blue aprons. She wears them at work.

'I kind of promised him,' I say. 'Too late now.' But Termite tilts his head back down, gives me his sideways look.

He can hold his head up now except for when he's tired. From the time I was a kid I thought his head was heavy because there was so much in it he couldn't tell or say. That everything had stayed in him, whether he recognized the pictures or not. That he'd kept all the words I couldn't call up, our mother's words and words about her. Words from before we were born, what I heard until I was three and forgot. Words about what house what road or street who was there how she looked and talked and why she sent us to Nonie. It's hard taking care of Termite but she kept him for a year, she tried. Why did she try or stop trying? And I was a normal kid she didn't keep, except I'm not normal, because I don't remember her. I've got my own big blank but no one can see it in the shape of my head, in how I speak or don't speak or don't move. It's like by the time he was born there was too much to know. It filled his head too full, then wiped it blank. If I said this to Nonie she'd say I like my own stories. These are birth defects, she'd tell me. No one knows why or what.

'Not too late,' Nonie says. 'We have most of a cake here, and a few leftover candles. Somebody celebrated at the restaurant today, with a piece of Charlie's lemon pie.' Nonie has a partly crushed box of those little skinny candles they give away free at bakeries.

'Pie is all wrong with candles,' Nick Tucci says. There are only three candles, but he's leaning forward, putting them on the cake. 'Should be nine, right? Each one of these counts for three years, Junior, so the flames gotta be extra high.' He lights them with his cigarette lighter, then he stands and picks up the plate and holds it just in front of Termite. Nonie and I get up and stand beside him, our faces either side of his, so close we touch, and we let the candles burn, then we blow, really slow, with Termite. The little flames flutter perfectly and go out just right, all at once.

I lean down close to him and whisper, in the powdery smell of his hair, 'Your birthday, Termite, every day.'

Every day, he says back to me, *every day, every day*. ☐

THE STEAM PEOPLE
Robin Grierson

Text by Ian Jack

Ian Jack

In *Tess of the d'Urbervilles*, published in 1891 but set in Wessex a few decades before that date, Thomas Hardy describes the coming of a steam engine to Flintcomb-Ash Farm at harvest time. The engine's job is to power the threshing machine. Tess's job is to stand on the threshing machine's platform and untie each bundle in the day-long procession of corn sheaves handed to her by her companion, Izz Huett, and then to pass the untied corn to the man feeding the revolving drum 'which whisked out every grain in one moment'.

That work has yet to begin. The tall-funnelled engine stands in the dawn light, hissing 'with a sustained hiss that spoke of strength very much in reserve'. And by the engine stands a steam man: 'a sooty and grimy embodiment of tallness, in a sort of trance, with a heap of coals by his side: it was the engineman.' Hardy writes that in his isolation the engineman looked like a misplaced creature from Tophet—a biblical reference; Tophet was a place near Gehenna where bonfires burned day and night and therefore symbolized hell. He had 'strayed into the pellucid smokelessness of this region of yellow grain and pale soil, with which he had nothing in common, to amaze and to discompose its aborigines'. He was 'in the agricultural world, but not of it. He served fire and smoke; these denizens of the fields served vegetation, weather, frost, and sun. He travelled with his engine from farm to farm, from county to county… He spoke in a strange northern accent… The long strap which ran from the driving wheel of his engine to the red thresher under the rick was the sole tie-line between agriculture and him.'

Steam railway-locomotives, steam ships, steam mills: all of these attracted writers, and sometimes—in the work, say, of Dickens, Zola, Kipling, Conrad, Twain—they appear as more than incidentals. But Hardy's is a rare writerly account of a different kind of steam machine, one that flourished in fields and farms throughout the world during the brief window—eighty years at most—between the age of muscle power, animal and human, and the coming of the internal combustion engine.

England invented and perfected the steam engine. By the 1830s, English farmers were surrounded in the world's first industrial nation by the evidence of what it could do in transport, manufacture and mining. Applying it to agriculture was a trickier question. Some large farms built stationary steam engines to thresh corn, saw timber and cut chaff, but farms worked by seasons; often the engine lay still and unemployed. A portable engine was the answer, hired by the farmer when he needed it, drawn by horse from farm to farm. By the late 1850s, the portable engine became self-propelled; steam rather than horses moved it down country lanes to the place where it would winnow the harvest. The new mobility gave it other uses. Self-propelled engines—traction engines—could be adapted to plough, tow farm carts, move circuses and fairgrounds around the country, roll metalled roads firm and flat.

Agricultural machinery makers in the marketing towns of eastern England built many thousands of them. One company alone (and not the largest), Clayton and Shuttleworth of Lincoln, claimed a total of 31,000 by the year 1897, and opened subsidiary plants in Vienna, Budapest, Prague and Kraków. In the United States, Jerome Increase Case (the 'Threshing King') built 36,000 between 1869 and 1928 at his plant in Racine on the Ohio river. (In 2001, one of these engines, lovingly but also carelessly preserved, blew up at a county fair in Medina, Ohio, killing five people and injuring forty more.)

For a time, they were ubiquitous. Pillars of their smoke rose above the Prairies and the plains of East Anglia. They ploughed the sugar beet fields of Germany and the cotton fields of Egypt. They levelled waste tips at South African diamond mines. In India, their ploughs cut through sunbaked clay. They broke up virgin land in Java and the lava soils of Italian vineyards. English aristocrats used them to dredge ornamental lakes. They were sent to Peru, Antigua, Australia, New Zealand, and to the Boer war. They can be seen in pictures of the Gallipoli landings, towing munitions from the beach, and at the Russian front in the same war, cutting trenches for the Tsar's army. Benito Mussolini never forgot the English traction engines he had seen as a boy and in 1932 ordered two especially powerful ones—fascist engines, built in Leeds—for his scheme to drain the Pontine marshes.

But by then the steam traction engine's heyday was over. As early as 1911, the Manitoba Steam Plow Trials (which were said to be 'the foremost agricultural event in the world') had been won by a petrol-engined tractor. England made its last traction engine in 1942, though its variant, the steamroller, had a renewed life as a flattener and repairer of bomber runways for a few years after.

Useless, redundant, they became loved. Their brass and steel, their history, attracted hobbyists and enthusiasts, men (though not solely men) who liked to mend, tinker and polish. In Britain, this enthusiasm is now fifty years old—a tradition in itself, known by its adherents as 'the traction engine movement'. Out of it have come clubs, societies, rallies, magazines, and around 2,500 preserved and working engines which in summer are shown off at steam fairs, when the skies of rural England are once again smudged by coal smoke and over the hedges you can hear steam whistles pooping.

In my copy of *Tess of the d'Urbervilles*, the introduction by P. N. Furbank notes that 'Tess, enslaved to the steam threshing machine, typifies traditional agriculture in its defeat'. In the context of a steam fair, it is odd to read that. Steam fairs, as well as displaying steam engines, are a great conglomeration of make-believe, of the long ago and far away, of what England thinks of as its traditional pursuits: bee-keeping, gypsy caravans, roundabouts, steam organs, clog-making, spoon-carving, coin jewellery, weaving, knot-tying, rabbit-keeping, pottery, biscuit, cake and fudge manufacture, home-made jams, meat pies, quiche and sausage rolls. In this world, the steam engine isn't Hardy's vile rupture of England's rural past but a vital part of its continuum, as 'traditional' now as a horse brass.

The biggest of these fairs, said to be the biggest of its kind in the world, takes place over five days every August in Dorset—Hardy's own county. It can attract five hundred steam engines and 250,000 people. It was there in 1992 that the photographer Robin Grierson, who started his working life as a garage fitter and knows machines, began to take pictures of steam engines, their owners and their audience. He has been photographing them ever since. The pictures on the following pages are a selection from his work—pictures of a popular but neglected slice of England now, as it exists, though of this fact it is sometimes hard to be sure. □

THE MONTESI SCANDAL

The Death of Wilma Montesi and the Birth of the Paparazzi in Fellini's Rome

Karen Pinkus

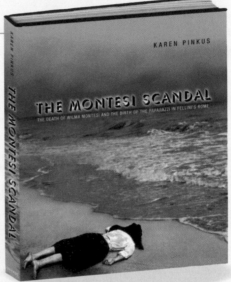

"While the police asserted that Wilma Montesi had died as a result of an accident, the press pursued its own independent quest for justice. On May 14, a Naples news-paper dropped a bombshell on Rome that would explode into 'the scandal of the century.'"
—Gabriel Garcia Marquez, *La Repubblica*, 1953

46 halftones ✦ Cloth $27.50

"Scholarly and entertaining at the same time. Reading Karen Pinkus's book is like attending your favorite class at college. You hardly realize that you're 'learning' because you're having such a good time. I remember going to see *La Dolce Vita* for the first time. I felt compelled to study the 'film' but I couldn't because I was too busy watching the 'movie.'"—George Romero

The University of Chicago Press
1427 East 60th Street, Chicago, IL 60637
www.press.uchicago.edu

THE TUTOR
Nell Freudenberger

S he was an American girl, but one who apparently kept Bombay time, because it was three-thirty when she arrived for their one o'clock appointment. It was a luxury to be able to blame someone else for his wasted afternoon, and Zubin was prepared to take full advantage of it. Then the girl knocked on his bedroom door.

He had been in the preparation business for four years, but Julia was his first foreign student. She was dressed more like a Spanish or an Italian girl than an American, in a sheer white blouse and tight jeans that sat very low on her hips, perhaps to show off the tiny diamond in her belly button. Her hair was shiny, reddish-brown— chestnut you would call it—and she'd ruined her hazel eyes with a heavy application of thick, black eyeliner.

'I have to get into Berkeley,' she told him.

It was typical for kids to fixate on one school. 'Why Berkeley?'

'Because it's in San Francisco.'

'Technically Berkeley's a separate city.'

'I know that,' Julia said. 'I was born in San Francisco.'

She glanced at the bookshelves that covered three walls of his room. He liked the kids he tutored to see them, although he knew his pride was irrelevant: most didn't know the difference between Spender and Spenser, or care.

'Have you *read* all of these?'

'Actually that's the best way to improve your verbal. It's much better to see the words in context.' He hated the idea of learning words from a list; it was like taking vitamin supplements in place of eating. But Julia looked discouraged, and so he added: 'Your dad says you're a math whiz, so we don't need to do that.'

'He said that?'

'You aren't?'

Julia shrugged. 'I just can't believe he said "whiz".'

'I'm paraphrasing,' Zubin said. 'What were your scores?'

'Five hundred and sixty verbal, 760 math.'

Zubin whistled. 'You scored higher than I did on the math.'

Julia smiled, as if she hadn't meant to, and looked down. 'My college counsellor says I need a really good essay. Then my verbal won't matter so much.' She dumped out the contents of an expensive-looking black leather knapsack, and handed him the application, which was loose and folded into squares. Her nails were bitten, and decorated with half-moons of pale pink polish.

'I'm such a bad writer though.' She was standing expectantly in front of him. Each time she took a breath, the diamond in her stomach flashed.

'I usually do lessons in the dining room,' Zubin said.

The only furniture in his parents' dining room was a polished mahogany table, covered with newspapers and magazines, and a matching sideboard—storage space for jars of pickle, bottles of Wild Turkey from his father's American friends, his mother's bridge trophies, and an enormous, very valuable Chinese porcelain vase, which the servants had filled with artificial flowers: red, yellow and salmon-coloured cloth roses beaded with artificial dew. On nights when he didn't go out, he preferred having his dinner served to him in his room; his parents did the same.

He sat down at the table, but Julia didn't join him. He read aloud from the form. 'Which book that you've read in the last two years has influenced you most, and why?'

Julia wandered over to the window.

'That sounds okay,' he encouraged her.

'I hate reading.'

'Talk about the place where you live, and what it means to you.' Zubin looked up from the application. 'There you go. That one's made for you.'

She'd been listening with her back to him, staring down Ridge Road toward the Hanging Garden. Now she turned around—did a little spin on the smooth tiles.

'Can we get coffee?'

'Do you want milk and sugar?'

Julia looked up, as if shyly. 'I want to go to Barista.'

'It's loud there.'

'I'll pay,' Julia said.

'Thanks. I can pay for my own coffee.'

Julia shrugged. 'Whatever—as long as I get my fix.'

Zubin couldn't help smiling.

'I need it five times a day. And if I don't get espresso and a cigarette first thing in the morning, I have to go back to bed.'

'Your parents know you smoke?'

'God, no. Our driver knows—he uses it as blackmail.' She smiled.

'No smoking is my dad's big rule.'

'What about your mom?'

'She went back to the States to find herself. I decided to stay with my dad,' Julia added, although he hadn't asked. 'He lets me go out.'

Zubin couldn't believe that any American father would let his teenage daughter go out at night in Bombay. 'Go out where?'

'My friends have parties. Or sometimes clubs—there's that new place, Fire and Ice.'

'You should be careful,' Zubin told her.

Julia smiled. 'That's so Indian.'

'Anyone would tell you to be careful—it's not like the States.'

'No,' Julia said.

He was surprised by the bitterness in her voice. 'You miss it.'

'I am missing it.'

'You mean now in particular?'

Julia was putting her things back into the knapsack haphazardly—phone, cigarettes, datebook, chapstick. She squinted at the window, as if the light were too bright. 'I mean, I don't even know what I'm missing.'

Homesickness was like any other illness: you couldn't remember it properly. You knew you'd had the flu, and that you'd suffered, but you didn't have access to the symptoms themselves: the chills, the swollen throat, the heavy ache in your arms and legs as if they'd been split open and something—sacks of rock—had been sewn up inside. He had been eighteen, and in America for only the second time. It was cold. The sweaters he'd bought in Bombay looked wrong—he saw that the first week—and they weren't warm enough anyway. He saw the same sweaters, of cheap, shiny wool, in too-bright colours, at the 'international' table in the Freshman Union. He would not sit there.

His room-mate saw him go out in his T-shirt and windcheater, and offered to loan him one of what seemed like dozens of sweaters: brown or black or wheat-coloured, the thickest, softest wool Zubin had ever seen. He went to the Harvard Coop, where they had a clothing section, and looked at the sweaters. He did the calculation several times: the sweaters were 'on sale' for eighty dollars, which worked out to roughly 3,300 rupees. If it had been a question of just one he might have managed, but you needed a minimum of three. When the salesperson came over, Zubin said that he was just looking around.

It snowed early that year.

'It gets like, how cold in the winter in India?' his room-mate Bennet asked.

Zubin didn't feel like explaining the varied geography of India, the mountains and the coasts. 'About sixty degrees Fahrenheit,' he said.

'*Man,*' said Bennet. Jason Bennet was a nice guy, an athlete from Natick, Massachusetts. He took Zubin to eat at the lacrosse table, where Zubin looked not just foreign, but as if he were another species—he weighed at least ten kilos less than the smallest guy, and felt hundreds of years older. He felt as if he were surrounded by enormous and powerful children. They were hungry, and then they were restless; they ran around and around in circles, and then they were tired. Five nights a week they'd pledged to keep sober; on the other two they drank systematically until they passed out.

He remembered the day in October that he'd accepted the sweater (it was raining) and how he'd waited until Jason left for practice before putting it on. He pulled the sweater over his head and saw, in the second of woolly darkness, his father. Or rather, he saw his father's face, floating in his mind's eye like the Cheshire Cat. The face was making an expression that Zubin remembered from the time he was ten, and had proudly revealed the thousand rupees he'd made by organizing a betting pool on the horse races among the boys in the fifth standard.

He'd resolved immediately to return the sweater, and then he had looked in the mirror. What he saw surprised him: someone small but good-looking, with fine features and dark, intense eyes, the kind of guy a girl, not just a girl from home but any girl—an American girl—might find attractive.

And he wanted one of those: there was no use pretending he didn't. He watched them from his first-floor window, as close as fish in an aquarium tank. They hurried past him, laughing and calling out to one another, in their boys' clothes: boots, T-shirts with cryptic messages, jeans worn low and tight across the hips. You thought of the panties underneath those jeans, and in the laundry room you often saw those panties: impossibly sheer, in incredible colours, occasionally, delightfully torn. The girls folding their laundry next to him were entirely different from the ones at home. They were clearly free to do whatever they wanted—a possibility that often hit him, in class or the library or on the historic brick walkways of the Radcliffe Quad, so intensely that he had to stop and take a deep breath, as if he were on the point of blacking out.

He wore Jason's sweater every day, and was often too warm; the classrooms were overheated and dry as furnaces. He almost never ran into Jason, who had an active and effortless social schedule to complement his rigorous athletic one. And so it was a surprise, one day in late October, to come back to the room and find his room-mate hunched miserably over a textbook at his desk.

'Midterms,' Jason said, by way of an explanation. Zubin went over and looked at the problem set, from an introductory physics class. He'd taken a similar class at Cathedral; now he laid out the equations and watched as Jason completed them, correcting his room-mate's mistakes as they went along. After the third problem Jason looked up.

'Man, thanks.' And then, as if it had just occurred to him. 'Hey, if you want to keep that—'

He had managed so completely to forget about the sweater that he almost didn't know what Jason meant.

'It's too small for me anyway.'

'No,' Zubin said.

'Seriously. I may have a couple of others too. Coach has been making us eat like hogs.'

'Thanks,' Zubin said. 'But I want something less preppy.'

Jason looked at him.

'No offence,' Zubin said. 'I've just been too fucking lazy. I'll go tomorrow.'

The next day he went back to the Coop with his almost-new textbooks in a bag. These were for his required classes (what they called the Core, or general knowledge), as well as organic chemistry. If you got to the reserve reading room at nine, the textbooks were almost always there. He told himself that the paperbacks for his nineteenth-century novel class weren't worth selling—he'd bought them used anyway—and when he took the rest of the books out and put them on the counter, he realized he had forgotten the *Norton Anthology of American Literature* in his dorm room. But the books came to $477.80 without it. He took the T downtown to a mall where he bought a down jacket for $300, as warm as a sleeping bag, the same thing the black kids wore. He got a wool watchman's cap with a Nike swoosh.

When he got home, Jason laughed. 'Dude, what happened? You're totally ghetto.' But there was approval in it. Folding the brown sweater on Jason's bed, Zubin felt strong and relieved, as if he had narrowly avoided a terrible mistake.

Julia had been having a dream about losing it. There was no sex in the dream; she couldn't remember whom she'd slept with, or when. All she experienced was the frustrating impossibility of getting it back, like watching an earring drop and scatter in the bathroom sink, roll and clink down the drain before she could put her hand on it. The relief she felt on waking up every time was like a warning.

She had almost lost it in Paris, before they moved. He was German, not French, gangly but still handsome, with brown eyes and blondish hair. His name was Markus. He was a year ahead of her at the American School and he already knew that he wanted to go back to Berlin for university, and then join the Peace Corps. On the phone at night, he tried to get her to come with him.

At dinner Julia mentioned this idea to her family.

'*You* in the Peace Corps?' said her sister Claudia, who was visiting from New York. 'I wonder if Agnès B. makes a safari line?'

When Claudia came home, she stayed with Julia on the fourth floor, in the *chambre de bonne* where she had twin beds and her Radiohead poster, all her CDs organized by record label and a very old stuffed monkey named Frank. The apartment was half a block from the Seine, in an old hotel on the Rue des Saint-Pères; in the living room were two antique chairs, upholstered in red-and-gold striped brocade, and a porcelain clock with shepherdesses on it. The chairs and the clock were Louis XVI, the rugs were from Tehran, and everything else was beige linen.

Claudia, who now lived with her boyfriend in a railroad apartment on the Lower East Side, liked to pretend she was poor. She talked about erratic hot water and rent control and cockroaches, and when she came to visit them in Paris she acted surprised, as if the houses she'd grown up in—first San Francisco, then Delhi, then Dallas, Moscow and Paris—hadn't been in the same kind of neighbourhood, with the same pair of Louis XIV chairs.

'I can't believe you have a Prada backpack,' she said to Julia. Claudia had been sitting at the table in the kitchen, drinking espresso and eating an orange indifferently, section by section. 'Mom's going crazy in her old age.'

'I bought it,' Julia said.

'Yeah but, with what?'

'I've been selling my body on the side—after school.'

Claudia rolled her eyes and took a sip of her espresso; she looked out the window into the little back garden. 'It's so *peaceful* here,' she said, proving something Julia already suspected: that her sister had no idea what was going on in their house.

It started when her father's best friend, Bernie, left Paris to take a job with a French wireless company in Bombay. He'd wanted Julia's father to leave with him, but even though her father complained all the time about the oil business, he wouldn't go. Julia heard him telling her mother that he was in the middle of an important deal.

'This is the biggest thing we've done. I love Bernie—but he's afraid of being successful. He's afraid of a couple of fat Russians.'

Somehow Bernie had managed to convince her mother that Bombay was a good idea. She would read the share price of the wireless company out loud from the newspaper in the mornings, while her father was making eggs. It was a strange reversal; in the past, all her mother had wanted was for her father to stay at home. The places he travelled had been a family joke, as if he were trying to outdo himself with the strangeness of the cities—Istanbul and Muscat eventually became Tbilisi, Ashkhabad, Tashkent. Now, when Julia had heard the strained way that her mother talked about Bernie and wireless communication, she had known she was hearing part of a larger argument—known enough to determine its size, if not its subject. It was like watching the exposed bit of a dangerous piece of driftwood, floating just above the surface of a river.

Soon after Claudia's visit, in the spring of Julia's freshman year, her parents gave her a choice. Her mother took her to Galeries Lafayette, and then to lunch at her favourite crêperie on the Ile Saint-Louis where, in between *galettes tomate-fromage* and *crêpe pomme-chantilly*, she told Julia about the divorce. She said she had found a two-bedroom apartment in the West Village: a 'feat', she called it.

'New York will be a fresh start—psychologically,' her mother said.

Nell Freudenberger

'There's a bedroom that's just yours, and we'll be a five-minute train ride from Claudie. There are wonderful girls' schools—I know you were really happy at Hockaday—'

'No I wasn't.'

'Or we can look at some co-ed schools. And I'm finally going to get to go back for my masters—' She leaned forward confidentially. 'We could both be graduating at the same time.'

'I want to go back to San Francisco.'

'We haven't lived in San Francisco since you were three.'

'So?'

The sympathetic look her mother gave her made Julia want to yank the tablecloth out from underneath their dishes, just to hear the glass breaking on the rustic stone floor.

'For right now that isn't possible,' her mother said. 'But there's no reason we can't talk again in a year.'

Julia had stopped being hungry, but she finished her mother's crêpe anyway. Recently her mother had stopped eating anything sweet; she said it 'irritated her stomach' but Julia knew the real reason was Dr Fabrol, who had an office on the Ile Saint-Louis very near the crêperie. Julia had been seeing Dr Fabrol once a week during the two years they'd been in Paris; his office was dark and tiny, with a rough brown rug and tropical plants which he misted from his chair with a plastic spritzer while Julia was talking. When he got excited he swallowed, making a clicking sound in the back of his throat.

In front of his desk Dr Fabrol kept a sandbox full of little plastic figures: trolls with brightly coloured hair, toy soldiers, and a little dollhouse people dressed in American clothes from the Fifties. He said that adults could learn a lot about themselves by playing '*les jeux des enfants*'. In one session, when Julia couldn't think of anything to say, she'd made a ring of soldiers in the sand, and then without looking at him, put the mother doll in the centre. She thought this might be over the top even for Dr Fabrol, but he started arranging things on his desk, pretending he was less interested than he was so that she would continue. She could hear him clicking.

The mother doll had yellow floss hair and a full figure and a red-and-white polka-dotted dress with a belt, like something Lucille Ball would wear. She looked nothing like Julia's mother—a fact that Dr Fabrol obviously knew, since Julia's mother came so often to pick

170

her up. Sometimes she would be carrying bags from the nearby shops; once she told them she'd just come from an exhibit at the new Islamic cultural centre. She brought Doctor Fabrol a postcard of a Phoenician sarcophagus.

'I think this was the piece you mentioned?' Her mother's voice was louder than necessary. 'I think you must have told me about it—the last time I was here to pick Julia up?'

'Could be, could be,' Dr Fabrol said, in his stupid accent. They both watched Julia as if she were a TV and they were waiting to find out about the weather. She couldn't believe how dumb they must have thought she was.

Her father asked her if she wanted to go for an early morning walk with their black labrador, Baxter, in the Tuileries. She would've said no—she wasn't a morning person—if she hadn't known what was going on from the lunch with her mother. They put their coats on in the dark hall with Baxter running around their legs, but by the time they left the apartment, the sun was coming up. The river threw off bright sparks. They crossed the bridge, and went through the archway into the courtyard of the Louvre. There were no tourists that early but a lot of people were walking or jogging on the paths above the fountain.

'Look at all these people,' her father said. 'A few years ago, they wouldn't have been awake. If they were awake they would've been having coffee and a cigarette. Which reminds me.'

Julia held the leash while her father took out his cigarettes. He wasn't fat but he was tall and pleasantly big. His eyes squeezed shut when he smiled, and he had a beard, mostly grey now, which he trimmed every evening before dinner with special scissors. When she was younger, she had looked at other fathers and felt sorry for their children; no one else's father looked like a father to her.

In the shade by the stone wall of the Tuileries, with his back to the flashing fountain, her father tapped the pack, lifted it to his mouth and pulled a cigarette out between his lips. He rummaged in the pocket of his brown corduroys for a box of the tiny wax matches he always brought back from India, a white swan on a red box. He cupped his hand, lit the cigarette and exhaled away from Julia. Then he took back Baxter's leash and said: 'Why San Francisco?'

She wasn't prepared. 'I don't know.' She could picture the broad stillness of the bay, like being inside a postcard. Was she remembering a postcard?

'It's quiet,' she said.

'I didn't know quiet was high on your list.'

She tried to think of something else.

'You know what I'd like?' her father asked suddenly. 'I'd like to watch the sunrise from the Golden Gate—do you remember doing that?'

'Yes,' Julia lied.

'I think you were in your stroller.' Her father grinned. 'That was when you were an early riser.'

'I could set my alarm.'

'You could set it,' her father teased her.

'I'm awake now,' she said.

Her father stopped to let Baxter nose around underneath one of the grey stone planters. He looked at the cigarette in his hand as if he didn't know what to do with it, dropped and stamped it out, half smoked.

'Can I have one?'

'Over my dead body.'

'I'm not sure I want to go to New York.'

'You want to stay here?' He said it lightly, as if it were a possibility.

'I want to go with you,' she said. As she said it, she knew how much she wanted it.

She could see him trying to say no. Their shadows were very sharp on the clean paving stones; above the bridge, the gold Mercury was almost too bright to look at.

'Just for the year and a half.'

'*Bombay*,' her father said.

'I liked India last time.'

Her father looked at her. 'You were six.'

'Why are you going?'

'Because I hate oil and I hate oilmen. And I hate these goddamn *kommersant*s. If I'd done it when Bernie first offered—' Her father stopped. 'You do not need to hear about this.'

Julia didn't need to hear about it; she already knew. Her father was taking the job in Bombay—doing exactly what her mother had wanted him to do—just as her parents were getting a divorce. The only explanation was that he'd found out about Dr Fabrol. Even though her mother was going to New York (where she would have to find another psychologist to help her get over Julia's), Julia could see how her father wouldn't want to stay in Paris. He would want to get as far away as possible.

Julia steered the conversation safely toward business: 'It's like, mobile phones, right?'

'It is mobile phones.' Her father smiled at her. 'Something you know about.'

'I'm not *that* bad.'

'No, you're not.'

They'd walked a circle in the shade, on the promenade above the park. Her father stopped, as if he wasn't sure whether he wanted to go around again.

'It's not even two years,' Julia said. There was relief just in saying it, the same kind she'd felt certain mornings before grade school, when her mother had touched her head and said *fever*.

Her father looked at the Pont Neuf; he seemed to be fighting with himself.

'I'd rather start over in college—with everybody else,' she added.

Her father was nodding slowly. 'That's something we could explain to your mother.'

As you got older, Zubin noticed, very occasionally a fantasy that you'd been having forever came true. It was disorienting, like waking up in a new and better apartment, remembering that you'd moved, but not quite believing that you would never go back to the old place.

That was the way it was with Tessa. Their first conversation was about William Gaddis; they had both read *Carpenter's Gothic*, and Zubin was halfway through *JR*. In fact he had never finished *JR*, but after the party he'd gone home and lay on his back in bed, semi-erect but postponing jerking off with the relaxed and pleasant anticipation of a sure thing, and turned fifty pages. He didn't retain much of the content of those pages the next morning, but he remembered having felt that Gaddis was an important part of what he'd called his 'literary pedigree', as he and Tessa gulped cold red wine in the historic, unheated offices of the campus literary magazine. He even told her that he'd started writing poems himself.

'Can I read them?' she asked. As if he could show those poems to anyone!

Tessa moved closer to him; their shoulders and their hips and their knees were pressed together.

'Sure,' he said. 'If you want.'

They had finished the wine. Zubin told her that books were a kind of religion for him, that when things seemed unbearable the only comfort he knew was to read. He did not tell her that he was more likely to read science fiction at those times than William Gaddis; he hardly remembered that himself.

'What do you want to do now?' he'd asked, as they stepped out on to the narrow street, where the wind was colder than anything he could have imagined at home. He thought she would say she had class in the morning, or that it was late, or that she was meeting her room-mate at eleven, and so it was a surprise to him when she turned and put her tongue in his mouth. The wind disappeared then, and everything was perfectly quiet. When she pulled away, her cheeks and the triangle of exposed skin between her scarf and her jacket were pink. Tessa hung her head, and in a whisper that was more exciting to him than any picture he had ever seen, print or film, said: 'Let's go back to your room for a bit.'

He was still writing to Asha then. She was a year below him in school, and her parents had been lenient because they socialized with his parents (and because Zubin was going to Harvard). They had allowed him to come over and have a cup of tea, and then to take Asha for a walk along Marine Drive, as long as he brought her back well before dark. Once they had walked up the stairs from Hughes Road to Hanging Garden and sat on one of the benches, where the clerks and shop-girls whispered to each other in the foliage. He had ignored her flicker of hesitation and pointed down at the sun setting over the city: the Spenta building with a pink foam of cloud behind it, like a second horizon above the bay. He said that he wouldn't change the worst of the concrete-block apartments, with their exposed pipes and hanging laundry and waterstained, crumbling facades, because of the way they set off plain Babulnath Temple, made its tinselled orange flag and bulbous dome rise spectacularly from the dense vegetation, like a spaceship landed on Malabar Hill.

He was talking like that because he wanted to kiss her, but he sometimes got carried away. And when he noticed her again he saw that she was almost crying with the strain of how to tell him that she had to get home *right now*. He pointed to the still-blue sky over the bay (although the light was fading and the people coming up the path were already dark shapes) and took her hand and together they climbed up to the streetlight, and turned left toward her parents' apartment. They dropped each other's hand automatically when they got to the driveway, but Asha was so relieved that, in the mirrored elevator on the way up, she closed her eyes and let him kiss her.

That kiss was the sum of Zubin's experience, when he lost it with Tessa on Jason Bennet's green futon. He would remember forever the way she pushed him away, knelt in front of him and, with her jeans unbuttoned, arched her back to unhook her bra and free what were still the breasts that Zubin held in his mind's eye: buoyant and pale with surprising long, dark nipples.

Clothed, Tessa's primary feature was her amazing acceptability; there was absolutely nothing wrong with the way she looked or dressed or the things she said at the meetings of the literary magazine. But when he tried to remember her face now, he came up with a white oval into which eyes, a nose and a pair of lips would surface only separately, like leftover Cheerios in a bowl of milk.

When he returned from the States the second time, Asha was married to a lawyer and living in Cusrow Baug. She had twin five-year-old boys, and a three-year-old girl. She had edited a book of essays by famous writers about Bombay. The first time he'd run into her, at a wine tasting at the Taj President, he'd asked her what she was doing and she did not say, like so many Bombay women he knew, that she was married and had three children. She said: 'Prostitution.' And when he looked blank, she laughed and said, 'I'm doing a book on prostitution now. Interviews and case histories of prostitutes in *Mumbai*.'

When their city and all of its streets had been renamed overnight, in '94, Zubin had had long discussions with Indian friends in New York about the political implications of the change. Now that he was back those debates seemed silly. The street signs were just something to notice once and shake your head at, like the sidewalks below them—constantly torn up and then abandoned for months.

175

His mother was delighted to have him back. 'We won't bother you,' she said. 'It will be like you have your own artist's loft.' 'Maybe I should start a salon,' Zubin joked. He was standing in the living room, a few weeks after he'd gotten back, helping himself from a bottle of Rémy Martin.

'Or a saloon,' his father remarked, passing through.

He didn't tell his parents that he was writing a book, mostly because only three of the thirty poems he'd begun were actually finished; that regrettable fact was not his fault, but the fault of the crow that lived on the sheet of tin that was patching the roof over his bedroom window. He'd learned to ignore the chainsaw from the new apartment block that was going up under spindly bamboo scaffolding, the hammering across the road, the twenty-four-hour traffic and the fishwallah who came through their apartment blocks between ten and ten-thirty every morning, carrying a steel case on his head and calling '*hell-o, hell-o, hell-o.*' These were routine sounds, but the crow was clever. It called at uneven intervals, so that just as Zubin was convinced it had gone away, it began again. The sound was mournful and rough, as depressing as a baby wailing; it sounded to Zubin like despair.

When he'd first got back to Bombay, he'd been embarrassed about the way his students' parents introduced him: 'BA from Harvard; Henry fellow at Oxford; PhD from Columbia.' He would correct them and say that he hadn't finished the PhD (in fact, he'd barely started his dissertation) when he quit. That honesty had made everyone unhappy, and had been bad for business. Now he said his dissertation was in progress. He told his students' parents that he wanted to spend a little time here, since he would probably end up in the States.

The parents assumed that he'd come back to get married. They pushed their children toward him, yelling at them: 'Listen to Zubin; he's done three degrees—two on scholarship—not lazy and spoiled like you. Aren't I paying enough for this tutoring?' They said it in Hindi, as if he couldn't understand.

The kids were rapt and attentive. They did the practice tests he assigned them; they wrote the essays and read the books. They didn't care about Harvard, Oxford and Columbia. They were thinking of Boston, London and New York. He could read their minds. The girls asked about particular shops; the boys wanted to know how many girlfriends he had had, and how far they'd been willing to go.

None of his students could believe he'd come back voluntarily. They asked him about it again and again. How could he tell them that he'd missed his bedroom? He had felt that if he could just get back *there*—the dark wood floor, the brick walls of books, the ancient roll-top desk from Chor Bazaar—something would fall back into place, not inside him but in front of him, like the lengths of replacement track you sometimes saw them fitting at night on dark sections of the Western Railway commuter line.

He had come home to write his book, but it wasn't going to be a book about Bombay. There were no mangoes in his poems, and no beggars, no cows or Hindu gods. What he wanted to write about was a moment of quiet. Sometimes sitting alone in his room there would be a few seconds, a silent pocket without the crow or the hammering or wheels on the macadam outside. Those were the moments he felt most himself; at the same time, he felt that he was paying for that peace very dearly—that life, his life, was rolling away outside.

'But why did you wait three years?' his mother asked. 'Why didn't you come home right away?'

When he thought about it now, he was surprised that it had taken only three years to extract himself from graduate school. He counted it among the more efficient periods of his life so far.

He saw Julia twice a week, on Tuesdays and Thursdays. One afternoon when his mother was hosting a bridge tournament, he went to her house for the first time. A servant showed him into her room and purposefully shut the door, as if he'd had instructions not to disturb them. It was only four o'clock but the blinds were drawn. The lights were on and the door to her bathroom was closed; he could hear the tap running. Zubin sat at a small, varnished desk. He might have been in any girl's room in America: stacks of magazines on the book shelf, tacked-up posters of bands he didn't know, shoes scattered across a pink rag-rug and pieces of pastel-coloured clothing crumpled in with the sheets of the bed. A pair of jeans was on the floor where she'd stepped out of them, and the denim held her shape: open, round and paler on the inside of the fabric.

Both doors opened at once. Zubin didn't know whether to look at the barefoot girl coming out of the bathroom, or the massive, bearded white man who had appeared from the hall.

'Hi Daddy,' Julia said. 'This is Zubin, my tutor.'

'We spoke on the phone, sir,' said Zubin, getting up.

Julia's father shook hands as if it were a quaint custom Zubin had insisted on. He sat down on his daughter's bed, and the springs protested. He looked at Zubin.

'What are you working on today?'

'*Dad.*'

'Yes.'

'He just got here.'

Julia's father held up one hand in defence. 'I'd be perfectly happy if you didn't get into college. Then you could just stay here.'

Julia rolled her eyes, a habit that struck Zubin as particularly American.

'We'll start working on her essay today.' Zubin turned to Julia: 'Did you do a draft?' He'd asked her the same thing twice a week for the past three, and he knew what the answer would be. He wouldn't have put her on the spot if he hadn't been so nervous himself. But Julia surprised him: 'I just finished.'

'What did you write about?' her father asked eagerly.

'The difficulties of being from a broken home.'

'Very interesting,' he said, without missing a beat.

'I couldn't have done it without you.'

'I try,' he said casually, as if this were the kind of conversation they had all the time. 'So maybe we don't even need Zubin—if you've already written your essay?'

Julia shook her head: 'It isn't good.'

Zubin felt he should say something. 'The new format of the SAT places much greater emphasis on writing skills.' He felt like an idiot.

Julia's father considered Zubin. 'You do this full-time?'

'Yes.'

'Did you always want to be a teacher?'

'I wanted to be a poet,' Zubin said. He could feel himself blushing but mostly he was surprised, that he had told these two strangers something he hadn't even told his parents.

'Do you write poems now?'

'Sometimes,' Zubin said.

'There are some good Marathi poets, aren't there?'

'That's not what I'm interested in.' Zubin thought he'd spoken too forcefully, but it didn't seem to bother Julia's father.

'I'll leave you two to work now. If you want, come to dinner some time—our cook makes terrible Continental food, because my daughter won't eat Indian.'

Zubin smiled. 'That sounds good—thank you, Sir.'

'Mark,' Julia's father said, closing the door gently behind him.

'Your dad seems cool.'

Julia was gathering up all of her clothes furiously from the bed and the floor. She opened her closet door—a light went on automatically—and threw them inside. Then she slammed it. He didn't know what he'd done wrong.

'Do you want me to take a look at what you have?'

'What?'

'Of the essay.'

'I didn't write an essay.'

'You said—'

Julia laughed. 'Yeah.'

'How do you expect to get into Berkeley?'

'You're going to write it.'

'I don't do that.' He sounded prim.

'I'll pay you.'

Zubin got up. 'I think we're finished.'

She took her hair out of the band and redid it, her arms above her head. He couldn't see any difference when she finished. 'A hundred dollars.'

'Why do you want me to write your essay?'

Suddenly Julia sank down on to the floor, hugging her knees. 'I have to get out of here.'

'You said that before.' He wasn't falling for the melodrama. 'I'll help you do it yourself.'

'A thousand. On top of the regular fee.'

Zubin stared. 'Where are you going to get that much money?'

'Half a *lakh*.'

'That calculation even I could have managed,' Zubin said, but she wasn't paying attention. She picked up a magazine off her night table, and flopped down on the bed. He had the feeling that she was giving him time to consider her offer and he found himself—in that sealed-off corner of his brain where these things happened—considering it.

With $200 a week, plus the $1,000 bonus, he easily could stop all the tutoring except Julia's. And with all of that time, there would be no excuse not to finish his manuscript. There were some prizes for first collections in England and America; they didn't pay a lot, but they published your book. Artists, he thought, did all kinds of things for their work. They made every kind of sacrifice—financial, personal, moral—so as not to compromise the only thing that was truly important.

'I'll make a deal with you,' Zubin said.

Julia looked bored.

'You try it first. If you get really stuck—then maybe. And I'll help you think of the idea.'

'They *give* you the idea,' she said. 'Remember?'

'I'll take you to a couple of places. We'll see which one strikes you.' This, he told himself, was hands-on education. Thanks to him, Julia would finally see the city where she had been living for nearly a year.

'Great,' said Julia sarcastically. 'Can we go to Elephanta?'

'Better than Elephanta.'

'To the Gateway of India? Will you buy me one of those big, spotted balloons?'

'Just wait,' said Zubin. 'There's some stuff you don't know about yet.'

They walked from his house past the Hanging Garden, to the small vegetable market in the lane above the Walkeshwar Temple. They went down a flight of uneven steps, past small, open electronic shops where men clustered around televisions waiting for the cricket scores. The path wound between low houses, painted pink or green, a primary school and a tiny, white temple with a marble courtyard and a black *nandi* draped in marigolds. Two vegetable vendors moved to the side to let them pass, swivelling their heads to look, each with one hand lightly poised on the flat basket balanced on her head. Inside the baskets, arranged in an elegant multicoloured whorl, were eggplants, mint, tomatoes, Chinese lettuces, okra, and the smooth white pumpkins called *dudhi*. Further on a poster man had laid out his wares on a frayed, blue tarpaulin: the usual movie stars and glossy deities, plus kittens, puppies and an enormous white baby, in a diaper and pink headband. Across the bottom of a composite photo—an English cottage superimposed on a Thai beach, in the shadow of Swiss mountains dusted with yellow and purple wild flowers and bisected by a torrential Amazonian waterfall—were the words, *Home is where. When you go there, they have to let you in.* Punctuation aside, it was difficult for Zubin to imagine a more depressing sentiment.

'You know what I hate?'

Zubin had a strange urge to touch her. It wasn't a sexual thing, he didn't think. He just wanted to take her hand. 'What?'

'Crows.'

Zubin smiled.

'You probably think they're poetic or something.'

'No.'

'Like Edgar Allen Poe.'

'That was a raven.'

'Edgar Allen Po*etic*.' She giggled.

'This kind of verbal play is encouraging,' Zubin said. 'If only you would apply it to your practice tests.'

'I can't concentrate at home,' Julia said. 'There are too many distractions.'

'Like what?' Julia's room was the quietest place he'd been in Bombay.

'My father.'

The steps opened suddenly on to the temple tank: a dark green square of water cut out of the stone. Below them, a schoolgirl in a purple jumper and a white blouse, her hair plaited with two red ribbons, was filling a brass jug. At the other end a labourer cleared muck from the bottom with an iron spade. His grandmother had brought him here when he was a kid. She had described the city as it had been: just the sea and the fishing villages clinging to the rocks, the lush, green hills, and in the hills these hive-shaped temples, surrounded by the tiny coloured houses of the priests. The concrete block apartments were still visible on the Malabar side of the tank, but if you faced the sea you could ignore them.

'My father keeps me locked up in a cage,' Julia said mournfully.

'Although he lets you out for Fire and Ice,' Zubin observed.

'He doesn't. He ignores it when I go to Fire and Ice. All he'd have to do is look in at night. I don't put pillows in the bed or anything.'

'He's probably trying to respect your privacy.'

'I'm his *kid*. I'm not supposed to have privacy.' She sat down suddenly on the steps, but she didn't seem upset. She shaded her eyes with her hand. He liked the way she looked, looking—more serious than he'd seen her before.

'Do you think it's beautiful here?' he asked.

The sun had gone behind the buildings, and was setting over the sea and the slum on the rocks above the water. There was an orange glaze over half the tank; the other, shadowed half was green and cold. Shocked-looking white ducks with orange feet stood in the shade, each facing a different direction, and on the opposite side two boys played an impossibly old-fashioned game, whooping as they rolled a worn-out bicycle tire along the steps with a stick. All around them bells were ringing.

'I think lots of things are beautiful,' Julia said slowly. 'If you see them at the right time. But you come back and the light is different, or someone's left some trash, or you're in a bad mood—or whatever. Everything gets ugly.'

'This is what your essay is about.' He didn't think before he said it; it just came to him.

'The Banganga Tank?'

'Beauty,' he said.

She frowned.

'It's your idea.'

She was trying not to show she was pleased. Her mouth turned up at the corners, and she scowled to hide it. 'I guess that's OK. I guess it doesn't really matter what you choose.'

Julia was a virgin, but Anouk wasn't. Anouk was Bernie's daughter; she lived in a fancy house behind a carved wooden gate, on one of the winding lanes at Cumbala Hill. Julia liked the ornamental garden, with brushed-steel plaques that identified the plants in English and Latin, and the blue ceramic pool full of lumpy-headed white-and-orange goldfish. Behind the goldfish pond was a cedar sauna, and it was in the sauna that it had happened. The boy wasn't especially cute, but he was distantly related to the royal house of Jodhpur. They'd only done it once; according to Anouk that was all it took, before you could consider yourself ready for a real boyfriend at university.

'It's something to get over with,' Anouk said. 'You simply hold your breath.' They were listening to the Shakira album in Anouk's room, which was covered with pictures of models from magazines. There were even a few pictures of Anouk, who was tall enough for print ads, but not to go to Europe and be on runways. She was also in a Colgate commercial that you saw on the Hindi stations. Being Anouk's best friend was the thing that saved Julia at the American School, where the kids talked about their fathers' jobs and their vacation houses even more than they had in Paris. At least at the school in Paris they'd gotten to take a lot of trips—to museums, the Bibliothèque Nationale, and Monet's house at Giverny.

There was no question of losing her virginity to any of the boys at school. Everyone would know about it the next day.

'You should have done it with Markus,' Anouk said, for the hundredth time, one afternoon when they were lying on the floor of her bedroom, flipping through magazines.

Julia sometimes thought the same thing; it was hard to describe why they hadn't done it. They'd talked about it, like they'd talked about everything, endlessly, late at night on the phone, as if they were the only people awake in the city. Markus was her best friend—still, when she was sad, he was the one she wanted to talk to—but when they kissed he put his tongue too far into her mouth and moved it around in a way that made her want to gag. He was grateful when she took off her top and let him put his hand underneath her bra, and sometimes she thought he was relieved too, when she said no to other things.

'You could write him,' Anouk suggested.

'I'd love him to come visit,' Julia allowed.

'Visit and come.'

'Gross.'

Anouk looked at her sternly. She had fair skin and short hair that flipped up underneath her ears. She had cat-shaped green eyes exactly like the ones in the picture of her French grandmother, which stared out of an ivory frame on a table in the hall.

'What about your tutor?'

Julia pretended to be horrified. 'Zubin?'

'He's cute, right?'

'He's about a million years older than us.'

'How old?'

'Twenty-nine, I think.'

Anouk went into her dresser and rummaged around. 'Just in case,' she said innocently, tossing Julia a little foil-wrapped packet.

This wasn't the way it was supposed to go—you weren't supposed to be the one who got the condom—but you weren't supposed to go to high school in Bombay, to live alone with your father, or to lose your virginity to your SAT tutor. She wondered if she and Zubin would do it on the mattress in his room, or if he would press her up against the wall, like in 9½ *Weeks*.

'You better call me, like, the second after,' Anouk instructed her.

She almost told Anouk about the virginity dream, and then didn't. She didn't really want to hear her friend's interpretation.

It was unclear where she and Markus would've done it, since at that time boys weren't allowed in her room. There were a lot of rules, particularly after her mother left. When she was out, around eleven, her father would message her mobile, something like: WHAT TIME, MISSY? or simply, ETA? If she didn't send one right back, he would call. She would roll her eyes, at the cafe or the party or the club, and say to Markus, 'My dad.'

'Well,' Markus would say. 'You're his daughter.'

When she came home, her father would be waiting on the couch with a book. He read the same books over and over, especially the ones by Russians. She would have to come in and give him a kiss, and if he smelled cigarettes he would ask to see her bag.

'You can't look in my bag,' she would say, and her father would hold out his hand. 'Everybody else smokes,' she told him. 'I can't help smelling like it.' She was always careful to give Markus her Dunhills before she went home.

'Don't you trust me?' she said sometimes (especially when she was drunk).

Her father smiled. 'No. I love you too much for that.'

It was pouring and the rain almost shrieked on Zubin's tin roof, which still hadn't been repaired. They were working on reading comprehension; a test two years ago had used Marvell's 'To His Coy Mistress'. Zubin preferred 'The Garden', but he'd had more success teaching 'To His Coy Mistress' to his students; they told him it seemed 'modern'. Many of his students seemed to think that sex was a relatively new invention.

'It's a persuasive poem,' Zubin said. 'In a way, it has something in common with an essay.'

Julia narrowed her eyes. 'What do you mean, persuasive?'

'He wants to sleep with her.'

'And she doesn't want to.'

'Right,' Zubin said.

'Is she a virgin?'

'You tell me.' Zubin remembered legions of teachers sing-songing exactly those words. 'Look at line twenty-eight.'

'That's disgusting.'

'Good,' he said. 'You understand it. That's what the poet wanted—to shock her a little.'

'That's so manipulative!'

It was amazing, he thought, the way Americans all embraced that kind of psychobabble. *Language* is manipulative, he wanted to tell her.

'I think it might have been very convincing,' he said instead.

'*Vegetable* love?'

'It's strange, and that's what makes it vivid. The so-called metaphysical poets are known for this kind of conceit.'

'That they were conceited?'

'Conceit,' Zubin said. 'Write this down.' He gave her the definition; he sounded conceited.

'*The sun is like a flower that blooms for just one hour,*' Julia said suddenly.

'That's the opposite,' Zubin said. 'A comparison so common that it doesn't mean anything—you see the difference?'

Julia nodded wearily. It was too hot in the room. Zubin got up and propped the window open with the wooden stop. Water sluiced off the dark, shiny leaves of the magnolia.

'What is that?'

'What?'

'That thing, about the sun.'

She kicked her foot petulantly against his desk. The hammering outside was like an echo, miraculously persisting in spite of the rain. 'Ray Bradbury,' she said finally. 'We read it in school.'

'I know that story,' Zubin said. 'With the kids on Venus. It rains for seven years, and then the sun comes out and they lock the girl in the closet. Why do they lock her up?'

'Because she's from Earth. She's the only one who's seen it.'

'The sun.'

Julia nodded. 'They're all jealous.'

People thought she could go out all the time because she was American. She let them think it. One night she decided to stop bothering with the outside stairs; she was wearing new jeans that her mother had sent her; purple cowboy boots and a sparkly silver halter top that showed off her stomach. She had a shawl for outside, but she didn't put it on right away. Her father was working in his study with the door cracked open.

The clock in the hall said 10.20. Her boots made a loud noise on the tiles.

'Hi,' her father called.

'Hi.'

'Where are you going?'

'A party.'

'Where?'

'Juhu.' She stepped into his study. 'On the beach.'

He put the book down and took off his glasses. 'Do you find that many people are doing Ecstasy—when you go to these parties?'

'Dad.'

'I'm not being critical—I read an article about it in *Time*. My interest is purely anthropological.'

'Yes,' Julia said. 'All the time. We're all on Ecstasy from the moment we wake up in the morning.'

'That's what I thought.'

'I have to go.'

'I don't want to keep you.' He smiled. 'Well I do, but—' Her father was charming; it was like a reflex.

'See you in the morning,' she said.

The worst thing was that her father *knew* she knew. He might have thought Julia knew even before she actually did; that was when he started letting her do things like go out at 10.30, and smoke on the staircase outside her bedroom. It was as if she'd entered into a kind of pact without knowing it; and by the time she found out why they were in Bombay for real, it was too late to change her mind.

It was Anouk who told her, one humid night when they were

having their tennis lesson at Willingdon. The air was so hazy that
Julia kept losing the ball in the sodium lights. They didn't notice
who'd come in and taken the last court next to the parking lot until
the lesson was over. Then Anouk said: 'Wow, look—*Papa!*' Bernie
lobbed the ball and waved; as they walked toward the other court,
Julia's father set up for an overhead and smashed the ball into the
net. He raised his fist in mock anger, and grinned at them.

'Good lesson?'

'Julia did well.'

'I did not.'

'Wait for Bernie to finish me off,' Julia's father said. 'Then we'll
take you home.'

'How much longer?'

'When we're finished,' said Bernie sharply.

'*On sort ce soir.*'

'*On va voir,*' her father said. Anouk started to say something and
stopped. She caught one ankle behind her back calmly, stretched, and
shifted her attention to Julia's father. 'How long?'

He smiled. 'Not more than twenty.'

They waited in the enclosure, behind a thin white net that was
meant to keep out the balls, but didn't, and ordered fresh lime sodas.

'We need an hour to get ready, at least.'

'I'm not going.'

'Yes you are.'

Anouk put her legs up on the table and Julia did the same and
they compared: Anouk's were longer and thinner, but Julia's had a
better shape. Julia's phone beeped.

'It's from Zubin.'

Anouk took the phone.

'It's just about my lesson.'

Anouk read Zubin's message in an English accent: CAN WE
SHIFT FROM FIVE TO SIX ON THURSDAY?

'He doesn't talk like that,' Julia said, but she knew what Anouk
meant. Zubin was the only person she knew who wrote SMS in full
sentences, without any abbreviations.

Anouk tipped her head back and shut her eyes. Her throat was
smooth and brown and underneath her sleeveless white top, her breasts
were outlined, the nipples pointing up. 'Tell him I'm hot for him.'

'You're a flirt.'

Anouk sat up and looked at the court. Now Bernie was serving. Both men had long, dark stains down the fronts of their shirts. A little bit of a breeze was coming from the trees behind the courts; Julia felt the sweat between her shoulders. She thought she'd gone too far, and she was glad when Anouk said, 'When are they going to be finished?'

'They'll be done in a second. I think they both just play 'cause the other one wants to.'

'What do you mean?'

'I mean, my dad never played in Paris.'

'Mine did,' Anouk said.

'So maybe he just likes playing with your dad.'

Anouk tilted her head to the side for a minute, as if she were thinking. 'He would have to though.'

The adrenaline from the fight they'd almost had, defused a minute before, came flooding back. She could feel her pulse in her wrists. 'What do you mean?'

Her friend opened her eyes wide. 'I mean, your dad's probably grateful.'

'Grateful for *what*?'

'The job.'

'He had a good job before.'

Anouk blinked incredulously. 'Are you serious?'

'He was the operations manager in Central Asia.'

'Was,' Anouk said.

'Yeah, well,' Julia said. 'He didn't want to go back to the States after my mom did.'

'My God,' Anouk said. 'That's what they told you?'

Julia looked at her. *Whatever you're going to say, don't say it.* But she didn't say anything.

'You have it backwards,' Anouk said. 'Your mother left because of what happened. She went to America, because she knew your father couldn't. There was an article about it in *Nefte Compass*—I couldn't read it, because it was in Russian, but my dad read it.' She lifted her beautiful eyes to Julia's. 'My dad said it wasn't fair. He said they shouldn't've called your dad a crook.'

'Four–five,' her father called. 'Your service.'

'But I guess your mom didn't understand that.'

Cars were inching out of the club. Julia could see the red brake lights between the purple blossoms of the hedge that separated the court from the drive.

'It doesn't matter,' Anouk said. 'You said he wouldn't have gone back anyway, so it doesn't matter whether he *could* have.'

A car backed up, beeping. Someone yelled directions in Hindi.

'And it didn't get reported in America or anything. My father says he's lucky he could still work in Europe—probably not in oil, but anything else. He doesn't want to go back to the States anyway— *alors, c'est pas grand chose.*'

The game had finished. Their fathers were collecting the balls from the corners of the court.

'Ready?' her father called, but Julia was already hurrying across the court. By the time she got out to the drive she was jogging, zigzagging through the cars clogging the lot, out into the hot night-time haze of the road. She was lucky to find an empty taxi. They pulled out into the mass of traffic in front of the Hagi Ali and stopped. The driver looked at her in the mirror for instructions.

'Malabar Hill,' she said. 'Hanging Garden.'

Zubin was actually working on the essay, sitting at his desk by the open window, when he heard his name. Or maybe hallucinated his name: a bad sign. But it wasn't his fault. His mother had given him a bottle of sambuca, which someone had brought her from the duty-free shop in the Frankfurt airport.

'I was thinking of giving it to the Mehtas but he's stopped drinking entirely. I could only think of you.'

'You're the person she thought would get the most use out of it,' his father contributed.

Now Zubin was having little drinks (really half drinks) as he tried to apply to college. He had decided that there would be nothing wrong with writing a first draft for Julia, as long as she put it in her own words later. The only problem was getting started. He remembered his own essay perfectly, unfortunately on an unrelated subject. He had written, much to his English teacher's dismay, about comic books.

'Why don't you write about growing up in Bombay? That will distinguish you from the other applicants,' she had suggested.

He hadn't wanted to distinguish himself from the other applicants, or rather, he'd wanted to distinguish himself in a much more distinctive way. He had an alumni interview with an expatriate American consultant working for Arthur Anderson in Bombay; the interviewer, who was young, Jewish and from New York, said it was the best college essay he'd ever read.

'Zu-bin.'

It was at least a relief that he wasn't hallucinating. She was standing below his window, holding a tennis racket. 'Hey Zubin— can I come up?'

'You have to come around the front,' he said.

'Will you come down and get me?'

He put a shirt over his T-shirt, and then took it off. He took the glass of sambuca to the bathroom sink to dump it, but he got distracted looking in the mirror (he should've shaved) and drained it instead.

He found Julia leaning against a tree, smoking. She held out the pack.

'I don't smoke.'

She sighed. 'Hardly anyone does any more.' She was wearing an extremely short white skirt. 'Is this a bad time?'

'Well—'

'I can go.'

'You can come up,' he said, a little too quickly. 'I'm not sure I can do antonyms now though.'

In his room Julia gravitated to the stereo. A Brahms piano quartet had come on.

'You probably aren't a Brahms person.'

She looked annoyed. 'How do *you* know?'

'I don't,' he said. 'Sorry—are you?'

Julia pretended to examine his books. 'I'm not very familiar with his work,' she said finally. 'So I couldn't really say.'

He felt like hugging her. He poured himself another sambuca instead. 'I'm sorry there's nowhere to sit.'

'I'm sorry I'm all gross from tennis.' She sat down on his mattress, which was at least covered with a blanket.

'Do you always smoke after tennis?' he couldn't help asking.

'It calms me down.'

'Still, you shouldn't—'

'I've been having this dream,' she said. She stretched her legs out in front of her and crossed her ankles. 'Actually it's kind of a nightmare.'

'Oh,' said Zubin. Students' nightmares were certainly among the things that should be discussed in the living room.

'Have you ever been to New Hampshire?'

'What?'

'I've been having this dream that I'm in New Hampshire. There's a frozen pond where you can skate outside.'

'That must be nice.'

'I saw it in a movie,' she admitted. 'But I think they have them—anyway. In the dream I'm not wearing skates. I'm walking out on to the pond, near the woods, and it's snowing. I'm walking on the ice but I'm not afraid—everything's really beautiful. And then I look down and there's this thing—this dark spot on the ice. There are some mushrooms growing, on the dark spot. I'm worried that someone skating will trip on them, so I bend down to pick them.'

Her head was bent now; she was peeling a bit of rubber from the sole of her sneaker.

'That's when I see the guy.'

'The guy.'

'The guy in the ice. He's alive, and even though he can't move, he sees me. He's looking up and reaching out his arms and just his fingers are coming up—just the tips of them through the ice. Like white mushrooms.'

'Jesus,' Zubin said.

She misunderstood. 'No—just a regular guy.'

'That's a bad dream.'

'Yeah well,' she said proudly. 'I thought maybe you could use it.'

'Sorry?'

'In the essay.'

Zubin poured himself another sambuca. 'I don't know if I can write the essay.'

'You have to.' Her expression changed instantly. 'I have the money—I could give you a cheque now even.'

'It's not the money.'

'Because it's dishonest?' she said in a small voice.

'I—' But he couldn't explain why he couldn't manage to write even a college essay, even to himself. 'I'm sorry.'

She looked as if she'd been about to say something else, and then changed her mind. 'Okay,' she said dejectedly. 'I'll think of something.'

She looked around for her racket, which she'd propped up against the bookshelf. He didn't want her to go yet.

'What kind of a guy is he?'

'Who?'

'The guy in the ice—is he your age?'

Julia shook her head. 'He's old.'

Zubin sat down on the bed, at what he judged was a companionable distance. 'Like a senior citizen?'

'No, but older than you.'

'Somewhere in that narrow window between me and senior citizenship.'

'You're not old,' she said seriously.

'Thank you.' The sambuca was making him feel great. They could just sit here, and get drunk and do nothing, and it would be fun, and there would be no consequences; he could stop worrying for tonight, and give himself a little break.

He was having that comforting thought when her head dropped lightly to his shoulder.

'Oh.'

'Is this okay?'

'It's okay, but—'

'I get so tired.'

'Because of the nightmares.'

She paused for a second, as if she was surprised he'd been paying attention. 'Yes,' she said. 'Exactly.'

'You want to lie down a minute?'

She jerked her head up—nervous all of a sudden. He liked it better than the flirty stuff she'd been doing before.

'Or I could get someone to take you home.'

She lay down and shut her eyes. He put his glass down carefully on the floor next to the bed. Then he put his hand out; her hair was very soft. He stroked her head and moved her hair away from her face. He adjusted the glass beads she always wore, and ran his hand lightly down her arm. He felt that he was in a position where there was no choice but to lift her up and kiss her very gently on the mouth.

'Julia.'

"Quite simply the most impressive literary magazine of its time."*

A one-year subscription to *Granta* is just $39.95. You save over $19 (more than 33%) off the bookshop price of $14.95 an issue. That's like getting a whole issue of *Granta*, **FREE!** (You save even more—up to $76—with a two- or three-year subscription.)

This is why nearly 70,000 discerning *Granta* readers—from every corner of the world—subscribe. Why not join them? Or give a subscription to a friend? It's a great gift: thoughtful, unusual and lasting.

*The Daily Telegraph

GRANTA BACK ISSUES

Every issue of *Granta* is in print, and available direct from *Granta* at significant discounts—because every issue is as vital and pertinent now as when it was first published. Some—like the 1983 and 1993 'Best of Young British Novelists' issues; and the 1996 'Best of Young American Novelists'—have become literary landmarks. Details of (and extracts from) these, and all of the other back issues since 1979, are available at our Web site, www.granta.com—where you can buy them at discounts of at least 25% and up to 55%

www.granta.com

She opened her eyes.

'I'm going to get someone to drive you home.'

She got up very quickly and smoothed her hair with her hand.

'Not that I wouldn't like you to stay, but I think—'

'Okay,' she said.

'I'll just get someone.' He yelled for the servant.

'I can get a taxi,' Julia said.

'I know you *can*,' he told her. For some reason, that made her smile.

In September she took the test. He woke up early that morning as if he were taking it, couldn't concentrate, and went to Barista, where he sat trying to read the same *India Today* article about regional literature for two hours. She wasn't the only one of his students taking the SAT today, but she was the one he thought of, at the 8.40 subject change, the 10.00 break, and at 11.25, when they would be warning them about the penalties for continuing to write after time was called. That afternoon he thought she would ring him to say how it had gone, but she didn't, and it wasn't until late that night that his phone beeped and her name came up: JULIA: VERBAL IS LIKE S-SPEARE: PLAY. It wasn't a perfect analogy, but he knew what she meant.

He didn't see Julia while the scores were being processed. Without the bonus he hadn't been able to give up his other clients, and the business was in one of its busy cycles; it seemed as if everyone in Bombay was dying to send their sixteen-year-old child halfway around the world to be educated. Each evening he thought he might hear her calling up from the street, but she never did, and he didn't feel he could phone without some pretence.

One rainy Thursday he gave a group lesson in a small room on the first floor of the David Sassoon library. The library always reminded him of Oxford, with its cracked chalkboards and termite-riddled seminar tables, and today in particular the soft, steady rain made him feel as if he were somewhere else. They were doing triangles (isosceles, equilateral, scalene) when all of a sudden one of the students interrupted and said: 'It stopped.'

Watery sun was gleaming through the lead glass windows. When he had dismissed the class, Zubin went upstairs to the reading room. He found Bradbury in a tattered ledger book and filled out a form. He waited while the librarian frowned at the call number, selected a key from a crowded ring, and, looking put-upon, sent an assistant into the reading room to find 'All Summer in a Day' in the locked glass case.

> It had been raining for seven years; thousands upon thousands of days compounded and filled from one end to the other with rain, with the drum and gush of water, with the sweet crystal fall of showers and the concussion of storms so heavy they were tidal waves come over the islands.

He'd forgotten that the girl in the story was a poet. She was different from the other children, and because it was a science fiction story (this was what he loved about science fiction) it wasn't an abstract difference. Her special sensitivity was explained by the fact that she had come to Venus from Earth only recently, on a rocket ship, and remembered the sun—it was like a penny—while her classmates did not.

Zubin sat by the window in the old seminar room, emptied of students, and luxuriated in a feeling of potential he hadn't had in a long time. He remembered when a moment of heightened contrast in his physical surroundings could produce this kind of elation; he could feel the essay wound up in him like thread. He would combine the Bradbury story with the idea Julia had had, that day at the tank. Beauty was something that was new to you. That was why tourists and children could see it better than other people, and it was the poet's job to keep seeing it the way the children and the tourists did.

He was glad he'd told her he couldn't do it because it would be that much more of a surprise when he handed her the pages. He felt noble. He was going to defraud the University of California for her gratis, as a gift.

He intended to be finished the day the scores came out and, for perhaps the first time in his life, he finished on the day he'd intended. He waited all day, but Julia didn't call. He thought she would've gone out that night to celebrate, but she didn't call the next day, or the next, and he started to worry that she'd been wrong about her verbal. Or she'd lied. He started to get scared that she'd choked— something that could happen to the best students, you could never tell which. After ten days without hearing from her, he rang her mobile.

'Oh yeah,' she said. 'I was going to call.'

'I have something for you,' he said. He didn't want to ask about the scores right away.

She sighed. 'My dad wants you to come to dinner anyway.'

'Okay,' Zubin said. 'I could bring it then.'

There was a long pause, in which he could hear traffic. 'Are you in the car?'

'Uh-huh,' she said. 'Hold on a second?' Her father said something and she groaned into the phone. 'My dad wants me to tell you my SAT scores.'

'Only if you want to.'

'Eight hundred math.'

'Wow.'

'And 690 verbal.'

'You're kidding.'

'Nope.'

'Is this the Julia who was too distracted to do her practice tests?'

'Maybe it was easy this year,' Julia said, but he could tell she was smiling.

'I don't believe you.'

'*Zubin*!' (He loved the way she added the extra stress.) 'I *swear*.'

They ate *coquilles St Jacques* by candlelight. Julia's father lit the candles himself, with a box of old-fashioned White Swan matches. Then he opened Zubin's wine and poured all three of them a full glass. Zubin took a sip; it seemed too sweet, especially with the seafood. 'A toast,' said Julia's father. 'To my daughter the genius.'

Zubin raised his glass. All week he'd felt an urgent need to see her; now that he was here he had a contented, peaceful feeling, only partly related to the two salty dogs he'd mixed for himself just before going out.

'Scallops are weird,' said Julia. 'Do they even have heads?'

'Did any of your students do better?' her father asked.

'Only one, I think.'

'Boy or girl?'

'Why does *that* matter?' Julia asked. She stood up suddenly: she was wearing a sundress made of blue-and-white printed Indian cotton, and she was barefoot. 'I'll be in my room if anyone needs me.'

Zubin started to get up.

'Sit,' Julia's father said. 'Finish your meal. Then you can do whatever you have to do.'

'I brought your essay—the revision of your essay,' Zubin corrected himself, but she didn't turn around. He watched her disappear down the hall to her bedroom: a pair of tan shoulders under thin, cotton straps.

'I first came to India in 1976,' her father was saying. 'I flew from Moscow to Paris to meet Julia's mom, and then we went to Italy and Greece. We were deciding between India and North Africa—finally we just tossed a coin.'

'Wow,' said Zubin. He was afraid Julia would go out before he could give her the essay.

'It was February and I'd been in Moscow for a year,' Julia's father said. 'So you can imagine what India was like for me. We were staying in this pension in Benares—Varanasi—and every night there were these incredible parties on the roof.

'One night we could see the burning ghats from where we were—hardly any electricity in the city, and then this big fire on the ghat, with the drums and the wailing. I'd never seen anything like that—the pieces of the body that they sent down the river, still burning.' He stopped and refilled their glasses. He didn't seem to mind the wine. 'Maybe they don't still do that?'

'I've never been to Benares.'

Julia's father laughed. 'Right,' he said. 'That's an old man's India now. And you're not writing about India, are you?'

Writing the essay, alone at night in his room, knowing she was out somewhere with her school friends, he'd had the feeling, the delusion really, that he could hear her. That while she was standing on the beach or dancing in a club, she was also telling him her life story: not the places she'd lived, which didn't matter, but the time in third grade when she was humiliated in front of the class; the boy who wrote his number on the inside of her wrist; the weather on the day her mother left for New York. He felt that her voice was coming in the open window with the noise of the motorbikes and the televisions and the crows, and all he was doing was hitting the keys.

Julia's father had asked a question about India.

'Sorry?' Zubin said.

He waved a hand dismissively in front of his face. 'You don't have to tell me—writers are private about these things. It's just that business guys like me—we're curious how you do it.'

'When I'm here, I want to write about America and when I'm in America, I always want to write about being here.' He wasn't slurring words, but he could hear himself emphasizing them: 'It would have made *sense* to stay there.'

'But you didn't.'

'I was homesick, I guess.'

'And now?'

Zubin didn't know what to say.

'Far be it from me, but I think it doesn't matter so much, whether you're here or there. You can bring your home with you.' Julia's father smiled. 'To some extent. And India's wonderful—even if it's not your first choice.'

It was easy if you were Julia's father. He had chosen India because he remembered seeing some dead bodies in a river. He had found it 'wonderful'. And that was what it was to be an American. Americans could go all over the world and still be Americans; they could live just the way they did at home and nobody wondered who they were, or why they were doing things the way they did.

'I'm sure you're right,' Zubin said politely.

Finally Julia's father pressed a buzzer and a servant appeared to clear the dishes. Julia's father pushed back his chair and stood up. Before disappearing into his study, he nodded formally and said something—whether 'Good night,' or 'Good luck,' Zubin couldn't tell.

Zubin was left with a servant, about his age, with big, southern features and stooped shoulders. The servant was wearing the brown uniform from another job: short pants and a shirt that was tight across his chest. He moved as if he'd been compensating for his height his whole life, as if he'd never had clothes that fit him.

'Do you work here every day?' Zubin asked in his school-book Marathi.

The young man looked up as if talking to Zubin was the last in a series of obstacles that lay between him and the end of his day.

'*Nahin,*' he said. '*Mangalwar ani guruwar.*'

Zubin smiled—they both worked on Tuesdays and Thursdays. 'Me too,' he said.

The servant didn't understand. He stood holding the plates,

waiting to see if Zubin was finished and scratching his left ankle with his right foot. His toes were round and splayed, with cracked nails and a glaucous coating of dry, white skin.

'Okay,' Zubin said. *'Bas.'*

Julia's room was, as he'd expected, empty. The lights were burning and the stereo was on (the disc had finished), but she'd left the window open; the bamboo shade sucked in and out. The mirror in the bathroom was steamed around the edges—she must've taken a shower before going out; there was the smell of some kind of fragrant soap and cigarettes.

He put the essay on the desk where she would see it. There were two Radiohead CDs, still in their plastic wrappers, and a detritus of pens and pencils, hairbands, fashion magazines—French *Vogue*, *Femina* and *YM*—gum wrappers, an OB tampon and a miniature brass abacus, with tiny ivory beads. There was also a diary with a pale blue paper cover.

The door to the hall was slightly open, but the house was absolutely quiet. It was not good to look at someone's journal, especially a teenage girl's. But there were things that would be worse—jerking off in her room, for example. It was a beautiful notebook with a heavy cardboard cover that made a satisfying sound when he opened it on the desk.

'It's empty.'

He flipped the diary closed but it was too late. She was climbing in through the window, lifting the shade with her hand.

'That's where I smoke,' she said. 'You should've checked.'

'I was just looking at the notebook,' Zubin said. 'I wouldn't have read what you'd written.'

'My hopes, dreams, fantasies. It would've been good for the essay.'

'I finished the essay.'

She stopped and stared at him. 'You wrote it?'

He pointed to the neatly stacked pages, a paper island in the clutter of the desk. Julia examined them, as if she didn't believe it.

'I thought you weren't going to?'

'If you already wrote one—'

'No,' she said. 'I tried but—' She gave him a beautiful smile. 'Do you want to stay while I read it?'

Zubin glanced at the door.

'My dad's in his study.'

He pretended to look through her CDs, which were organized in a zippered binder, and snuck glances at her while she read. She sat down on her bed with her back against the wall, one foot underneath her. As she read she lifted her necklace and put it in her mouth, he thought unconsciously. She frowned at the page.

It was better if she didn't like it, Zubin thought. He knew it was good, but having written it was wrong. There were all these other kids who'd done the applications themselves.

Julia laughed.

'What?' he said, but she just shook her head and kept going.

'I'm just going to use your loo,' Zubin said.

He used it almost blindly, without looking in the mirror. Her towel was hanging over the edge of the counter, but he dried his hands on his shirt. He was drunker than he'd thought. When he came out she had folded the three pages into a small square, as if she were getting ready to throw them away.

Julia shook her head. 'You did it.'

'It's okay?'

Julia shook her head. 'It's perfect—it's spooky. How do you even know about this stuff?'

'I was a teenager—not a girl teenager, but you know.'

She shook her head. 'About being an American I mean? How do you know about that?'

She asked the same way she might ask who wrote *The Fairie Queene* or the meaning of the word 'synecdoche'.

Because I am not any different, he wanted to tell her. He wanted to grab her shoulders: *If we are what we want, I am the same as you.*

But she wasn't looking at him. Her eyes were like marbles he'd had as a child, striated brown and gold. They moved over the pages he'd written as if they were hers, as if she were about to tear one up and put it in her mouth.

'This part,' Julia said. 'About forgetting where you are? D'you know, that *happens* to me? Sometimes coming home I almost say the wrong street—the one in Paris, or in Moscow when we used to have to say "*Pushkinskaya*".'

Her skirt was all twisted around her legs.

'Keep it,' he said.

'I'll write you a cheque.'

'It's a present,' Zubin told her.

'Really?'

He nodded. When she smiled she looked like a kid. 'I wish I could do something for *you.*'

Zubin decided that it was time to leave.

Julia put on a CD—a female vocalist with a heavy bass line. 'This is too sappy for daytime,' she said. Then she started to dance. She was not a good dancer. He watched her fluttering her hands in front of her face, stamping her feet, and knew, the same way he always knew these things, that he wasn't going anywhere at all.

'You know what I hate?'

'What?'

'Boys who can't kiss.'

'All right,' Zubin said. 'You come here.'

Her bed smelled like the soap—lilac. It was amazing, the way girls smelled, and it was amazing to put his arm under her and take off each thin strap and push the dress down around her waist. She made him turn off the lamp but there was a street lamp outside; he touched her in the artificial light. She looked as if she were trying to remember something.

'Is everything okay?'

She nodded.

'Because we can stop.'

'Do you have something?'

It took him a second to figure out what she meant. 'Oh,' he said. 'No—that's good I guess.'

'I have one.'

'You do?'

She nodded.

'Still. That doesn't mean we have to.'

'I want to.'

'Are you sure?'

'If you do.'

'If I do—yes.' He took a breath. 'I want to.'

She was looking at him very seriously.

'This isn't—' he said.

'Of course not.'

'Because you seem a little nervous.'

'I'm just thinking,' she said. Her underwear was light blue, and it didn't quite cover her tan line.

'About what?'

'America.'

'What about it?'

She had amazing gorgeous perfect new breasts. There was nothing else to say about them.

'I can't wait,' she said, and he decided to pretend she was talking about this.

Julia was relieved when he left and she could lie in bed alone and think about it. Especially the beginning part of it: she didn't know kissing could be like that—sexy and calm at the same time, the way it was in movies that were not *9½ Weeks*. She was surprised she didn't feel worse; she didn't feel regretful at all, except that she wished she'd thought of something to say afterwards. *I wish I didn't have to go*, was what he had said, but he put on his shoes very quickly. She hadn't been sure whether she should get up or not, and in the end she waited until she heard the front door shut behind him. Then she got up and put on a T-shirt and pyjama bottoms, and went into the bathroom to wash her face. If she'd told him it was her first time, he would've stayed longer, probably, but she'd read enough magazines to know that you couldn't tell them that. Still, she wished he'd touched her hair the way he had the other night, when she'd gone over to his house and invented a nightmare.

Zubin had left the Ray Bradbury book on her desk. She'd thanked him, but she wasn't planning to read it again. Sometimes when you went back you were disappointed, and she liked the rocket ship the way she remembered it, with silver tail fins and a red lacquer shell. She could picture herself taking off in that ship—at first like an airplane, above the hill and the tank and the bay with its necklace of lights—and then straight up, beyond the sound barrier. People would stand on the beach to watch the launch: her father, Anouk and Bernie, everyone from school, and even Claudie and her mother and Dr Fabrol. They would yell up to her, but the yells would be like the tails of comets, crusty blocks of ice and dust that rose and split in silent, white explosions.

She liked Zubin's essay too, although she wasn't sure about the way he'd combined the two topics; she hoped they weren't going to take points off. Or the part where he talked about all the different perspectives she'd gotten from living in different cities, and how she just needed one place where she could think about those things and articulate what they meant to her. She wasn't interested in 'articulating'. She just wanted to get moving.

Zubin walked all the way up Nepean Sea Road, but when he got to the top of the hill he wasn't tired. He turned right and passed his building, not quite ready to go in, and continued in the Walkeshwar direction. The market was empty. The electronics shops were shuttered and the 'Just Orange' advertisements twisted like kites in the dark. There was the rich, rotted smell of vegetable waste, but almost no other trash. Foreigners marvelled at the way Indians didn't waste anything, but of course that wasn't by choice. Only a few useless things flapped and flattened themselves against the broad, stone steps: squares of folded newsprint from the vendors' baskets, and smashed matchbooks—extinct brands whose labels still appeared underfoot: 'export quality premium safety matches' in fancy script.

At first he thought the tank was deserted, but a man in shorts was standing on the other side, next to a small white dog with stand-up, triangular ears. Zubin picked a vantage point on the steps out of the moonlight, sat down and looked out at the water. There was something different about the tank at night. It was partly the quiet; in between the traffic sounds a breeze crackled the leaves of a few, desiccated trees, growing between the paving stones. The night intensified the contrast, so that the stones took on a kind of sepia, sharpened the shadows and gave the carved and whitewashed temple pillars an appropriate patina of magic. You could cheat for a moment in this light and see the old city, like taking a photograph with black-and-white film.

The dog barked, ran up two steps and turned expectantly toward the tank. Zubin didn't see the man until his slick, seal head surfaced in the black water. Each stroke broke the black glass; his hands made eddies of light in the disturbed surface. For just a moment, even the apartment blocks were beautiful. □

AN EDUCATION
Lynn Barber

Lynn Barber, 1961

One day in 1992 I went to work as usual at the *Independent on Sunday* and the doorman handed me a message slip and said, 'This man has been phoning all night.' The message said, 'Ring Alan Green,' and gave a Jerusalem number. Now, as it happened, Alan Green, the Director of Public Prosecutions, was front page news that week because he had been caught kerb-crawling prostitutes in the King's Cross area. And it is a mark of how crazed with self-importance I was at the time that I immediately thought, 'Oh good. The DPP wants me to interview him.' What more natural than that he should want to give an exclusive to the hottest interviewer in London? I didn't even pause to wonder why he was in Jerusalem. So I rang the Jerusalem number and said, 'Can I speak to Alan Green?' And this horrible cooing voice at the other end said, 'Minn! Bubl has been pining for you all these years.' I dropped the phone like a burning coal and didn't speak again all day.

I met Alan Green—my Alan Green, not the Director of Public Prosecutions—in 1960 when I was sixteen and he was—he said twenty-seven, but probably in his late thirties. I was waiting for a bus home to Twickenham after a rehearsal at Richmond Little Theatre, when a sleek maroon car drew up and a man with a big cigar in his mouth leaned over to the passenger window and said, 'Want a lift?' Of course my parents had told me, my teachers had told me, everyone had told me, never to accept lifts from strange men but at that stage he didn't seem strange, and I hopped in. I liked the smell of his cigar and the leather seats. He asked where I wanted to go and I said Clifden Road, and he said Fine. I told him I had never seen a car like this before, and he said it was a Bristol, and very few were made. He told me lots of facts about Bristols as we cruised— Bristols always cruised—towards Twickenham.

He had a funny accent—later, when I knew him better, I realized it was the accent he used for posh—but I asked if he was foreign. He said, 'Only if you count Jews as foreign.' Well of course I did. I had never consciously met a Jew; I didn't think we had them at my school. But I said politely, 'Are you Jewish? I never would have guessed.' (I meant he didn't have the hooked nose, the greasy ringlets, the straggly beard of Shylock in the school play.) He said he had lived in Israel when he was 'your age'. I wondered what he thought my age was: I hoped he thought nineteen. But then when he said, 'Fancy a coffee?' I foolishly answered, 'No, I have to be home by ten—my father will kill me if I'm late.' 'School tomorrow?' he asked lightly, and, speechless with fury at myself, I could only nod. So then he drove me to my house, and said, 'Can I take you out for coffee another evening?'

My life might have turned out differently if I had just said No. But I was not quite rude enough. Instead, I said I was very busy rehearsing a play which meant that unfortunately I had no free evenings. He asked what play, and I said *The Lady's Not for Burning* at Richmond Little Theatre. Arriving for the first night a couple of weeks later, I found an enormous bouquet in the dressing room addressed to me. The other actresses, all grown-ups, were mewing with envy and saying, 'Those flowers must have cost a fortune.' When I left the theatre, hours later, I saw the Bristol parked outside and went over to say thank you. He said, 'Can't we have our coffee now?' and I said no, because I was late again, but he could drive me home. I wasn't exactly rushing headlong into this relationship; he was far too old for me to think of as a boyfriend. On the other hand, I had always fantasized about having an older man, someone even more sophisticated than me, to impress the little squirts of Hampton Grammar. So I agreed to go out with him on Friday week, though I warned that he would have to undergo a grilling from my father.

My father's grillings were notorious among the Hampton Grammar boys. He wanted to know what marks they got at O level, what A levels they were taking, what universities they were applying to. He practically made them sit an IQ test before they could take me to the flicks. But this time, for once, my father made no fuss at all. He asked where Alan and I had met; I said at Richmond Little Theatre, and that was that. He seemed genuinely impressed by Alan, and even volunteered that we could stay out till midnight, an hour after my normal weekend curfew. So our meeting for coffee turned into dinner, and with my father's blessing.

Alan took me to an Italian place on Marylebone High Street and of course I was dazzled. I had never been to a proper restaurant before, only to tea rooms with my parents. I didn't understand the menu, but I loved the big pepper grinders and the heavy cutlery, the crêpes Suzette and the champagne. I was also dazzled by Alan's conversation. Again, I understood very little of it, partly because his accent was so strange, but also because it ranged across places and activities I could hardly imagine. My knowledge of the world was based on Shakespeare, Jane Austen, George Eliot and the Brontës and none of them had a word to say about living on a kibbutz or making Molotov cocktails. I felt I had nothing to bring to the conversational feast and blushed when Alan urged me to tell him about my schoolfriends, my teachers, my prize-winning essays. I didn't realize then that my being a schoolgirl was a large part of my attraction.

Over the next few weeks, it became an accepted thing that Alan would turn up on Friday or Saturday nights to take me to 'the West End'. Sometimes we went to the Chelsea Classic to see foreign films; sometimes he took me to concerts at the Wigmore or Royal Festival Hall, but mostly we went to restaurants. The choice of restaurants seemed to be dictated by mysterious visits Alan had to make on the way. He would say, 'I've just got to pop into Empress Gate,' and would disappear into one of the white cliff-like houses while I would wait in the car. Sometimes the waiting was very long, and I learned to take a book on all our dates. Once, I asked if I could come in with him, but he said, 'No, this is business,' and I never asked again.

Besides taking me out at weekends, Alan would sometimes drop in during the week when he said he was 'just passing'. (Why was he passing Twickenham? Where was he going? I never asked.) On these occasions, he would stay chatting to my parents, sometimes for an hour or more, about news or politics—subjects of no interest to me. Often the three of them were so busy talking they didn't even notice if I left the room. I found this extraordinary. It was quite unprecedented in our house for me not to be the centre of attention.

Perhaps I should explain about my parents. I was their only child and their only mutual interest. They had no relatives in London, and no friends who ever came to the house—my father had his bridge club (he was a county champion), my mother her amateur dramatics, but all they talked about at home was me, and specifically my school work. My father often quoted Charles Kingsley's line 'Be good, sweet maid, and let who can be clever' but he said it sarcastically—he wanted me to be clever, and let who can be good. My parents had been brought up as Primitive Methodists but by the time they had me their religion was education, education, education. I had been reared from the cradle to pass every possible exam, gain every possible scholarship, and go to university—Cambridge if I was mathematically inclined like my father, or Oxford if I proved to be 'artistic' like my mother. By the age of sixteen, when I met Alan, I was well on track. I had a scholarship at a fee-paying school, Lady Eleanor Holles, I had a royal flush of O levels, and my teachers predicted that I would easily win a place at Oxford to read English. But still my parents fretted and worried. Their big fear was that my Latin would 'let me down'.

My parents were first generation immigrants to the middle class. My father was a Lancashire mill-worker's son, who had taken a law degree at night school and risen high in the civil service. He was formidably intelligent but socially untamed. He still said, 'Side the pots' in his broad Lancashire accent—a source of deep annoyance to my mother and me. We also sighed over his habit of leaving the house with bits of paper on his face when he cut himself shaving. My mother was, in my view, more civilized, even glamorous. She had lovely black wavy hair, hazel eyes and a peachy complexion. But my father and I quietly agreed that she had only a beta plus or even beta minus brain. Nevertheless, she had somehow parlayed a frivolous diploma in speech and drama into a part-time job teaching English at grammar school, then a full-time job, then head of English. I always found it shocking that she could be head of English while privately preferring Georgette Heyer to Jane Austen, and Walter de la Mare to Wordsworth, and occasionally thought of writing to the education authorities to denounce her. It was only because I didn't, I felt, that she was able to continue her remorseless rise through the educational hierarchy.

My parents both earned good salaries, but my father could never shake off his desperate childhood fear of poverty, and was eternally saving for 'a rainy day'. (In the exceptionally wet winter of 2000, when their house was flooded to a depth of six inches, I cheerily remarked to my father, 'Well it looks like your rainy day has finally come'. Despite his being blind by this stage, in his mid-eighties, and handicapped by water lapping round his ankles, he still tried to wade across the room to hit me.) His great fear was fecklessness, which seemed to mean any form of fun. Thus—why did I want to have a Christmas tree? Terrible waste of time, money, all those pine needles buggering the vacuum cleaner and ruining the carpet. 'For fun,' I told him, and watched him almost die of apoplexy on the spot. He regarded any form of social life as time-wasting—to him my mother's involvement in amateur dramatics was feckless and profligate. But this must have been one of the very few subjects on which she 'dug her heels in' and when my mother dug her heels in, my father knew to retreat.

All my rows were with my father—I remember my teens, before Alan appeared, as one long row with my father. My mother was a passive, occasionally tearful, spectator. Sometimes when he hit me ('What you need is a clip around the ear') she would intervene, and often after a particularly loud shouting match, when I had stormed up to my room, she would come sidling up with a hot drink and biscuit as a peace offering. 'Can't you be more tactful?' she would urge. 'Why do you *have* to enrage him?' But I despised her peace-making, always too little and too late, and once told her, 'Look, Mum, if you're really on my side, you'll divorce him; otherwise shut up.' She shut up and went away.

This was the tight little family that Alan was to penetrate and eventually shatter. He represented everything my parents most feared—he was not one of us, he was Jewish and cosmopolitan, practically a foreigner! He wore sweaters and suede shoes; he drove a pointlessly expensive car; he didn't go to work in an office; he was vague about where he went to school and, worst of all, boasted that he had been educated in 'the university of life'—not a teaching establishment my parents recognized. And yet, inexplicably, they liked him. In fact, they liked him more than I ever liked him, perhaps because he took great pains to make them like him. He brought my mother flowers and my father wine; he taught them to play backgammon; he chatted to them endlessly and seemed genuinely interested in their views. I suppose it made a change for them from always talking about me.

Yet none of us ever really knew a thing about him. I think my parents once asked where he lived and he said 'South Kensington' but that was it. I never had a phone number for him, still less an address. As for what he did, he was 'a property developer'—a term I suspect meant as little to my parents as it did to me. I knew it was somehow connected with these visits he had to make, the great bunches of keys he carried, the piles of surveyors' reports and auction catalogues in the back of his car, and the occasional evenings when he had to 'meet Perec' which meant cruising around Bayswater looking for Perec (Peter) Rachman's Roller parked outside one of his clubs. Rachman would later give his name to Rachmanism when the press exposed him as the worst of London's exploitative landlords but at that time he was just one of Alan's many mysterious business colleagues.

Alan was adept at not answering questions, but actually he rarely needed to, because I never asked them. The extent to which I never asked him questions is astonishing in retrospect—I blame Albert Camus. My normal instinct was to bombard people with questions, to ask about every detail of their lives, even to intrude into their silences with, 'What are you thinking?' But just around the time I met Alan I became an Existentialist, and one of the rules of existentialism as practised by me and my disciples at Lady Eleanor Holles School was that you never asked questions. Asking questions showed that you were naive and bourgeois; not asking questions showed that you were sophisticated and French. I badly wanted to be sophisticated. And, as it happened, this suited Alan fine. My role in the relationship was to be the schoolgirl ice maiden, implacable, ungrateful, unresponsive to everything he said or did. To ask questions would have shown that I was interested in him, even that I cared, and neither of us really wanted that.

Alan established early on that I was a virgin, and seemed quite happy about it. He asked when I intended to lose my virginity and I said, 'Seventeen', and he agreed this was the ideal age. He said it was important not to lose my virginity in some inept fumble with a grubby schoolboy, but with a sophisticated older man. I heartily agreed—though, unlike him, I had no particular older man in mind. He certainly didn't seem like a groper. I was used to Hampton Grammar boys who turned into octopuses in the cinema dark, clamping damp tentacles to your breast. Alan never did that. Instead, he kissed me long and gently and said, 'I love to look into your eyes.' Eventually, one night he said, 'I'd love to see your breasts,' so I grudgingly unbuttoned my blouse and allowed him to peep inside my bra. But this was still well within the Lady Eleanor Holles dating code—by rights, given the number of hot dinners he'd bought me, he could really have taken my bra right off.

And then my parents threw me into bed with him. One day, on one of his drop-in visits, Alan said he was going to Wales next weekend to visit some friends and could I go with him? I confidently expected my parents to say no—to go *away*, overnight, with a man I barely knew?—but instead they said yes, though my father added jocularly, 'Separate rooms of course.' 'Of course,' said Alan. So off we went for the first of many dirty weekends. I hated Wales, hated the grim hotel, the sour looks when Alan signed us in. We shared a room of course, and shared a bed, but Alan only kissed me and said, 'Save it till you're seventeen.' After that, there were many more weekends—Paris, Amsterdam, Bruges, and often Sark in the Channel Islands because Alan liked the hotel there, and I liked stocking up on my exciting new discovery, Sobranie Black Russian cigarettes. They brought my sophistication on by leaps and bounds.

As my seventeenth birthday approached, I knew that my debt of dinners and weekends could only be erased by 'giving' Alan my virginity. He talked for weeks beforehand about when, where, how it should be achieved. He thought Rome, or maybe Venice; I thought as near as possible to Twickenham, in case I bled. In the end, it was a new trendy circular hotel—the Ariel?—by Heathrow airport, where we spent the night before an early morning flight to somewhere or other, I forget. He wanted to do a practice run with a banana—he had brought a banana specially. I said, 'Oh, for heaven's sake!' and told him to do it properly. He talked a lot about how he hoped Minn would do Bubl the honour of welcoming him into her home. Somewhere in the middle of the talking, he was inside me, and it was over. I thought, 'Oh well, that was easy. Perhaps now I can get a proper boyfriend.'

(I think the word that best describes my entire sex life with Alan is negligible. I never experienced even a glimmer of an orgasm while I was with him. He was a far from ardent lover—he seemed to enjoy waffling about Minn and Bubl more than actually doing anything. And whereas my games mistress was always bellowing across the changing room, 'But you said it was your period *last* week!' Alan always took my word for it when I said that Minn was 'indisposed'. So although I spent many nights in bed with Alan, usually in foreign hotel rooms, very little ever happened.)

The affair—if it was an affair—drifted on, partly because no proper boyfriends showed up, partly because I had become used to my strange double life of schoolgirl swot during the week, restaurant-going, foreign-travelling sophisticate at weekends. And this life had alienated me from my schoolfriends—if they said, 'Are you coming to Eel Pie Jazz Club on Saturday?' I would say, 'No, I'm going to Paris with Alan.' Of course my friends all clamoured to meet Alan but I never let them. I was afraid of something—afraid perhaps that they would 'see through him', see, not the James Bond figure I had depicted, but this rather short, rather ugly, long-faced, splay-footed man who talked in different accents and lied about his age, whose stories didn't add up.

Because by now—a year into the relationship—I realized that there was a lot I didn't know about Alan. I knew his cars (he had several Bristols), and the restaurants and clubs he frequented, but I still didn't know where he lived. He took me to a succession of flats which he said were his, but often they were full of gonks and women's clothes and he didn't know where the light switches were. So these were other people's flats, or sometimes empty flats, in Bayswater, South Kensington, Gloucester Road. He seemed to have a limitless supply of them.

Where did I imagine he lived? Incredible as it seems now—but this is a reminder of how young I was—I imagined that he lived with his parents but was ashamed to tell me. I pictured this ancient couple in some East End slum performing strange rituals in Yiddish. The fact that he told me his parents were well off and lived in Cricklewood was neither here nor there: I preferred my version. I suspect this is always the way with con men—they don't even have to construct a whole story, their victims fill in the gaps, reconcile the irreconcilables—their victims do most of the work. Alan hardly had to con me at all, because I was so busy conning myself.

But by now there was a compelling reason for staying with Alan—I was in love. Not with Alan, obviously, but with his business partner Danny and his girlfriend Helen. I loved them both equally. I loved their beauty, I loved their airy flat in Bedford Square where there were pre-Raphaelites on the walls and harpsichord music on the hi-fi. At that time, few people in Britain admired the Pre-Raphaelites but Danny was one of the first, and I eagerly followed. He lent me books on Rossetti and Burne-Jones and Millais, and sometimes flattered me

Lynn Barber, 1962

by showing me illustrations in auction catalogues and saying, 'What do you think? Should I make a bid?' I found it easy to talk to Danny; I could chatter away to him whereas with Alan I only sulked.

Helen was a different matter. She drifted around silently, exquisitely, a soulful Burne-Jones damsel half hidden in her cloud of red-gold hair. At first, I was so much in awe of her beauty I could barely speak to her. But gradually I came to realize that her silence was often a cover for not knowing what to say and that actually— I hardly liked to use the word about my goddess—she was thick. I was terrified that one day Danny would find out. And there were sometimes hints from Alan that Danny's interest in Helen might be waning, that there could be other girlfriends. Knowing this, keeping this secret, made me feel that it was crucial for me to go on seeing Helen, to protect her, because one day, when I was just a little older and more sophisticated, we could be best friends.

Alan always refused to talk about business to me ('Oh, you don't want to know about that, Minn') but Danny had no such inhibitions. He loved telling me funny stories about the seething world of dodgy property dealers—the scams, the auction rings, the way the auctioneers sometimes tried to keep out the 'Stamford Hill cowboys' by holding auctions on Yom Kippur or other holy days, and then the sight of all these Hasidic Jews in mufflers and dark glasses trying to bid without being seen. Or the great scam whereby they sold Judah Binstock a quarter acre of Ealing Common, without him realizing that the quarter acre was only two yards wide. Through Danny, I learned how Perec Rachman had seemingly solved the problem of 'stats'— statutory or sitting tenants—who were the bane of Sixties property developers. The law gave them the right to stay in their flats at a fixed rent for life if they wanted—and they had a habit of living an awfully long time. But Rachman had certain robust methods, such as carrying out building works all round them, or taking the roof off, or 'putting in the schwartzes' (West Indians) or filling the rest of the house with prostitutes, which made stats eager to move.

So I gathered from Danny that the property business in which Alan was involved was not entirely honest. But my first hint of other forms of dishonesty came about fifteen months into the relationship when I went to a bookshop on Richmond Green. Alan had taken me there several times to buy me books of Jewish history and the works of Isaac Bashevis Singer—I accepted them gratefully, though I never read them. But on this occasion, I went alone and the book dealer, who was normally so friendly, said, 'Where's your friend?'

'What friend?'

'Alan Prewalski.'

'I don't know anyone of that name,' I said truthfully.

'Well, whatever he calls himself. Tell him I'm fed up with his bouncing cheques—I've reported him to the police.'

That evening I said to Alan—'Do you know anyone called Prewalski?'

'Yes—my mother, my grandparents, why?'

I told him what the book dealer had said.

Alan said, 'Well don't go in there again. Or if you do, don't tell him you've seen me. Say we've broken up.'

'But what did he mean about the bouncing cheques?'

'How should I know? Don't worry about it.'

So that was a hint, or more than a hint. Then in Cambridge there was unmistakable proof. He and Danny had gone into Cambridge in a big way and were buying up a street called Bateman Street, so we often stayed there. One weekend I was moaning—I was always moaning—'I'm bored with Bateman Street' and Danny said, 'So am I—let's drive to the country,' so we drove out towards Newmarket. At a place called Six Mile Bottom, I saw a thatched cottage with a FOR SALE sign outside. 'Look, how pretty,' I said, 'Why can't you two buy nice places like that instead of horrible old slums?' 'Perhaps we can,' said Alan, sliding the Bristol to a stop—'Fancy it, Danny?' 'Why not?' So Alan parked the car and we all marched up to the door. An old lady answered it: 'The agent didn't tell me you were coming.' 'Oh dear, oh dear,' said Danny, 'how very remiss of him.' She must have liked his posh accent, which was so much more convincing than Alan's, because she said, 'Well, come in anyway—I'll show you round.'

The cottage was full, overfull, of antique furniture: I found it gloomy and was bored within minutes. But Alan and Danny both seemed enchanted and kept admiring the beams, the polished floorboards, the pictures, the furniture. Having been rather crabby, the owner blossomed into friendliness and invited us to stay for coffee. While she was making it, Alan asked if he could go upstairs to the bathroom. A few minutes later I saw him going out to the car carrying something. Then he joined us for coffee and, after half an hour chatting, we left. In the car, Danny said, 'Got it?'

Alan nodded.

'Speed?'

'Pretty sure.'

'Got what?' I said.

'So was that your dream cottage?' said Danny. 'Will you and Alan live there happily ever after?'

'No,' I said, 'I found it gloomy.'

They both laughed. 'You're so difficult to please.'

Danny said he must get back to Bateman Street. I was still furious with him for laughing at me, so I said, 'You promised me a day in the country—I'm not going back.' Danny said we could drop him in Newmarket so we took him to the station, then went to a hotel for lunch. We were having a rather lugubrious meal when two men came into the dining room and one pointed the other towards our table. The man introduced himself as a detective. He said, 'We've had a complaint from a Mrs so-and-so of Six Mile Bottom. She says two men and a girl visited her cottage this morning and afterwards she noticed that a valuable antique map by Speed was missing from one of the bedrooms.' 'Oh, *Alan!*' I said. He shot me a look. 'Perhaps we could have this conversation outside,' he suggested. He went outside with the policeman. I waited a few minutes and then went to the Ladies, and from the Ladies, walked out the back door and away down the street. I had just enough money for a bus to Cambridge, and ran panting to find Danny in Bateman Street. 'Alan's been arrested!' I told him. 'He stole a map from that old lady!'

'I'm sure there was a misunderstanding,' he said smoothly. 'I'll sort it out. Why don't you take the train back to London?'

'I don't have any money!' I wailed.

He handed me a ten-pound note. 'Don't worry about Alan,' he told me. I didn't intend to: I hoped he was in prison.

He wasn't of course; he bounced round to Clifden Road a few days later and took me out to dinner. 'How could you *steal* from an old lady?'

'I didn't steal. She asked me to have the map valued.'

'No she didn't, I was with you.'

'All right, she didn't ask me. But I recognized that the map was by Speed and I thought if I got it valued for her, it would be a nice surprise.'

I knew he was lying, but I let it go. I said: 'If you ever really stole something, I would leave you.'

He said, 'I know you would, Minn.'

But actually I knew he had stolen something and I didn't leave him, so we were both lying.

Soon afterwards, I did try to leave him. I was bored. I was bored with the sex, and especially Minn and Bubl, I was bored with the endless driving round, the waiting while he ran his mysterious errands, the long heavy meals in restaurants, the tussles in strange bedrooms, the fact that we never met anyone except Danny and Helen. I loved the evenings in Bedford Square when Danny played the harpsichord and Helen showed me her new clothes, but now they spent most of their time in Cambridge and Alan was never going to Cambridge again. I told Alan, 'We're finished—I've got to concentrate on my A levels.' He said, 'We're not finished. I'll come for you when you've done your A levels.'

On the evening I finished sitting my A levels, Alan took me out to dinner and proposed. I had wanted him to propose, as proof of my power, but I had absolutely no intention of accepting because of course I was going to Oxford. Eighteen years of my life had been dedicated to this end, so it was quite impertinent of him to suggest my giving it up. I relayed the news to my parents the next morning as a great joke—'Guess what? Alan proposed! He wants me to marry him this summer!' To my complete disbelief, my father said, 'Why not?' *Why not?* Had he suddenly gone demented? 'Because then I couldn't go to Oxford.' My father said, 'Well—is that the end of the world? Look,' he went on, 'You've been going out with him for two years; he's obviously serious, he's a good man; don't mess him around.' I turned to my mother incredulously but she shook her head. 'You don't need to go to university if you've got a good husband.'

This was 1962, well before the advent of feminism. But even so, I felt a sense of utter betrayal, as if I'd spent eighteen years in a convent and then the Mother Superior had said, 'Of course, you know, God doesn't exist.' I couldn't believe my parents could abandon the idea of Oxford. But apparently they could and over the next few days they argued it every meal time—good husbands don't grow on trees, you're lucky to get this one ('And you not even in the family way!'), why go to university if you don't need to? Alan meanwhile was taking me to see houses, asking where I wanted to live when we were married. I couldn't resist telling my schoolfriends, 'I'm engaged!' And they were all wildly excited and thrilled for me, and said, 'You'll never have to do Latin again!' Even so, I was queasy—I'd always liked the sound of Oxford, I even liked writing essays, I wasn't so keen to give up the idea. But my parents, especially my father, put great pressure on me. Why go to Oxford if I could marry Alan? And, they reminded me, I'd been saying all along that I couldn't face another term at school.

This was true. In those days, if you were aiming for Oxford or Cambridge, you had to stay at school an extra term after A levels to prepare for the entrance exams. I was dreading it because Miss R. Garwood Scott, the headmistress, had flatly refused to make me a prefect and, while all the other Oxbridge candidates could spend their time in the prefects' room, I would be left roaming the corridors or slouching round the playing field on my own, without any gang to protect me. But Miss R. Garwood Scott was adamant that I would never be a prefect even if I stayed at school a hundred years—I was a troublemaker, a bad influence, guilty of dumb insolence and making pupils laugh at teachers. I put a brave face on it, but I knew the next term was going to be the loneliest three months of my life. But then there was the glittering prize of Oxford at the end of it—I never doubted I would get in—and I had resolved it was a price I was willing to pay.

Events overtook me in the last few days of term. Miss R. Garwood Scott somehow got wind of my engagement and summoned me to see her. Was it true I was engaged? Yes, I said, but I would still like to take the Oxford exams. She was ruthless. I could either be engaged or take the exams but not both. When was the wedding and which church would it be in? Not in church, I said, because my fiancé was Jewish. Jewish! She looked aghast—'Don't you realize that the Jews killed Our Lord?' I stared at her. 'So I won't take the Oxford exams,' I said. My little gang was waiting for me outside her study. 'I told her I was leaving,' I announced. 'She tried to persuade me to

stay but I refused.' They all congratulated me and begged to be
bridesmaids. Then I went to the bogs and cried my eyes out.

I told my parents: 'I'm not going to Oxford, I'm marrying Alan.'
'Oh good!' they said. 'Wonderful.' When Alan came that evening,
they made lots of happy jokes about not losing a daughter but
gaining a son. Alan chuckled and waved his hands about, poured
drinks and proposed toasts—but I caught the flash of panic in his
eyes. A few days later, probably no more than a week later, we were
in the Bristol on our way to dinner when he said he just needed to
pop into one of his flats to have a word with a tenant. Fine, I said,
I'll wait in the car. As soon as he went inside the house, I opened
the glove compartment and started going through the letters and bills
he kept in there. It was something I could have done on any one of
a hundred occasions before—I knew he kept correspondence in the
glove compartment, I knew the glove compartment was unlocked,
I was often waiting in the car alone and had no scruples about
reading other people's letters. So why had I never done it before? And
why did it seem the most obvious thing in the world to do now?
Anyway the result was instantaneous. There were a dozen or more
letters addressed to Alan Green, with a Twickenham address. And
two bank statements addressed to Mr and Mrs Alan Green with the
same address.

I behaved quite normally that evening though at the end, when
he asked if Minn would welcome a visit from Bubl I replied
smoothly that she was indisposed. By that stage, I was at least as
good a liar as Alan. As soon as I got home, I looked in the phone
book—and why had I never thought of doing *that* before?—and sure
enough found an A. Green with a Popesgrove (Twickenham) number,
and the address I'd seen on the letters. It was only about half a mile
from my house, I actually passed it every day on the bus to school.
I spent the night plotting and rehearsing what I would say, working
out scripts for all eventualities. When I finally rang the number the
next morning, it was all over in seconds. A woman answered. 'Mrs
Green?' I said. 'Yes.' 'I'm ringing about the Bristol your husband
advertised for sale.' 'Oh,' she said, 'is he selling it? He's not here now
but he's usually back about six.' That was enough or more than
enough—I could hear a child crying in the background.

I took the train to Waterloo, and walked all the way to Bedford

Square. Helen was in, and guessed as soon as she saw me—'You've found out?'

'Yes,' I said—'It's not just that he's married—he *lives* with her. And there's a child.'

'Two, actually.'

'Why didn't you tell me?'

'I'm sorry. I wanted to. The other night when you said you were engaged, I told Danny we *must* tell you, but he said Alan would never forgive us.'

This was—what?—my third, fourth, fifth betrayal by adults? And I had really thought Helen was my friend.

'What was Alan planning to do?' I asked her. 'Commit bigamy?'

'Yes,' she said soberly. 'That's exactly what he intended to do. He felt he'd lose you if he didn't. He loves you very much you know.'

I went home and raged at my parents—'You did this. *You* made me go out with him, *you* made me get engaged.' My parents were white with shock—unlike me, they had no inkling before that Alan was dishonest. My mother cried. When Alan came that evening, my father went to the door and tried to punch him. I heard him shouting, 'You've ruined her life!' From my bedroom window, I saw Alan sitting in the Bristol outside with his shoulders shaking. Then my father strode down the front path and kicked the car as hard as he could, and Alan drove away. I found the sight of my father kicking the car hilarious and wanted to shout out of the window, 'Scratch it, Dad! Scratch the bodywork—that'll *really* upset him!'

It was a strange summer. My parents were grieving and still in deep shock. I, the less deceived, was faking far more sorrow than I felt. After all, I never loved him whereas I think perhaps they did. I stayed in my room playing César Franck's Symphony in D minor very loudly day after day. My main emotion was rage, followed by puzzlement about what to do next. I had no plans for the summer or—now—for the rest of my life. When my A level results came, I not only got the top marks I fully expected in English and French, but also—*mirabile dictu*—top marks in Latin. I slapped the letter on the breakfast table and said, 'You see? I *could* have gone to Oxford.'

My father took the day off work, probably for the first time in his life, and went to see Miss R. Garwood Scott. God knows what humble pie he had to eat—and he hated humble pie—but he came back with a grim face and a huge concession. She had agreed I could be entered for the Oxford exams as a Lady Eleanor Holles pupil, and I could sit the exams at school. But she was adamant that I could not attend the school—it was up to him to arrange private tutorials. Mum and Dad talked far into the night about how they would find a tutor, and how they would pay. A day or two later—presumably at Miss R. Garwood Scott's instigation—one of my English teachers rang and volunteered to be my tutor. She even offered to teach me for free, though I think my father insisted on paying. So I spent that autumn writing essays and going to tutorials, working hard and feeling lonely. My parents were in such deep grief that meal times were silent. Once or twice I saw the Bristol parked at the end of the street, but I was never remotely tempted to go to it.

One day that winter, sitting at my bedroom table writing an essay, I saw a woman walking slowly along the street looking at our house. I guessed immediately that she was Alan Green's wife. She was prettier than I'd imagined her, but of course mumsy and old. A few minutes later she walked back again and came up the path. My mother must have been watching from the downstairs window because she shouted to me, 'Stay in your room,' and then fetched the woman in. They talked for about half an hour. My mother wouldn't tell me afterwards what Mrs Green had said—with her typical beta brain logic she said it was none of my business. But she couldn't resist saying, with strange malice, 'You weren't the first, you know. He had other girlfriends before you. Anyway,' she went on, 'he's in prison now—best place for him.' For a moment, I thought she meant he was in prison for having girlfriends, but Mum said no—he'd been caught bouncing cheques. He was charged with three offences, asked for 190 others to be taken into account, and was sentenced to six months.

I sat the Oxford exams, I went for interviews, I was accepted by St Anne's. In my second term at Oxford, one of the nuns at the convent where I boarded handed me a note which she said a man had brought. It said 'Bubl respectfully requests the pleasure of the company of Minn for dinner at the Randolph Hotel tonight at 8.' I tore it up in front of the nun. 'Don't ever let that man in,' I told her, 'He's a con man.' I went round to Merton to tell my boyfriend Dick and he said, 'Well,

I'd like to meet him—let's go to the Randolph.' So we did. Alan was sitting in the lobby—on time, for once in his life—looking older, tireder, seedier than I remembered. His face lit up when he saw me and fell when I said, 'This is my boyfriend, Dick.' Alan said politely, 'Won't you please both stay to dinner as my guests?' 'How are you going to pay for it?' I snapped and Dick looked at me with horror— he had never heard me use that tone before. Alan silently withdrew a large roll of banknotes from his pocket and I nodded, okay.

Dick was enchanted by Alan. He loved his Israeli kibbutz stories, his fishing with dynamite stories, his Molotov cocktail stories. I had heard them all before, except his new prison stories. Alan said that when he got out of prison, he headed immediately for Sark—and here he cast me such a doe-eyed soppy look I almost spat—but he was rearrested as soon as he got off the plane in Jersey, because he had passed some dud cheques in the Channel Islands which were not 'taken into account'. As Dick walked me back to my convent, he said, 'I see why you were taken in by him—he's quite a charmer, isn't he?' 'No,' I said furiously, 'he's a disgusting criminal con-man and don't you *dare* say you like him!'

Was Alan a con man? Well, he was a liar and a thief who used charm as his jemmy to break into my parents' house and steal their most treasured possession, which was me. Of course Oxford, and time, would have stolen me away eventually, but Alan made it happen almost overnight. Until our 'engagement', I'd thought my parents were ignorant about many things (fashion, for instance, and Existentialism, and why Jane Austen was better than Georgette Heyer) but I accepted their moral authority unquestioningly. So when they casually dropped the educational evangelism they'd sold me for eighteen years and told me I should skip Oxford to marry Alan, I thought, 'I'm never going to take your advice about anything ever again.' And when he turned out to be married, it was as if, tacitly, they concurred. From then on, whenever I told them my plans, their only response was a penitent, 'You know best.'

What did I get from Alan? An education—the thing my parents always wanted me to have. I learned a lot in my two years with Alan. I learned about expensive restaurants and posh hotels and foreign travel, I learned about antiques and Bergman films and classical music. All this was useful when I went to Oxford—I could read a menu, I could recognize a finger bowl, I could follow an opera, I was not a complete hick. But actually there was a much bigger bonus than that. My experience with Alan entirely cured my craving for sophistication. By the time I got to Oxford I wanted nothing more than to meet kind, decent, conventional boys my own age, no matter if they were gauche or virgins. I would marry one eventually and stay married all my life and for that, I suppose, I have Alan to thank.

But there were other lessons Alan taught me that I regret learning. I learned not to trust people; I learned not to believe what they say but to watch what they do; I learned to suspect that anyone and everyone is capable of 'living a lie'. I came to believe that other people—even when you think you know them well—are ultimately unknowable. Learning all this was a good basis for my subsequent career as an interviewer, but not, I think, for life. It made me too wary, too cautious, too ungiving. So that when, thirty years later, I heard that 'Minn!' on the phone from Jerusalem, I hated him more, not less, for all the intervening years. □

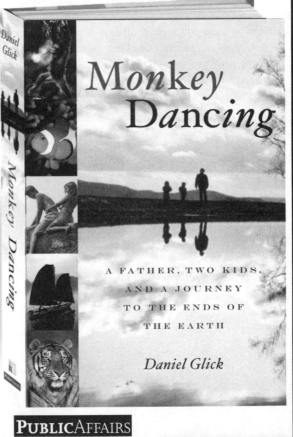

GRANTA

THE KITE TRICK
Bill Gaston

'This Tofino,' pronounced Uncle Phil, from his bed, first cigarette of the day bouncing unlit in his lips, 'is a freakish place.'

It was warm and lovely out and the cause of his declaration, yesterday having been stormy and cold. 'Hilariously cold,' he had said, not laughing. 'Mid May?' He'd also found it freakish that you could always hear the roar of waves, the constant roar of waves. 'Cheers, mate.'

Philip liked how his Uncle Phil thanked him. His uncle's namesake, he had fetched the cigarettes from the condo's living room, the kind of chore he'd been happily performing for two days, wanting to get to know his English uncle, his only uncle, whom he got to see once each year. Interesting, these notions of 'relative', 'English'. And Uncle Phil was entertaining in ways Philip's parents certainly weren't. Those expressions of his, for instance the way he sighed and said under his breath, 'deep carnival', pronouncing the second word like the French might. What did Uncle Phil mean by that?

From the doorway Philip watched his uncle suck absently on his cigarette, take it out to discover its unlit end then swear and lurch out of bed with more energy than he would show all day. Philip's mother wouldn't let Uncle Phil smoke inside the rented condo because of the children.

Uncle Phil still wore the bathing suit he'd worn last evening in the hot tub. He had the kind of body, Philip noted, that you expected of an Englishman, especially a musician, in that it was without defined muscle. Even his uncle's tan seemed not very attached to its skin, and mismatched to the pale tone underneath. Philip had to agree with his mother, whom he'd overheard telling his father, 'Your brother's two years younger and looks ten years older.' She'd said it accusingly, and Philip knew this had to do with his uncle's lifestyle. Or, as she put it, 'How your brother lives.'

'We did it backwards, darling,' Uncle Phil shouted again to Aunt Sally, who didn't hear because she was out at the car 'searching the boot' for sunscreen. By backwards he meant they shouldn't have gone to Jamaica before Canada, because 'the other way round wouldn't have felt so freaking frigid. Next year we do cold *then* hot.' Uncle Phil said 'freaking' a lot and slipped occasionally. At each slip Philip's mother closed her eyes, and once took his father away for a talk.

They sat eating breakfast quickly, all seven of them, Philip's little sister and brother racing to lick jam off their toast before they were told to stop. Philip's mother was impatient at the stove, waiting for the bacon to cook. Uncle Phil always wanted bacon, crispy bacon. Philip enjoyed the way his uncle defended his sins; earlier this morning, announcing that she was off to the resort store and what would people like for breakfast, his mother had been shocked by Uncle Phil's, 'Any deeply sustaining pork product!' booming from behind his closed bedroom door. There was something so English in what he said, sly like *Winnie-the-Pooh* was sly.

The idea this morning was that Philip's mother and father and Aunt Sally would go whale-watching while Uncle Phil took the three kids to the main beach to enjoy the warm day. At twelve, Philip was old enough to appreciate the rather undramatic grey whales surfacing to breathe, but he got seasick even on calm water and in any case he had to help, as his father put it, 'poor Uncle Phil look after the hordes'. Uncle Phil did look grateful that Philip was staying behind. He and Aunt Sally had no children—another side of Uncle Phil that seemed to rub his mother wrong.

Eating bacon, pretending to try to entice the adults away from whale-watching, Uncle Phil said, 'You're actually choosing the big grey blobs over the kite trick?' He refused to tell anyone what the trick was, though Aunt Sally nodded while she confirmed, 'It's a good one.'

After breakfast, his parents and Aunt Sally gone, Philip stood in the bedroom doorway again to watch his uncle pull a canvas hunting-vest over a bright red long-sleeved T-shirt and clutch himself, saying '*Brrrrr*'. He enjoyed being watched. His hair was always wild, standing up in strands which shifted comically as he moved. He would stay the whole day in that hunting vest—it had bullet holders and was apparently the real thing. On its back was a big yin-yang symbol, though two shades of blue rather than the typical black and white. Philip knew what it meant—it meant opposites that made a whole. Though odd on a hunting vest it was one of the more sensible ornaments. He hated it when people said ying-yang. He hated people who used 'phenomena' as the singular even more.

Philip backed out of the room when his uncle found a lighter in a vest pocket. But the smell of smoke followed him, almost instantly it seemed, as he walked past his sister and brother to open a window and the door to the patio. Though he performed these acts of ventilation quietly he felt awkward, a sissy in his mother's camp. Plus it was clear that these openings simply pulled the smoke more quickly out of Uncle Phil's bedroom and on into everyone's noses. No matter what he did, Philip's mother would smell it, and tonight there would be more hissing out in the parking lot.

'So,' said Uncle Phil, ambling out of the bedroom with cigarette blazing, unaware of his rebellion. 'This famous "Long Beach". Will it have a mosh pit?'

'For sure.' Ever since his uncle found out that Philip knew what a mosh pit was, and that his mother and father didn't, he talked this way. So does this famous 'grade seven' of yours have a mosh pit? So does this so-called 'seafood restaurant' we're off to have a mosh pit? Philip and his uncle refused to reveal to the others what a mosh pit was. Aunt Sally, who had tattoos, would just sit quietly smiling. Philip could tell she didn't want to be here. Her eyes were steady with waiting. She was younger than Uncle Phil, and Philip knew they weren't really married, though they had been together for as long as he could remember. Uncle Phil sometimes called her 'Aunt Silly', which sounded funny mostly because 'aunt' rhymed with 'want'. It made Sasha and Tommy laugh, especially when Aunt Silly pulled a face to match, but it also confused them, because their parents never made fun like that in front of children.

Leaving for the whale-watching, his mother had taken Philip aside, both his shoulders under her hands, steering him into the rhododendron grove bordering the parking lot.

'You are going to a beach with a Very. Strong. Undertow,' she'd said. '*Adults* drown there. *Never* let Tommy and Sasha out of your sight. Do *not* let them go in over their ankles. Today is *sand*castles.' She looked over her glasses toward the condo and raised her eyebrows. '*You* are the boss.' She squeezed his shoulders and repeated, '*You*.'

Which was all fine except it made Philip resent his mother even more. He hadn't liked it, while they checked in, hearing her insist to his father that they pay the entire rental on the condo because then they would 'have more control'. Most of all he resented her for standing in the way of him and Uncle Phil. It was becoming clear to him that you could have a special feeling for relatives, beyond seeing the play of genes. This year, Philip had come to understand that Uncle Phil visited each year not just to see his only brother but also, more and more, to see him too. The way he'd hugged him second at the airport, the way he said, '*Hello*, Namesake.'

Philip liked this about his uncle, this potential and blossoming uncle-ness. Though already familiar with the word, he had reviewed 'avuncular' in his OED.

It was a twenty-minute drive to Long Beach and Uncle Phil did only one joke about driving on the wrong side of the road, veering over the double-yellow line when there was no other car in sight, then a goofy 'Oops!' and gently veering them back. Philip's brother and sister were thrilled, though only Sasha, eight, had any sense of there being a left or a right side to anything.

'I *can't* believe in one month you'll be thirteen.' He said it 'thir*deen*' with a weight that did make it seem important. Uncle Phil gave him a wink. 'Thir*deen* is when it begins, mate.'

Philip sat saying nothing. He smiled like his aunt smiled, tired and knowing. He knew what his uncle was on about. But he knew even better that, as far as 'it' went, next year would be no different than this one.

'You have some fun but you keep up those famous straight As of yours. All right? Get all yer girlfriends to help ya?'

'Sure.'

'Promise?'

'Sure.'

'You really got one hundred per cent in maths?'

'I guess.' Actually 105, this impossible score due to his teacher's inane dangling of bonus.points.

'*And* science?'

'I guess.'

'*And* wankology?'

Philip smiled and stared straight ahead. He really wanted to be praised for his reading, which was, of course, untestable.

'Jesus, you know, you're a loner just like your dad.' When Philip didn't respond, Uncle Phil added, 'Which is not a bad thing, not a bad thing at all.'

'What do you mean,' Philip asked, 'when you say, "deep carni*val*"? What does that mean, exactly?'

'It means—' Uncle Phil stared into the road and tried hard for his nephew. '—it means, the strange and colourful activity of human meat.

230

That's what it means. Exactly.' He looked over at Philip. 'Get it?'
'I guess.'

The parking lot was nearly empty of cars. Anyone on this beach
that planed vastly off to the right was swallowed up in its sheer size.
Philip could see what might be a beach umbrella a half mile away.
There was someone in blue-and-yellow walking the haze and hard
sand of low tide but you couldn't tell if they were one person or two.
Other than that, a small dog poked about the huge bleached logs
that storms had tossed, over the years, at the foot of the forest.

'This is *brilliant*,' said Uncle Phil, standing with hands on hips,
taking it in, having almost to shout over the roar of surf. 'There's
no one *here*! *Look* at this! You don't get this where your father and
I come from!' The breeze put his hair back, flat for once.

Sasha and Tommy sat anguished in the car. Tommy bounced.
Uncle Phil finally understood their set faces.

'Yes! You can get out!' He raised his hands over his head, astounded
that they would still be sitting there. 'Out! Run off! It's a beach!'

'Stay close!' Philip shouted at their backs. 'Sasha—keep Tommy
with you. We'll catch up.'

Uncle Phil opened the trunk and emptied it of towels, lunch pack,
kite. He asked Philip if they should bring the shovel and Philip told
him how good it was for sandcastles, how it let you build something
sizeable. He liked using words like 'sizeable' around Uncle Phil for
the way they made him comically startle and say something like, 'My
namesake's a freaking intellectual.'

At the edge of the parking lot Uncle Phil stopped in the breeze to
take in the scope of what he was about to enter. He seemed almost
nervous. Something in his uncle's hesitation made Philip proud that
he lived in Canada: empty and powerful, dangerous even. Philip
hadn't been to Long Beach for two years. He liked it well enough,
though the water was useless. It was so cold, like it had melted only
seconds before. It numbed you completely.

'Your father didn't tell me! This is brilliant!'

His father seemed critical of Uncle Phil too, though he smiled
warmly when he spoke of his little brother. This was him yearning
for England and his own boyhood—so Philip's mother explained it
to Philip. His father had left England for Canada at eighteen, going
to university, to become a civil servant with Canada Post. Uncle Phil

stayed in London and, as his father put it, had never grown up. Philip recalled his mother's face when, a few months ago, she happened upon a reality show on TV. A long-haired old guy was stuttering his words. She had declared with sarcastic revelation to Philip's father, 'Your brother wishes he were *Ozzy Osbourne*.'

Uncle Phil used to play in bands—he was a bass player, mostly a session musician. His main claims to fame were his 'jams' with certain rock stars Philip had actually heard of. He'd been listening to the stories since he was born. Uncle Phil had been on stage with Elton John, once, and with Phil Collins for a whole European tour, and once with Denny Laine of Wings, formerly of the Moody Blues. He'd played on two tracks of Charlie Watts's solo album, though neither track made the final cut. He was on an entire Ian Dury live album and apparently you could see him on the cover. There were others his father could list, plus plenty more stories about musicians that weren't about music. Phil 'knew the *first* guy who found Hendrix in the morning'. He himself had 'bodily saved a mature but severely pissed Richard Starkey from taking out an entire table loaded with pints.'

It had been twenty years since Uncle Phil had played in a band. Since then he'd been 'in production', meaning he made the CDs, though Philip wasn't clear exactly what his uncle did, other than know lots of musicians. When asked, he joked, 'It's music politics. I'm the *party organizer*.' Philip had just last week overheard his mother describing him to his father as an 'elderly gopher', and his father had shaken his head while agreeing. Lending the visit an air of illegality that Philip found thrilling, his mother had added, 'He'd better not be bringing anything in from Jamaica.' His father assured her his brother wouldn't. Philip loved hearing his father's moderate English accent spice up whenever he talked about Uncle Phil. He could almost picture his father as a boy, having fun.

Another thing his father said about his brother, sounding as English as could be, was, 'I can tell he's still fantastically lonely.'

They walked a fair way, Uncle Phil wanting to 'go past any people'. So eager was he on this point that for a distance he carried Tommy and the basket at the same time, and when they arrived he was exhausted and he dropped both abruptly. Tommy landed on his side and looked to Philip to see if he was supposed to cry.

Uncle Phil began immediately to unpack and assemble his kite. The breeze, he said, was brilliantly steady. Philip was sent up into the driftwood logs for a chunk of wood 'the size of your own leg'. When he returned with one, Uncle Phil moved them from the soft part of the beach down to the hard-packed, low-tide sand. Tommy proudly dragged the shovel.

'Is the tide coming in?' asked Sasha, gazing out at the froth of breakers, its roar and roiling mist.

'Yes,' Philip answered, trying to sound a warning, though he wasn't sure. The sand was cold and damp on his feet, and as hard as a floor. 'And it comes in quickly. When I say it's time to move, we move.'

But Sasha only wanted to hear that it was coming in. 'Save the Queen! We can play Save the Queen!' A game they played with tides, it involved a queen—a stick or a shell or moulded sand—around which you built a sandcastle and fortress walls and outer walls and moats, all in an effort to keep the rising tide from getting in and drowning her. When the first surging flat tongues reached the moats and filled them, and then licked at the walls, which then began to crumble, the inevitable was upon you and so was the wonderful frenzy and panic to heap as much sand as fast as possible to shore up breaching walls. Last year at a gentler beach Sasha had actually lain down and used her body to plug a crumbling wall, screaming in hopeless joy, because the water just came and came, eventually breaking through and washing up to the sand queen's feet—and down she came, dissolving—an outcome always known but always pretended against—otherwise there would be no reason to the game at all. Eventually they would simply give up and stand there breathing hard, open-mouthed and slack-faced, staring at the dying.

'Just let me get my kite up and then we'll save the freaking queen.' The two smaller children were waiting for him. Still puffing from the walk, Uncle Phil sat down twice for a cigarette while he got his kite trick set up. From a thermos he sipped what Philip knew to be gin. When Tommy ran up to his uncle for a sip he was rebuffed with a laughing, 'You don't want any of this, luv.'

The kite was egg shaped, with a Union Jack design on both sides. Against the monotones of sand and water, the colours of this design looked truly unnatural, bizarre even, and Philip fancied that high in the sky was the only place for it.

His uncle got the kite together and laid it on the ground, pinnning it down with one foot for it really was quite breezy. He asked Philip to dig him a leg-sized hole and Philip shovelled until told to stop, about two feet down. Uncle Phil tied some clear fishing-line to the long stake, placed it in the hole and buried it, with the invisible line protruding. He tied the fishing line to the kite-string handle. It was easy to get the kite airborne—cigarette in mouth, Uncle Phil looked almost athletic running five steps and tossing it aloft—and soon the kite was sitting hard in the sky one hundred feet above them. At this point Uncle Phil let go of it completely.

The trick involved what you didn't see. With the hole smoothed over, what you did see was a kite and its string and its handle, suspended in mid-air, six feet off the ground, held by no one.

Uncle Phil twanged the fishing line, which was taut and holding invisibly well. He slapped sand from his hands. Staring at the eerie floating handle, not the soaring kite, he asked, 'So what d'ya think?' He gazed up and down the beach for passers-by, though there weren't any. 'They'll think we brought our pet ghost,' he said, and laughed lightly.

Sasha asked if they could play Save the Queen now.

It was Sasha who began constructing walls around Uncle Phil as he sat there on the sand admiring his kite trick. It was also Sasha who demanded that they had to 'bury him all except for his head' when she decided that this 'king' was way too big. Uncle Phil climbed stoically into the long hole that was as deep as Philip could make it. His uncle shouted as he sat, declaring it was 'freaking ice' but loudly assuring himself it would warm up.

'You have to keep me in supplies,' he told Philip, meaning his gin and cigarettes. He looked funny, padded collar of the hunting vest framing his jaws, hair weak in the breeze, cigarette bobbing as he talked. Classic disembodied head. Tommy enjoyed his task of leaning in with the thermos cup and getting the drink past the cigarette and into his uncle's mouth. Philip had to admit to pride not only at lighting a first cigarette but learning to light one in the wind. Uncle Phil was a good teacher. 'The trick,' he said, 'is to cup your hand as close as you can to the flame without burning yourself. The thing is finding that quarter inch.'

Because this time the queen, or in this case, king was a person, the walls had to be higher, the moats deeper. Sasha and Tommy dug and pushed and moulded to keep their buried uncle from the calamity that roared ever closer as it pounded out clouds of mist that turned the blue day cold, backed by ocean that filled the horizon and that your stomach knew never stopped.

Placing the latest cigarette in his uncle's lips, which reached out for it in a less than attractive way, Philip decided against telling him that his lips were turning purple. If the game ended now, with the wave surges not yet at the first moats, his brother and sister would be upset. Also Uncle Phil was still energetic with chatter. Because of the nearing surf, he had to shout. He was a sight. Sasha had draped his head with a seaweed crown, a frond of which flipped wind-blown against one cheek.

'...because it isn't English anymore, it's Euro or brown. Now I *love* brown. Little Richard's my hero, mate. And I *had* my Ravi Shankar period. I mean we've never had music of our own unless you want to include fucking *skiffle*.' He laughed and Philip didn't know why, but his uncle was talking fast and not really noticing anyone. His teeth were chattering. 'See you had Elvis translate black for us and these were the first invaders, which we digested and sent back as the Stones and Yardbirds and R & B whomevers, you catch my drift, but now you've sent us Britney and it makes me, it truly makes me hostile. All we can send you back this time is a big fucking bucket of *sweets*.' He laughed again, and coughed. 'Jesus, it's really cold in here.' Then he put his nose in the air to call out again, rolling the *r*, for 'Brrrandy!', at which Tommy said, 'Yay!', ceased his scooping and, stepping carefully over the battlements, hurried in with the thermos of gin. Tommy's offering was unsteady and Uncle Phil shivered as he drank, and some dripped off his chin.

'I've met Sting. You know Sting, right?'

'No.'

'Proof that *unbridled ambition* is all a bloke really truly needs, plus an instinct to go Hollywood at *the first ring of the freaking bell*. Sure he's *hand*some but...'

Uncle Phil wasn't talking to anyone but himself any more and

Philip wished he would stop. An eagle was up in the snag behind them and at Philip's pointing Uncle Phil tried turning to look, but not really, and on he talked. Now three ravens—Philip's favourite bird—came to chase the eagle off and take its place in the trees, and though the ocean was loud he wanted his uncle to hear their croaks and screams and other sounds, especially the one exactly like a hugely amplified drop of water landing in a pool in the depths of a cave: *Plooink*. Sometimes ravens would make this sound back and forth, using different tones that seemed to mean something or sounded intentionally funny, and Philip wanted to tell his uncle that at such times it was possible to believe that these birds carried the spirits of dead Native elders who, it seemed, were comedians.

When a surging tongue from a big wave travelled up with a hiss, leapt over two moats and knocked through the first wall as if it weren't there, it was almost like this was a signal to Uncle Phil. He lifted his head, straining to rise above the sand.

'It's—it's *very cold actually*.' He laughed, but he wasn't smiling. He seemed embarrassed. 'I think I—Philip? Well I don't think I can feel my... Actually, I think I have to—Phil?'

Uncle Phil's voice trailed off. He gritted his teeth and stretched his blue lips out away from them. His gums were grey. In the middle of that he appeared to go to sleep.

Philip could see that, barely halfway to the parking area, Sasha and Tommy had slowed to a walk. There were a few people moving about near the cars. Philip couldn't see their arms so he knew they couldn't see his either and he stopped waving. He had tried one steady scream but it was nothing, he could barely hear it himself in the roar of the surf that was so close now.

At first the children had dug out Uncle Phil's arms and tried pulling, but it was obvious that they weren't moving him at all. They dug some more, and got him clear to the waist, but still he wouldn't budge, and now Tommy had to kneel behind and struggle to keep Uncle Phil's head propped out of the flats of wave that rushed in and submersed Tommy to his chest. Sasha fell face down to plug a breached wall, like two years ago, but this time there were no screams of delight, just barely heard coughs of, 'Quick, quick.' Tommy, big-eyed and grim, knew his uncle wasn't playing and that this panic had something to do with time. A bigger, quicker wave came in and Tommy lost his grip on his uncle's head and shoulders and Uncle Phil stayed under for a while because Philip was off feeling for the shovel. When the wave receded and his head reappeared and not being able to breathe didn't seem to have troubled him, that's when Sasha and Tommy saw it for real and started crying, and that's when Philip told them to run to the parking lot for help.

Philip knelt holding his uncle's head up as the waves came in and went out. It was loud, and exhausting, and hard to know the true passing of time—maybe fifteen minutes went by before Tommy and Sasha reached the parking lot. By now the surges were up to Philip's chin, and his uncle's head was underwater half the time anyway, so finally Philip mumbled several words he couldn't hear himself mumble, let his uncle's head fall, and walked backwards, watching, to higher ground.

Philip knew he had miscalculated in some way. He had failed at something huge, something beyond him, and he wondered what his mother would say, and what Aunt Sally would say, and when she would leave them and return to England. Would she stay with them tonight, or go to a motel? Tomorrow there would be no crispy bacon. His father no longer had a brother.

He stood ankle-deep and blank as each wave hit, his uncle mounding the clear rushing water like a boulder under the surface of a fast, broad river, a river that slowed to a stop and reversed before running over the boulder in the other direction. Each time the water receded and Uncle Phil appeared, Philip looked for signs of revival, but nothing changed, except for the strand of seaweed rearranged at his uncle's neck and shoulders, and his thin hair which itself seemed like a pathetic variety of seaweed. Then a new wave hit, and then another, and Philip had to backstep to higher and higher beach until, deep carnival, all he could see of this relative was, just to the right, his kite trick.   □

PASSOVER
IN BAGHDAD
Tim Judah

The Great Synagogue, Baghdad, 1910

Baghdad was not the most obvious place to celebrate Passover. Saddam had fallen barely a week before it began, looters were rampaging through the city, dozens of buildings were on fire and Islamic hardliners were arming militias. What's more, in a city of almost five million people there were only a handful of Jews left.

Until the Second World War roughly a quarter of Baghdad's population was Jewish. In June 1941, following a Nazi-inspired coup, 179 Jews died and almost a thousand were wounded in a pogrom while the police and army stood by. Until 1948 there were still 150,000 Jews in Iraq but by 1951, after the Israeli government had organized airlifts, the vast majority of them had left. The government placed severe restrictions on those who stayed. Even so, a community of some six thousand lingered on. But now, according to those that remain, their numbers add up to the grand total of thirty-four people.

While most Iraqi Jews left for Israel after its creation in 1948, significant numbers also made their way to Britain and the US, especially those from the middle classes—the Saatchi family, for example. Some wealthy Iraqi Jews did remain in the country after 1951, knowing that to leave was to lose everything: Jews who emigrated were stripped, not just of their citizenship, but also of all their property and other assets. In the end, however, their wealth could not protect them and indeed often made them targets for murder and blackmail. So they left too, for Israel, Britain, Holland and Canada.

Today it is hard to imagine that so many Jews once lived here. But if you look carefully in parts of town that used to be Jewish, like Bataween, on the east bank of the Tigris, or around Rashid Street, a bustling commercial area, you can still see brickwork patterned into Stars of David. You can also see places where moulded stars have been hacked away. What you can't see are the stories.

Although the majority of Iraqi Jews left in 1950 and 1951 in fact they had been emigrating for a lot longer than this. In the eighteenth century Baghdadi Jews began to make their way to India and beyond, which is the beginning of my story. My father was born in 1924 in Calcutta and this was his background. He came to Britain when he was four and, except for a single holiday a few years ago, he never went back. When he returned from the holiday he told us a surprising anecdote. Several times he had wanted to ask for something and on each occasion a Hindi word he had no idea that he knew popped out of his mouth. The words had lain dormant, lodged somewhere deep in his mind, for seventy years or so.

When he died in November 2002 he was buried in strict accordance with Sephardi tradition. At the Hoop Lane cemetery in Golders Green in London all the tombstones on one side stand upright, that is, in the Ashkenazi or European way, and all the Sephardi tombs are flat, in the oriental and Middle-Eastern Jewish way. The night before we buried him we wrote some notes for the rabbi to help him in his oration and in them we described how proud my father had been of his Baghdadi Jewish heritage.

My father's family left Baghdad or Aleppo or all the other Middle Eastern cities they traced their roots to during the late nineteenth century. They left behind the rotting corners of the Ottoman Empire and headed for the great commercial hubs of the British Empire and beyond: Bombay, Calcutta, Singapore, Hong Kong and Shanghai. Some left even earlier than this. On my grandmother's side, David Sassoon, founder of a prodigious commercial dynasty, fled Baghdad in about 1829 before eventually settling in Bombay.

When I was growing up, 'Baghdad' was a place that lurked like those Hindi words deep in family memory, but it was no more present than this. After all, no one in my family had actually been there. My grandmother herself had been born in Calcutta.

And yet from my childhood I remember what I now realize were echoes, faint ripples of Baghdad, which still survived. My father and grandmother played backgammon and would laugh *inshallah*— 'God willing'—when something was to be wished for. When we break the fast at Yom Kippur we still eat pomegranates. In Baghdad during the war I found myself eating the same food we used to eat, and sometimes still do on high holy days in London, such as chicken with okra or ladies' fingers. Iraqis would say, 'Do you know what that is?' and I would tell them I did—but never why.

I had gone to Baghdad to report the war for the *Economist* and the *New York Review of Books*. But of course I also had my own personal reasons for wanting to be there. Before I left, I joked that I was going to be the first Judah—of my family anyway—back in Baghdad for more than a century. But being Jewish, especially in Saddam's Iraq, was hardly something you wanted to advertise, and from the visa application onwards—which demanded the applicant's religion—I said nothing about the subject. When my government translator, discussing her views on foreigners, said, 'of course, we hate the Jews,' then added generously, 'you know, I think that even among the Jews there might be some good people,' I just nodded and kept my mouth shut. It had taken me ten months to get a visa and now, with war about to break out, I had no intention of being expelled.

As a foreign correspondent I spent more than a decade covering the Balkan wars and their aftermath. But after September 11 no one was interested in the Balkans any more. I realized I would have to start working in Arab and Muslim Middle Eastern countries, something I had always shied away from previously. Being Jewish and with an obviously Jewish name meant I was nervous both personally and professionally. Of course there are many Jewish correspondents who cover the Middle East, but how you feel about covering this story and whether your own feelings might somehow cloud your objectivity can only be an individual decision.

But when I got to Afghanistan in October 2001, I was surprised to find I felt quite relaxed. Sometimes I was asked if I was an infidel and once, if I was 'thinking of Jesus'. To this I replied with a cautious 'sometimes', and the man who asked me the question seemed happy to leave it there.

Then I went to Iran and no one asked me anything. When I got back, though, I had lunch with the press attaché at the Iranian Embassy who spent the meal complaining about the pieces I'd written. As we finished eating he said, 'and, anyway what does "Judah" mean?'

'Nothing, it's just a name,' I said.

Looking straight at me, he said, 'Because in Farsi it means "Jewish".'

Just before going to Baghdad, I went to Jordan and people began to ask questions. 'Judah? Judah? What sort of a name is that?' they asked. But every time, before I had a chance to reply, they said, 'so you must be from here and have Arab family?' I was startled—'Judah' is, after all, just an anglicization of the Hebrew 'Yehuda'. But now it turned out that there was a prominent Jordanian–Palestinian family whose name was pronounced, if not transliterated, in exactly the same way as mine. It made me feel less nervous.

Tim Judah

On the night of March 11, I crossed the border into Iraq, the country where my ancestors lived for 2,500 years. Here I was—the first Judah back. I felt absolutely nothing. Perhaps the feeling will come, I told myself.

This was not, anyway, the right moment for personal reflection or for hunting down my roots or, in fact, for mentioning anything Jewish in any context at all. Every few days foreign journalists were being expelled. Some were arrested and jailed. I needed to be careful. I limited myself to sending a few emails to friends and relatives asking them if they had any relevant information that I could use once things were safe.

The bombing campaign began on March 20. The Americans reached Firdos Square, just by the Palestine Hotel (where the foreign press were based) on the afternoon of April 9. For the next few days I was busy with work, but then I realized that if I wanted to do Passover in Baghdad I had better get organized. Before the bombing had ended I had received an email from a friend of a friend of a friend in London asking me if I could try and find their elderly mother and aunt. They were desperate for news. All the telephone exchanges had just been bombed, but I had a satellite phone.

I asked my driver to take me to the address they'd given me, but he refused. It was too late in the day and besides, he said, Bataween market was full of 'Ali Babas' or robbers and he did not want to risk his life or his car. The next day I got another car. The house turned out to be only a few minutes drive from the Palestine Hotel. To avert attention I told him to park further away, down the street. The house stood alone in a street covered, like much of the rest of the city, in rubbish. The people on the balcony of the low-rise block opposite watched me, an obvious foreigner, with interest.

After I banged on the door it opened a crack and an old lady peeped out. 'My name is Tim Judah,' I explained, 'I am from London and I have a message from your family.' She stared at me. I said in a whisper, 'My name is Judah—*Yehuda! Yehuda!*—Let me in!' Cautiously she opened the door.

The old ladies, Um Daoud ('Mother of Daoud') and her sister Mariam, were still suspicious. I explained that I had come with a message from Um Daoud's daughter who had asked me to find out if they were alive and, if so, how they were. Did they have enough food and money? I sat awkwardly on a sofa in the front room, which was a jumble of furniture and bags. Mariam paced about; Um Daoud, sitting in a chair with a rug over her knees, looked thin and drawn. She reminded me of my grandmother, who used to sit in just the same way, with the same sort of rug tucked over her lap. 'You are Jewish?' one of them asked, suspiciously. 'Yes, yes,' I said, I hoped not too impatiently. I could feel the tension in the room subside.

'We are frightened,' said Um Daoud. 'Thank you for coming, but we are Jews and they will come and ask who you are and we will have trouble. Please tell the family we are okay.' I explained that the war was over, that there was no more Mukhabbarat (secret police), and no government. Saddam was finished. Um Daoud shot back instantly, 'There are thousands of Saddams in this country. Did anyone see you come? You had better go.'

The eve of Passover, the Seder night, when Jews recount the story of the coming out of Egypt, was the very next day. I wondered if Um Daoud and her sister, or the Baghdadi Jewish community, had any plans. 'It is the eve of Passover tomorrow,' I said hopefully. 'Are you doing something? Have you got Matzah?'

They looked at me as if I was mad. 'No! We are frightened, we are not doing anything.'

Two days later it was the first day of Passover. I went to the Meir Tweg synagogue, the only synagogue left in Baghdad. It was hidden behind a high wall, close to where the old ladies lived. Unless you knew what you were looking for you would never find it. There is nothing on the outside to identify the building or the compound as a synagogue.

I banged on the steel door. Eventually a young man, whom I later learned was the Muslim caretaker, peered out and gestured to me that the synagogue was closed and that I should go away. When I insisted that I wanted to come in, he popped his head out of the door, checked to see if anyone was looking and then pointed at his watch and told me to come back later.

By now the friend of the friend of the friend was passing on more messages from families in Britain and elsewhere desperate for news of their relatives in Baghdad. I got a new driver and set out to hunt for them. 'You,' said the driver suspiciously. 'What religion?' 'Christian,' I replied, as matter-of-factly as I could, and on we drove.

After I'd banged for several minutes at the gates of one house in a predominantly middle-class and Christian part of the city an old lady, Victoria, finally appeared on its flat roof. 'Who are you?' she quavered. I tried to explain, but even though she spoke English I didn't think it was a good idea to be shouting my business in front of the whole street. 'Please come down,' I pleaded. 'But I don't know you,' she remonstrated. Eventually Victoria tottered to the gate. Her alsatian was working himself into a frenzy. 'Neither my son nor my daughter are here, come back tomorrow,' she said.

That evening a surprising new email arrived from the friend of the friend of the friend.

> plans for airlift r underway for those who r ready to move immediately. no need for passports. if you have the chance please explain that this is a chance which cannot be repeated for a while. our estimates that only 15 people r ready to move out with no hesitation. the children of the two old ladies are begging them to just leave if the chance presents itself.

No more explanations were forthcoming. Exactly who was organizing this airlift? Where would the plane take these people to? When would they leave? How much warning would people be given? I was not told. All I was asked to do (by whom exactly?—even this was unclear and I decided not to enquire too deeply) was to find the city's Jews and ask them a simple question: 'If you have the chance to go in a week or two—leaving everything behind—will you go?'

Suddenly my job had changed. Passover was taking an unexpected turn. As my colleagues started to look around for new angles and stories, I began to hide. I did not want anyone to ask me what I was doing, and I particularly didn't want anyone to ask me if I knew anything about the remnant of the Jewish community in Baghdad.

The next day I found Ishak and Yusef and their mother, Sara. Ishak was forty-three and Yusef thirty-six; during the bombing I turned forty-one. I felt a kind of instant familiarity with them; after all it was only a twist of fate which made me the visitor and them the visited and not the other way around. Ishak was a businessman and Yusef worked as a jeweller while also studying for a doctorate in linguistics. They both spoke English and while they had been keeping a low profile during the bombing, they were not as frightened as the old people I'd met.

Yusef told me that he was not surprised to see me. 'The other day I dreamt that someone, like an angel, or from the Red Cross, would come to visit us soon and ask us whether we wanted to leave.' I asked them if they *did* want to leave, because the people organizing the airlift needed to know. They began to shower me with questions. 'If we leave now, can we come back later to sell our property? Can we leave without passports?'

I went back to my hotel to give them time to think. When I returned to the house the next day, Sara began to cry. She had had a dream that her husband, who had died the previous year, had implored her 'not to leave him'. But the brothers argued that there was little point in staying as, apart from anything else, there were no Jewish girls to marry. What future was there for them in Iraq? Surely the future was grandchildren?

With Ishak acting as my guide, driving a 1960 Ford Zodiac that his father had imported, we managed to hunt down more of the Jewish community. We got past the steel door of the synagogue and found two old men who lived in rooms beside it. They seemed quite happy. One of them, unshaven, sunning himself in his pyjamas, looked exactly like my father just before he died. They told me they did not want to go anywhere and asked me to send their love to their families and to tell them they were fine. We sent a message to the head of the community asking him to come and meet us, but when we went back to the synagogue the next day, the guardian informed Ishak, in Arabic, 'He doesn't want to see him. Tell him he is out of Baghdad.' Ishak said, 'He is frightened.'

I went to ask Um Daoud and Mariam what they wanted to do. 'After you were here last time they came and broke down the door,' they told me. I was alarmed: perhaps the Mukhabbarat was not finished after all? I saw that the door had been barricaded to keep it upright. But it wasn't the Mukhabbarat, as it turned out. Someone, acting through malice or confusion, had told the Americans that there were two armed men holed up in the women's house. So seven American soldiers carried out a raid. Um Daoud said, 'They were looking for two men with swords, but I told them, "I will tell you the truth, we are just two Jewish girls here!"' The Americans had returned the next day with a military ration-pack as a gift to say sorry.

When I asked the women if they wanted to leave they said that they did. But then they told Ishak in Arabic that they did not.

Over the next few days I ferried news back and forth between families in Iraq and abroad explaining what was—or what was not— happening. I exchanged many emails with the friend of the friend of the friend. I found two women in their thirties and their elderly uncle. Unlike the other people I'd met they had no close family abroad, spoke only Arabic and were not the remnant of an educated and wealthy class. Chickens ran through their smoke-blackened house. With no close family in Britain or Holland or anywhere else, their only option was Israel. One woman wanted to go, the other two did not. The old man gave me the address of a cousin in New York whom he had last heard from in 1985. He clung to this, evidently believing that if only the man could be found he would send for them and everything would be all right.

As they dithered I asked them what they wanted me to tell the organizers of the airlift. They told me they wanted to stay. Ishak was outraged. 'You will be corrupted or they will make you convert,' he told them. Then he said to me, 'Once a man in a desert found people who were dying of thirst. They said, "give us water!" so he did. Then they said, "this is warm, we want cold water!" So the man could do nothing and left them. So let's go. They are crazy.'

Ishak told me people's stories as we searched. 'There,' said Ishak, passing one house, 'lived a family of two girls and two boys and their parents. There was also a sister, in Lebanon. It was 1972. At eight o'clock in the morning one of the girls went to school but when she came back in the afternoon she found men from the Mukhabbarat there including Khairallah Tulfah. You know who he was? Saddam's uncle. There was blood on the floor. "What happened? What happened?" shouted the girl. They told her, "Your family left for Iran." She said, "Without me? Look, here are their passports." She was about seventeen years old. Then she said, "Please give me some money," because the police had stolen everything in the house, jewellery, everything precious. "I want to live," she told them but they told her they had nothing. She became half-crazy. Our community and our parents gave her money and made contact with her sister and she left.'

As we passed another house Ishak said, 'Here was another family who were very wealthy and killed for their money. There was a man aged sixty or sixty-five. He married a young girl, Jewish, very beautiful. He owned three factories. He bought her a car but the Mukhabbarat would come after her and stop her. "Give us a kiss," they'd say. Once she went to stay with her sister and the Mukhabbarat went to the husband and cut off his ears and the tip of his nose. When the wife heard she came back. This was in 1973. Then, four or five days later, the Mukhabbarat came back and took them. Later a friend of my father who worked in the Mukhabbarat told him that they dissolved his body in acid. I don't know what happened to the girl. No one ever heard of her again.'

All the time I kept thinking how fortunate I had been that my ancestors had decided that there was not much of a future to be had in Baghdad. But why were these people, even if they were only a handful, still here in 2003? Everyone I asked came up with something but most of their reasons were unclear. It was a painful question to answer. Why had they decided to stay when their parents, brothers, sisters and almost everyone else they knew had left, either by the end of 1951 or whenever there had been other opportunities to leave since then?

Victoria's daughter, Rahel, a thirty-eight-year-old doctor who lived with her mother, told me, as we drove to find her elderly aunt, 'I blame my parents. They lost every chance to go.' Her colleagues at the surgery had put up a calendar on the wall to taunt her, with a slogan from Saddam: "Damn, damn the dirty Jews!".

When I asked Victoria about her story, she told me that her father had died, before the Second World War, when she was very young. Her sister didn't work and had never married. She was therefore responsible for looking after both her mother and her sister. In 1951, when she was still a medical student, she had wanted to leave. 'I wanted to go and arranged everything for us to go to Israel. But my mother refused and so did my sister. I was angry, but I loved my mother and did not want her to know that I was angry.' After she married there had been opportunities to leave in the early 1960s and then in the early 1970s but her mother refused again, as did her husband. Property had been a problem. Those who left before 1951 had been allowed to take the equivalent of twenty US dollars with them. They lost their property and were stripped of their citizenship. The same thing happened to those who left after them.

After this, periods of repression came and went. There were periods when Jews were arrested and disappeared and certain jobs were barred for Jews. Among the worst of times was that which followed the 1967 Six Day War when Ahmed Hassan al-Bakr, who became president in 1968, used the issue of Israel to distract Iraqis from domestic concerns. In this period in particular being Jewish was dangerous and there was both official and unofficial harassment. Saddam was al-Bakr's deputy and increasingly the real power-broker. He finally assumed the presidency himself in July 1979. There were so few Jews left in Iraq by this point that the president could play a more subtle game. Saddam needed Western support for his war against Iran, and presented himself as a protector of minorities, mostly Christian. But at the same time he played the Palestinian card to garner support in the Arab world and also borrowed increasingly from the rhetoric of the Islamists. His official media frequently spewed out virulent anti-Semitism.

Back in 1969, at the height of al-Bakr's rule, fourteen men, nine of them Jewish, were hanged in Tahrir Square after show trials in which they were accused of spying for Israel. Iraqi radio called on people to come out to celebrate and up to half a million did. 'Come and enjoy the feast!' it said. 'Death to Israel! Death to all traitors!' chanted the people. That evening Victoria talked her husband into taking her up to the square. 'Their necks were as long as this,' she said, indicating her forearm. She wrote down some of the men's names for me. She crooked her body and said, 'They were hanging like this.' I asked her what happened next. 'I cried,' she said.

'And your husband?'

'He said nothing.'

Victoria told me several times, 'I pray to God that when the Messiah comes he will not revive him [Bakr]. *I always pray to God about this.*'

I asked Victoria if, if she could turn the clock back to 1951, she would have left, whatever her mother and sister had said. She just smiled and said, 'I don't know. I can't imagine this.'

Victoria's house, like the other houses I had visited, was ramshackle. It contained several large old fridges and there were piles of clothing and bric-a-brac in various rooms. I had the impression, in all of these houses, that the reason for the mess, the reason these houses were in need of paint and work, wasn't just lack of money. It was as though an argument had raged on and off for sixty years among the people who had lived in these rooms about whether they should stay or go. Why bother to invest in your house, if you might one day leave and the law stated that Jews who left Iraq could not sell their property?

I asked Um Daoud why she had stayed. I knew from the emails she was getting and I was reading to her that she had almost a dozen grandchildren abroad—but she had never seen them. She pointed at her sister with a quick, low, stabbing movement.

Sara, the mother of Ishak and Yusef, told me her story. She was born in 1938 in Al Kifl, a little town about an hour and a half's drive south of Baghdad. There had been a community of 250 Jews there. When Israel was created, she told me, the Jews were happy, and behind closed doors at least, they celebrated. But then the atmosphere began to change. There were anti-Jewish demonstrations, Jews began to be arrested, restrictions were placed on them by the government and they no longer felt safe. Also they believed Israel was the Promised Land. In 1950 and 1951 most of the community left. They went by bus from Al Kifl to Baghdad, from where they flew to Cyprus and from there, to Israel. In 1951 Sara was thirteen years old. I asked her what she remembered of people leaving, 'They were crying,' she said, 'they were remembering the good times with their neighbours.'

At home there were fights. Her mother would ask her father: 'Why do you want to leave us with the Muslims? Aren't you afraid of our destiny?' He maintained that he was successful in Iraq, that he made good money. He sold clothes and silks. 'We were afraid,' said Sara, 'but we used to take our mother's side. I would cry but my father was stubborn and despotic.' In the end, she said, 'he did not want to hear anything about going. I loved him as a father but he was a dictator.'

Suddenly all the Jews had left Al Kifl, and Sara's family were the only ones left. They moved to Baghdad. In 1959 Sara married and the story began again. Her husband was Jewish and had been a communist. After 1951 he left the party and pursued his career as a lawyer, although with difficulty after new anti-Jewish restrictions were enforced in the early 1960s. For the whole of the marriage the question hung in the air, but Sara's husband always refused to go. He loved his country and wanted to die there. Sara explained, 'The same problem that we had had with my father reappeared again with my husband. I would say, "what about our sons? They will need to get married," and he would say, just as a Muslim Iraqi would have done: "It is the will of God."'

Sara told me that in Al Kifl her family had lived next to the shrine of Ezekiel the Prophet. Every year thousands of Jews would come to make a pilgrimage there. A couple of days before I talked to Sara I had visited the nearby town of Karbala. Here I had seen tens of thousands of Shiite Muslims beating their breasts and heads and converging on the golden domed mosques of the city to mourn the Imam Hussein who had died there in AD 680. At the height of the pilgrimage there may have been up to a million pilgrims in Kerbala at any one time.

I asked Sara when the Jews would make their pilgrimage and she said that it used to take place in the week after Passover. In fact, she said—scrabbling through a Jewish calendar—it would have to be done by, well, tomorrow.

We began to debate. Would the road be safe? What about the Shiites? A day or two before, one of the Shia leaders had been arrested by the Americans, and his followers had been protesting, writing slogans in blood on the road outside the Palestine Hotel. But we decided to try and go anyway.

We set off the next morning. The road was open and there were no checkpoints. American military convoys jostled for space with the rest of the traffic. When we got to Al Kifl we made our way to the shrine, behind the old, covered market. Because it was Friday, the Muslim day of prayer, the shops were shut and just as we got there a Shiite imam was leading his flock into the tomb to pray. He politely told Sara to put on a headscarf. We went to have lunch while the prayers took place. Ishak was nervous and did not feel safe. Men ambled around with Kalashnikovs. There had been fighting with the Americans here and the main street was pockmarked with bullet holes. Outside the little restaurant were three mini vans with coffins strapped to their roofs. They were Shi'a being taken for burial at their nearby holy city of Najaf.

When we went back, prayers had not yet finished. We sat outside a teahouse in the covered market while inside a group of men watched a DVD chronicling the crimes of Saddam. Sara told me that until 1951 about five thousand Jews used to come to Al Kifl during Passover week. And people still came after 1951, at least until 1967, after which it grew too dangerous. Then in 1984 a group of twenty Jews had come from Baghdad and in 1989 Sara, her family and another family had come, but no Jews to her knowledge had made the pilgrimage since then.

We wandered back to the gate of the shrine and met a young man who was waiting there for his father. He told us, without being asked, that the market used to belong to Jews and added that now Indians and Iranians came to pray at the shrine. I asked if Jews came too and he said, 'I don't know, because I don't know what they look like.'

Before the Jews left Al Kifl the Jews and the Shiites had shared the shrine. They would come at different times of day and steer clear of it on one another's holy days.

Inside the shrine was the tomb of the Prophet Ezekiel. There were still Hebrew inscriptions on the walls. The tomb was surrounded by a large wooden covering, like a sarcophagus. We lit candles and the guardian, who realized from the way we talked and acted that we were Jewish, opened a tiny door at the bottom of the covering. By crouching down we could see the actual, concrete-covered tomb. It had Hebrew script on one end. The guardian told us he would welcome the Jews to come back to pray here. Sara walked around and kissed the corners of the tomb.

Later Sara told me she was both exhilarated and saddened by what we had done. The past, she said, her childhood in Al Kifl, had seemed 'like yesterday'. But now perhaps this would be her last visit.

On the way back to Baghdad we stopped at the ruins of Babylon. Much of the ancient city was reconstructed under Saddam, the rest is crumbling walls in dips and mounds and the whole site is dominated by one of his nearby palaces. A few American soldiers were mooching about, some guarding the site, some tourists.

This was where this story began, and this was where it was

ending. In 606 BC the Babylonians brought the first group of Jews from Judah into exile here. In 597 BC King Nebuchadnezzar brought several thousand more, including Ezekiel. Ezekiel told his people that, following the destruction of Jerusalem, the exiles were the hope of Israel's redemption. When the time was right, God would lead them back to the Promised Land.

I left Iraq on May 1. The planned airlift still hadn't happened and the people who were supposed to be organizing it—exactly who they were was still unclear—had started to argue that airlifting a handful of people was not only unnecessary but might even be 'bad for the Jews'. Bad for those who would be left behind, and bad politics in a region—and world, even—that already believes that one of the main reasons for the war was to help Israel. Those that wanted to go would be helped to do so individually.

As Sara and Ishak and I drove back to Baghdad I tried to imagine my ancestors here. At home my father had always told me that we came to Iraq with the exiles of 597 BC. (How did he know this, I had always wondered.) I tried to picture my forebears, in the fields or perhaps in the shops or the market, but I couldn't. A cold grey dust filled the air. Wrecked cars and burnt-out tanks littered the road back to Baghdad. On either side were dried-out, churned-up fields and the remains of unfinished concrete buildings. So my ancestors lived here for 2,500 years? So what? My pilgrimage was over. I will never need to do it again.   ☐

To protect those that remain in Baghdad I have changed their names.

NOTES ON CONTRIBUTORS

Lynn Barber is an interviewer for the London *Observer*. She has won five British Press Awards. Two books of her interviews, *Mostly Men* and *Demon Barber*, are published by Viking. She lives with her family in north London.

Kathryn Chetkovich's collection of short stories, *Friendly Fire*, is published by the University of Iowa Press. She lives in Boulder Creek, California, and New York.

Nell Freudenberger's short-story collection, *Lucky Girls*, will be published by Ecco Press in the US in August, and by Picador in the UK next year. She lives in New York.

Bill Gaston's novels include *The Good Body* which is published by Stoddart in Canada and HarperCollins in the US and *The Cameraman* (Raincoast). His most recent collection of short stories, *Mount Appetite*, was nominated for the Giller Prize. His forthcoming novel, *Sointula*, will be published by Raincoast in 2004. He teaches at the University of Victoria.

Simon Gray's plays include *Butley*, *Otherwise Engaged*, *Quatermaine's Terms* and *Japes*. 'The Smoking Diaries' is taken from a forthcoming volume of his diaries which will be published by Granta Books next year.

Robin Grierson was born in County Durham in 1962. His photographs can be seen in the Victoria & Albert Museum's permanent collection in London. He is working on a book about steam fairs.

Tim Judah is a freelance reporter and writer. He is the author of *Kosovo: War and Revenge* and *The Serbs: History, Myth and the Destruction of Yugoslavia*, both published by Yale University Press.

J. Robert Lennon's novels are *The Funnies*, *The Light of Falling Stars* (Granta/Riverhead) and *On the Night Plain* (Granta/Picador USA) 'Five Cats and Three Women' is taken from his fourth novel, *Mailman*, which will be published this autumn by Granta Books in the UK and by W. W. Norton in the US. He lives in Ithaca, New York.

Paul Murray was born in 1975 in Dublin, where he continues to live. His first novel, *An Evening of Long Goodbyes*, is published by Hamish Hamilton in the UK and will be published by Random House in the US in January 2004.

Jayne Anne Phillips is the author of two collections of stories, *Fast Lanes* (Vintage/Faber), and *Black Tickets* (Delta/Faber), and three novels; *Motherkind* (Knopf/Jonathan Cape), which was nominated for the 2001 Orange Prize, *Shelter* (Delta/Faber) and *Machine Dreams* (Vintage/Faber). 'Termite's Birthday, 1959' is taken from *Termite*, a novel-in-progress.